D0404421

AMERICAN
FOLKLORE
SCHOLARSHIP

Folkloristics

ALAN DUNDES, GENERAL EDITOR

AMERICAN FOLKLORE SCHOLARSHIP

A Dialogue of Dissent

ROSEMARY LÉVY ZUMWALT

Indiana University Press

BLOOMINGTON AND INDIANAPOLIS

1888-89
AMERICAN
FOLKLORE
SOCIETY
CENTENNIAL
1988-89

© 1988 by Rosemary Lévy Zumwalt
All rights reserved

No part of this book may be reproduced or utilized in any form or by
any means, electronic or mechanical, including photocopying and
recording, or by any information storage and retrieval system, without
permission in writing from the publisher. The Association of American
University Presses' Resolution on Permissions constitutes the only
exception to this prohibition.

Manufactured in the United States of America
Library of Congress Cataloging-in-Publication Data

Zumwalt, Rosemary Lévy, 1944–
American folklore scholarship.

(Folkloristics)
Bibliography: p.
Includes index.
1. Folklore—United States—History.   I. Title.
II. Series.
GR48.Z86   1988   398'.0973   87-45408
ISBN 0-253-31738-X
ISBN 0-253-20472-0 (pbk.)
1 2 3 4 5   92 91 90 89 88

To my mother and father

CONTENTS

Foreword

The Indiana *Folkloristics* series is intended to demonstrate the highest levels of scholarship in the study of folklore. While the majority of books in the series will be concerned with individual genres, several of the titles will treat special areas in folklore theory and method. This volume, *American Folklore Scholarship*, which inaugurates the series, is an incisive historical account of the development of folkloristics in the United States.

A discipline may be said to have achieved its niche in the academy when its history has been documented. This being so, the study of folklore in the United States may achieve such status through the publication of Zumwalt's thorough and detailed chronicle of the beginnings and development of serious folklore study by American scholars. Her judicious combination of the published record and un-published archival materials, especially the correspondence of many of the pioneering figures of the field, gives a remarkable account of the emergence of the academic study of folklore. The biographical facts, the intellectual genealogies of both "literary" and "anthropological" folklorists, and the continuing influence of the American Folklore Society, founded in 1888, are all presented as integral parts of the history of modern American folkloristics. Some of this information is not easily accessible to the casual inquirer and Zumwalt has performed a real service in both unearthing significant letters and bringing together a mass of diverse materials under one cover.

The central argument of the volume is that part-time folklorists of the past, be they ballad scholars in English departments or myth scholars in anthropology departments, have given way to full-time folklorists who have little patience with divisive debates over the respective merits of "literary" versus "anthropological" approaches to folklore data. Scholars who consider themselves folklorists first are less concerned than their predecessors, most of whom were born in the nineteenth century, with their allegiance to literary or anthropological warring camps. The struggle between literary and anthropological paradigms in the development of folkloristics in the United States is a historical fact, as Zumwalt's painstaking research shows. But at the same time, her even-handed treatment of the two rival factions may serve to end once and for all this unnecessary and often debilitating conflict. In that sense, this book may help unify folklorists of various persuasions and encourage them to address the major theoretical and methodological issues in folklore research, issues that are inherent in folklore itself and that are independent of the particular academic affiliation of the folklorist.

I am convinced that this useful survey of American folkloristics will not only be required reading for all graduate students in folkore in the United States, but that it will acquaint many non-folklorists with intimate details of the founding of folklore as an academic discipline. Nowhere else is it possible to learn so much about Francis James Child, Franz Boas, William Wells Newell, and many others responsible for the establishment and growth of the study of folklore. Zumwalt succeeds admirably in discussing both individuals and ideas.

Born in Decatur, Georgia, Rosemary Lévy Zumwalt was educated in California. She earned a B.A. in anthropology with honors at the University of California, Santa Cruz, in 1972, and it was there she was introduced to folklore by Professor Gary Gossen. She completed her M.A. in folkfore at Berkeley in 1978, writing her thesis on French folklorist Arnold van Gennep. Her doctorate in anthropology was also at Berkeley and her dissertation was an earlier version of the present book. Throughout her career, she has been especially fascinated by the intellectual history of folklore and folklorists, particularly in the late nineteenth and early twentieth centuries. Since 1983, she has taught in the Department of Anthropology and Sociology at Davidson College in North Carolina.

Perhaps in the future, some energetic scholar will undertake the task of writing a history of folkloristics worldwide. Such a scholar will have to rely on the standard histories of folklore research in individual countries. One of the sources for that work will surely be this volume. And as American folklorists take pleasure in celebrating the centennial of the American Folklore Society in 1988, they may also feel justifiable pride in having this survey of American folklore scholarship to stand on the same shelf as such works as: Inger M. Boberg, *Folkemindeforskningens Historie* (1953); Juan Alfonso Carrizo, *Historia del Folklore Argentino* (1953); Giuseppe Cocchiara, *Storia degli studi delle tradizioni popolari in Italia* (1947); Richard M. Dorson, *The British Folklorists: A History* (1968); Ruth Finnegan, *Oral Literature in Africa* (1970); Jouko Hautala, *Finnish Folklore Research 1828–1918* (1968); Michael Herzfeld, *Ours Once More: Folklore, Ideology, and the Making of Greece* (1982); Chang-tai Hung, *Going to the People: Chinese Intellectuals and Folk Literature, 1918–1937* (1985); Mazharul Islam, *A History of Folktale Collections in India and Pakistan* (1970); Gustav Jungebauer, *Geschichte der deutschen Volkskunde* (1931); Leopold Schmidt, *Geschichte der Österreichischen Volkskunde* (1951); and Gheorghe Vrabie, *Folcloristica română* (1968).

All folklorists, whatever their genre specialization, if any, and whatever their academic affiliation, if any, ought to find this pioneering historical overview of great interest. One cannot function in the future effectively without knowing the past. Zumwalt has made available for the first time much of the intriguing past of American folklore scholarship.

Alan Dundes

Preface

Writing an intellectual history necessitates choosing an angle, a perspective. One takes a slice of the past and scrutinizes a portion of the events that occurred during this time frame. In this work, the perspective on the past will reveal the conflict between the literary and the anthropological folklorists. The period of consideration will span the years from 1888, when the American Folklore Society was founded, to the early 1940s, when the anthropological control of the *Journal of American Folklore* was ended. At this time, anthropologists largely "abandoned" folklore. This had to do with a series of events: the reorganization of the American Folklore Society in 1940; and the deaths of Elsie Clews Parsons, the patron and scholar, in 1941, of Franz Boas in 1942, and of Ruth Benedict in 1948. Additionally, new concerns developed in anthropology. Radcliffe-Brown had had a crucial impact on American anthropology during his years at the University of Chicago in the 1930s, which resulted in an increasing emphasis on the study of social structure and kinship. World War II brought with it a series of new approaches, including acculturation studies. Most importantly, however, an anti-Boasian sentiment resulted in the rejection of much of the explicit directions of Boas's work. Included in this was a de-emphasis on the importance of studying folklore.

This withdrawal of anthropologists from folklore studies is illustrated in a letter from Anna Gayton to A. Irving Hallowell written in 1946:

Dear Pete:

When Fred Eggan asked me to be the spokesman for "Folklore" in his symposium on the fields of anthropology, he suggested that I "plant" a couple of copies of my talk with people who might start discussion.

Since the two points I am emphasizing—need for comparative work and need for improved psychological techniques—are interests of yours I am hoping you may care to respond in some way concerning them. I think you are one of the very few anthropologists who understands the methods and the values in both the old analytic-comparative studies and the new psychological interests in native mythology.

The paper as a whole is very dull, as any brief talk has to be. And since the bulk of anthropologists really does not know what goes on in the folklore society any more, I felt the introductory background should be given.

(Hallowell Papers, Gayton to Hallowell, 12/18/1946)

Thus, four years after the death of Boas, as stated by Gayton, the anthropologists no longer knew what was happening in the American Folklore Society.

During this same period, the literary folklorists took an increasingly active role in the American Folklore Society and the *Journal of American Folklore*. A subtle but telling sign of a shift in identity began to appear in the correspondence of the late 1930s and early 1940s. References were made to *the folklorists*—and these were those who studied folklore from a literary perspective.

At the center of the conflict between the literary and the anthropological folklorists were concerns of professionalism, science, and discipline. The core of the issue had to do not with theory, not with what the anthropological and the literary people did with folklore—this, as will be shown, was remarkably similar—but rather with professionalism. Folklore served the purpose of the anthropologists solely within the frame of a careful, scientific approach. Further, it could be used to strengthen their professional base, as a source for publication in the *Journal of American Folklore* and a means of organizational power in the American Folklore Society. In truth, for a period of over half a century, the anthropologists formed a united front within the society; and the literary people either maintained a defensive stance, or withdrew from the society. For the literary folklorists, folklore reached its efflorescence in their courses and in their writings.

In choice lies omission; by selecting a perspective on the past, others are necessarily put aside. There is frustration in this, for one is aware that the angle on the past, while vitally necessary as a frame for the myriad events, means also that many things will lie outside the realm of consideration. This is not to say that other perspectives are unimportant or insignificant. There were vital concerns that arose during the period under study—these include the popularist movement in folklore and the development of folklife studies and of public sector folklore. There are also important events that occurred after the period selected for this study: the development of graduate programs in folklore, the activities of the American Folklore Society after the 1941 accords, especially during the critical period of the 1940s, and the growth of folklore as a separate discipline. These and other areas are crucial for the development of American folklore scholarship. They are also, necessarily, outside the frame I have selected.

The singular in history has given way to the plural. Just as Franz Boas changed Tylor's culture to the plural, so has history been restated as histories. Kenneth Bock, influenced by his mentor, Frederick Teggart, wrote on the *Acceptance of Histories*. In the plural, the word "histories" emphasizes that there is more than one story to be told, more than one series of events unfolding from the past—that, indeed, the past is made up of a multiplicity of events which defies neat, uniform categorization. Throughout this work, I have been concerned with the complexity of historical developments. It has not been my intent to minimize the forces at work. This would lead to what David Fischer refers to as the chronic fallacy, a "listing of facts that relate to each other only in calendric succession." As Dan Ben-Amos (1973, 114) says, remarking on Fischer's concept, this yields "a chronicle but not a history of folklore."[1] Thomas Kuhn also refers to such a tendency to simplify the history of science by presenting it as a unified development. As he remarks, "Scientists are not, of course, the only group that tends to see its discipline's past developing linearly towards its present vantage. The temptation to write history backward is both omnipresent and perennial" (Kuhn 1970a, 138).

George Stocking cautions against reading the past in terms of present concerns. Such a perspective is part of what I call the "forerunner syndrome," where one looks to the past to find the point of origin for the present theory. As Stocking says, we are all in search of the putative founders of our disciplines. The search yields a reward; once we have found our ancestors and seminal theoreticians, we have legitimacy. Intellectual genealogy when predicated on such presentist concerns traces a linear view of history without the dimension of time. Continuity, Stocking says, can be equated with atemporality. From the point of origin, developments continue in an unbroken line to the present, and the assumption is made that "one may enter into direct debate with the figures of the past" (Stocking 1974, 511). Stocking suggests that instead of attempting to read the past in the present, one should accept the past on its own terms. Discontinuity, he says, is as important as continuity. This he explains with the metaphor of stacked pie plates: rather than a straight arrow of uninterrupted linear development, a history might be viewed

> as a series of pie plates stacked somewhat irregularly one upon another. The irregularity is important, for the pie plates themselves have thickness in time— what we are in fact investigating as intellectual historians are "contexts of assumption" which exist through time in complex interrelation with each other.
>
> (Stocking 1974, 513)

I have also attempted in the research and writing of this history to portray the "native view" of the events. This, of course, is the angle of perspective adopted by ethnographers. As Clifford Geertz (1976, 228) in " 'From the Native's Point of View' " says, "The trick is to figure out what the devil they think they are up to." The same can be said of historical research. In this case, one must pay close attention to the precise words and specific concerns of the people involved. This can be done by a careful reading and frequent reference of their letters and works. And it is from the native's own view—from Newell and Boas, Tozzer and Kittredge, Parsons and Taylor—that the concern with the literary and the anthropological emerges. In this sense, they have selected the frame of inquiry; I have followed the threads of tension.

The focus, then, has been on the schism in folklore studies between the literary and the anthropological. The view has been sharpened by the framework of the development of disciplines. In chapter 1, general remarks on the development of discipline and identity are presented, along with a review of Kuhn's notion of disciplinary matrix. Chapter 2 carves out the field and scope of folklore studies and considers the significance of William Wells Newell's intitial statement in the *Journal of American Folklore*. Chapter 3 examines the schism in folklore studies as manifested in organizational terms. Chapters 4 and 5 discuss the literary and the anthropological folklorists. Chapter 6 compares the methods and theory of the literary and the anthropological folklorists and draws out the shared, underlying approach to the material. Finally, chapter 7 tugs on the intellectual threads to see the tension in contemporary folklore theory which is a remnant of the earlier division.

I am grateful to my friends and colleagues in folklore and anthropology who have given me their help and encouragement throughout the course of this work. In folklore, I have been guided by Alan Dundes, and it is to him that I owe so much. His enthusiasm for folklore is boundless, and his demands for rigor in research are exacting. Together they make him a model professor and scholar. It has been his encouragement and support of my research that has sustained me. John Howland Rowe has helped shape my work in the history of anthropology. With his quiet, learned advice, I am always reminded of the importance of careful documentary research and critical thinking. Kenneth Bock gave generously of his balanced, reasoned views. Roger Abrahams offered a careful reading of a first draft. His comments, as always, were both encouraging and helpful. Dan Ben-Amos has been supportive of my work and most kind in offering research suggestions. Florence Baer has shared time and ideas. Susan Dwyer-Shick counseled me in the early stages of my research. Elizabeth Simons has listened to me talk about the ideas that have taken shape in this work, and has, in her inimitable style, asked the crucial question, which startled me and then helped me to refocus my work. Judith Justice has shown always a gentle kindness. Janice Weingrod has offered me sustenance at all times.

During my research, I have touched the lives and works of many outstanding scholars who have shaped the course of folklore studies in the United States. Deeply did I feel the deaths of two leading folklorists, William Bascom and Richard Dorson. With their simultaneous passing on September 11, 1981, the present became the past; an era ended. As a student of folklore, I have necessarily been influenced by Richard Dorson. His dedication to the discipline of folklore I do so admire. As a student of William Bascom, I have benefited from his reasoned scholarship and I have appreciated his gentle ways. He remains a force and an inspiration in my work.

The following institutions were crucial for the archival research that I conducted, and I am most grateful to their fine professional staff: the Bancroft Library (University of California, Berkeley), the American Philosophical Society Library, the University of Pennsylvania Folklore and Folklife Archives, and the University of Georgia Library. I would especially like to thank J. Stephen Catlett and Elizabeth Carroll-Horrocks of the American Philosophical Society for their tireless efforts to aid me in my research.

The archival work was supported with a generous grant from Davidson College. I thank especially T. C. Price Zimmermann, Vice-President for Academic Affairs and Dean of the Faculty, and J. Nicholas Burnett, Associate Dean of the Faculty, for their support of my research.

To my family I owe endless thanks. They have each given me a part of themselves which has been a motivational force. My husband, Isaac Jack Lévy, has been patient and endlessly helpful. My daughter, Heather Allyson Elrick, has been, as always, enthusiastic and supportive. My father, Eugene Victor Zumwalt, and my mother, Dorothy Guy Zumwalt, have been, in the course of this work as in my life, my source of strength. It is to my parents that this work is dedicated.

Rosemary Lévy Zumwalt

AMERICAN
FOLKLORE
SCHOLARSHIP

ONE

Discipline and Identity

In 1888, George Lyman Kittredge became a faculty member at Harvard; Francis James Child was working on the *English and Scottish Popular Ballads;* Franz Boas published *The Central Eskimo;* and William Wells Newell succeeded in founding the American Folklore Society in Cambridge, Massachusetts. Perhaps it was a coincidence that these events should occur in the same year. More likely it was the confluence of forces and ideas at work during the 1880s, a dynamic time when new disciplines and organizations were being established. This creative energy carried over into the 1890s. Battles were waged over definitional disputes, disciplinary domains, and organizational boundaries. Strong, colorful personalities matched the challenge and fought with zeal to hold their positions.

A conflict in American folklore scholarship that emerged at this time, and was to continue in future decades, was the split between the literary folklorists and the anthropological folklorists. As a vortex for issues of power and control, territory and knowledge, status and prestige, the schism has had a formative influence on the development of folklore in the United States. To place these concerns in a broader context, they must be linked to the development of academic disciplines and the establishment of professional identity.

Not enjoying the supposed tranquility of the ivory tower, leaders of nascent disciplines have done battle to establish boundaries, to claim territory, and to chart the direction of the undertaking. The battle has been at times an intellectual blood-letting; at other times, a maneuvering of forces. Not for feeble souls of indecisive vision, it has required fortitude, a certain singleness of purpose, and dedication. The founding of disciplines has been intimately bound to the development of professionalism, which requires an increase of specialization, a standardization of training, a focus on research, a thrust toward institutionalization, and, at times, a claim to the legitimizing power of science.

The movement toward professionalism has been coupled with a movement away from amateurism. In place of the gentleman scholar who pursued numerous interests there came the specialist who focused intensively on one field of knowledge. This transition from the amateur to the specialist was highlighted in J. P. Lesley's 1885 presidential retirement address

1

to the American Association for the Advancement of Science. Lesley surveyed his 50 year involvement in science:

> Science was then an early morning stroll with sympathetic friends, uncritical and inexpert, to whom suggestions were as good as gospel truths. Then such a reunion as this tonight was a sort of picnic-party at some picturesque place on the shore of the unknown, hilarious and convivial.
>
> All that has passed way. The sun of science now rides high in heaven, and floods the earth with hot and dusty light. What was once play has turned to serious toil. . . . The few and early risers have become a multitude.
>
> (Daniels 1967, 156)

When an intellectual endeavor was viewed as a hobby, it was not requisite to receive payment. As George Daniels discusses in "The Pure-Science Ideal and Democratic Culture," in the mid-nineteenth century certain distinguished scientists refused government reimbursement for their services: one, because he was already engaged in the study of natural history and viewed it as unethical to receive additional payment; and another, to protest the necessity for entering into a contractual agreement with a government committee, "bargaining like a handiman for intellectual labor."[1] Charles Sanders Peirce decided against a scientific undertaking because "a saven is supposed to be doing that which he most delights to do, and he does it as the impulse of his rational nature directs and simply in order to satisfy his intellectual desires." Peirce concluded that "it would be unreasonable for people to pay a man for simply doing what he liked, and that science was therefore meant for leisure" (Daniels 1967, 1700).[2] However, while the amateurs were willing to work for free, the specialists would be paid. Full-time work had to be accompanied by a dependable, though not necessarily lavish, salary.

Inherent in the shift at the turn of the century from the nonacademic research of the nineteenth century—sponsored as it was by museums, by benefactors, or by the federal government—to the fledgling university departments, was a competition for limited teaching positions, dwindling research funds, and professional recognition. (See also Thoresen 1975a; Daniels 1967; Hinsley 1981.) Also part of this organizational shift was the change in learned societies from regional, isolated groups, to national, specialized groups (Oleson and Voss 1979, vii).

This realignment of power and reorganization of knowledge was definitely tied to the growth of professionalism and the eclipse of the amateur. Yet, in "The Matrix of Specialization," John Higman (1979, 4) stresses the main element was not simply the reorganization of professions, but rather the specialization which so markedly increased in the second half of the nineteenth century. The identity of the academic came from specialized research which was judged by a community of disciplinary peers (Oleson and Voss 1979, xii). In the introduction to *The Organization of Knowledge in Modern America, 1860–1920,* Oleson and Voss represent the change from the local and the amateur to the national and the professional:

In the American order of learning, the displacement of regional societies of "generalists" by these national associations of specialists signaled the coming of age of self-conscious communities of peer groups, intent on securing for themselves and their branch of learning an identity and status that transcended institutional boundaries. (Oleson and Voss 1979, xiv)

In addition to changes in the professional power structure, the latter part of the nineteenth and the first part of the twentieth century exhibit a movement toward scientism, a view that science had the answer for the modern world.[3] As W. J. McGee stated it in 1898:

America has become a nation of science. There is no industry, from agriculture to architecture, that is not shaped by research and its results; there is not one of our fifteen millions of families that does not enjoy the benefits of scientific advancement; there is no law on our statutes, no motive in our conduct that has not been made juster by the straightforward and unselfish habit of thought fostered by scientific achievements. (McGee 1898, 320)

Yet science—defined here as a systematized body of knowledge and the techniques for acquiring it—did not spring full-blown into the nineteenth century. Scientific study had been an important part of the intellectual life of the seventeenth and the eighteenth centuries. It was viewed as one way of extending the knowledge of God's works (Rosenberg 1961, 2). But in the latter part of the nineteenth century and the first part of the twentieth, science became equated with fact, with pure knowledge. If it was scientific, it was true. This equation of science with truth is part of the metaphor of science. As Charles Rosenberg writes in *No Other Gods, On Science and American Social Thought*, "Science has lent American social thought a vocabulary and a supply of images; it has served as a source of metaphor and . . . the similes of science have variously suggested, explained, justified, even helped dictate social categories and values" (Rosenberg 1961, 1). Additionally, science became equated with professionalism. It was associated with dispassionate inquiry, rejection of preconceived notions, a free and open mind. A scientific approach also entailed systematic inquiry and persistent study. Scientific rigor and thoroughness were to be the mark of the professional.

The latter part of the nineteenth and the first part of the twentieth century was a period of growth in science, of the establishment of rational scientific methods of study for numerous disciplines. And it was definitely a time for the social sciences to claim a place in academia. This did not occur without a complex struggle and shifting among the disciplines of social science and the humanities. For the consideration at hand, it was not a simple head-on conflict between those in anthropology and those in literature over the affiliation of folklore studies, but rather a struggle among various disciplines to carve up and claim intellectual domains. (See Miller 1975; Becker 1971; Shils 1972.) Perhaps for the social scientists, this process was facilitated by the lack of unity among those in the humanities. As

Oleson and Voss (1979, xv) note, the humanities were "the oldest subjects in the curriculum, yet the last to develop a sense of identity as a concrete grouping of academic disciplines."[4]

However, this trend toward scientism was not an intellectual one-way street. The end of the nineteenth century was the time when the intellectual framework was right for a focus on science as an answer to modern problems. But this is not to say that other intellectual frameworks were suddenly dropped. A unilinear intellectual theory is not suggested here. Instead, the complexity of the situation must be acknowledged. Within anthropology itself there was continuing discussion about the relationship of the discipline to science and humanities. Kroeber, Radin, Benedict, and Sapir stressed the link with humanities. Boas and Lowie worked within a scientific frame. So the shifting forces of what C. P. Snow (1964) has called the two cultures of science and humanities were not merely external to disciplines but featured in the process of self-definition. Certainly Alfred Louis Kroeber gave voice to this when he remarked, "Being the kind of anthropologist who is 40% natural history in bent and 40% humanities, I know little about 'social science' . . ." (Kroeber Papers, Kroeber to Berelson, 9/16/1956). It is this tension between science and the humanities—more specifically, in the case of this study, between anthropology and literature—that brings forth the dialogue of dissent and sets up the battleground for institutionalization of new disciplines.

It is possible to view the struggle for professional territory and for identity within the frame of the disciplinary matrix. As explained in "Post script—1969," Thomas Kuhn chose the term " 'disciplinary' because it refers to the common possession of the practitioners of a particular discipline [and] 'matrix' because it is composed of ordered elements . . ." (Kuhn 1970b, 182). He lists four components: (1) symbolic generalizations which are not questioned by members of the group, (2) shared commitment to beliefs or models, (3) accepted values which extend to a wider community than do the previous two categories, and (4) exemplars, or "the concrete problem-solutions that students encounter from the start of their scientific education" (1970b, 182, 184, 187).

For the establishment and continuation of such a community, Kuhn posits, it is necessary for "the practitioners of a scientific speciality" to have had "similar educations and professional initiations." They must be exposed to a shared body of technical information. "Usually the boundaries of that standard literature mark the limits of a scientific subject matter, and each community ordinarily has a subject matter of its own." Through similar training and study, these people also pursue "a set of shared goals, including the training of their successors" (Kuhn 1970b, 177). Kuhn designates the markers for community membership as "subject of highest degree, membership in professional societies, and journals read." To isolate even more specialized groups, he includes the "attendance at special conferences . . . the distribution of draft manuscripts or galley proofs prior to publication, and . . . formal and informal communication networks" (Kuhn 1970b, 177–78).

Due to the common body of literature and the shared training, communication is facilitated within the scientific community. However, Kuhn adds, because different scientific communities are concerned with other problems, "professional communication across group lines is sometimes arduous, often results in misunderstanding, and may, if pursued, evoke significant and previously unsuspected disagreement" (Kuhn 1970b, 177).

According to Kuhn's concept of disciplinary matrix, the establishment of intellectual boundaries requires a statement of field. The continuation of the group depends on the socialization to the shared values and commitments, and the passing on of the body of knowledge, whether this be symbolic generalizations and exemplars, or another agreed upon corpus of information. Validation of the group is achieved through its professional societies, conferences, and journals. Indeed, as Kuhn emphasizes, the "recognition of the existence of a uniquely professional group and acceptance of its role as the exclusive arbiter of professional achievement" is so vital that the entire professional identity is linked to it. Kuhn continues:

> The group's members as individuals and by virtue of their shared training and experience, must be seen as the sole possessors of the rules of the game or of some equivalent basis for unequivocal judgments. To doubt that they shared some such basis for evaluations would be to admit the existence of incompatible standards of scientific achievement. (Kuhn 1970a, 168)

What is included as part of the disciplinary matrix also delineates what will be excluded. And the establishment of intellectual territory must be accompanied by its defense from encroachment of others who would also like to stake their claim. Thus, conflicts between professional groups can result from differing interpretations of what comprises the disciplinary matrix.

As Kuhn remarks, when people are striving for the inclusion of a discipline as a science, "great energy is invested, great passion aroused, and the outsider is at a loss to know why" (Kuhn 1970a, 159). Much of the controversy is generated due to a concern for scientific status. And the conflict over definitions—in essense, what is to be included or excluded in the discipline—dissolves "when the groups that now doubt their own status achieve consensus about their past and present accomplishments" (Kuhn 1970a, 159–60).

In the nineteenth century when folklore was established as a subject worthy of investigation, the orientation of American scholars to the study of folklore was greatly influenced by the presence of the American Indian. The collection of American Indian mythology was deemed a proper enterprise for folklorists. (See Dundes 1966a; Newell 1888a.) On the Continent, the study of folklore was defined as the study of the peasant populations of Europe while the study of American Indians or other non-European peoples who were classified as savages or primitives was considered to be the domain of the ethnologists. The differing orientation was critical for the development of American folklore scholarship since it designated the study of native peoples as a suitable subject for folklore as well as for anthropology.

The shared field and divided loyalties lead to definitional disputes between the literary folklorists and the anthropological folklorists. Anthropologists, in carving out their discipline, developed a more restricted definition of folklore than did those in literature, but a more inclusive view of the folk. Folklore was given a specific place within anthropology, that of oral literature. Anthropologists, who traditionally worked in cultures without writing, could not designate folklore as that which is oral since that would include all aspects of the culture. As Voegelin elaborated, orally transmitted prose and verse forms were "myths and tales, jests and anecdotes, dramas and dramatic dialogs, prayers and formulas, speeches, puns, riddles, proverbs, and song and chant texts" (Voegelin 1949–50, 403). Bascom simply designated it verbal art. The folk could be Euro-American, Afro-American, or American Indian (Newell 1888a), though the anthropological folklorist usually studied the latter to the exclusion of the two former groups. The literary definition was more inclusive in subject matter, but more limited as to who comprised the folk. For the literary folklorists, folklore was part of the unlettered tradition within literate European and Euro-American societies. This included verbal art *and* traditional lifeways. As Archer Taylor said,

> It may be traditional tools and physical objects like fences or knots, hot cross buns, or Easter eggs; traditional ornamentation like the Walls of Troy; or traditional symbols like the swastika. It may be traditional procedures like throwing salt over one's shoulder or knocking on wood. It may be traditional beliefs like the notion that elder is good for ailments of the eye. All of these are folklore.
>
> (Taylor 1965, 34)

Francis Lee Utley remarked on the dispute between the literary folklorists and the anthropological folklorists over the definition of folklore. He said, though he had "no quarrel" with Bascom's delineation of folklore for the anthropologist as verbal art, he thought Bascom "through a courteous desire not to favor anthropology over 'humanistic' folklore" acquiesced too quickly to the protests that greeted his definition. "At the time [1955] I told him privately that 'the anthropologist's way of pigeonholing is a satisfactory one,' and added that 'all a definition can do is help us to work better; nature has no fixed categories unless one is a Platonist' " (Utley 1965, 12). However, for the folklorists battling for influence in the discipline, Utley's definitional pigeonholes held keys of power. One could not afford to be either sanguine about content or magnanimous about territory.

A difference between the literary folklorists and the anthropological folklorists was in their choice of folk. For the literary approach, the folk were a part of a marginal society that was dependent on a larger society. As Robert Redfield described it, this was the little tradition within the great tradition. For the anthropological approach, the folk were part of non-Western, small-scale societies. Significantly, the anthropological folklorists merely by the choice of the group to be studied had succeeded in broadening the concept of folk to include a non-European component.

There emerges here a seeming contradiction. For the literary folklorists, the field of study was broad. Folklore could include all aspects of the traditional lifeways of the people. It held promise of an ethnography of the folk. For the anthropological folklorists, folklore was verbal art or oral literature. Thus, one might surmise that the literary folklorists adopted an anthropological approach, and the anthropological folklorists adopted a literary one. To gain a perspective on this, one must anchor the approaches in the disciplinary matrix. The anthropological folklorists centered their work on the concept of culture. Folklore could be only a portion of the culture. The literary folklorists, whose scholarly world was written literature, could open the domain of the folk to unwritten tradition, the lifeways of the people. Where the anthropological folklorists were exclusive in material considered, the literary folklorists were inclusive. However, where the literary folklorists were narrow in their consideration of the folk group, the anthropological folklorists broadened the concept of folk. The contemporary American approach to the study of folklore combines the expansive aspects of both. Thus, from the literary comes the focus on traditional lifeways, and from the anthropological comes the inclusive concept of folk.

The stark division between the literary and the anthropological has diminished since the appearance of the professional folklorist. The first Ph.D. in folklore was awarded to Warren Roberts in 1953 from Indiana University. Presently there are four programs in the United States that grant doctorates in folklore. In 1949, Stith Thompson succeeded in establishing the first doctoral degree program at Indiana University (Dorson 1973b, 193), which operated as an interdepartmental committee with faculty located in departments of anthropology, English, history, Slavic languages and literature, Spanish, and linguistics (Dorson 1963a, 444). As Dorson noted, in 1962, "Indiana University made its first appointment entirely within its folklore programme" to Jerome R. Mintz, who had an Indiana doctorate in folklore (Dorson 1963a, 443). In 1963, the Folklore Institute achieved departmental status (Dorson 1972c, 3; 1973b, 193; Baker 1971). The Department of Folklore and Folklife at the University of Ponnoyl vania, known as the Folklore Program, was empowered to grant a doctoral degree in the academic year of 1962–1963 (Ben-Amos 1983; Dorson 1963a, 442). The Center for Intercultural Studies in Folklore and Oral History at the University of Texas, Austin announced the beginning of its program in 1971. And the Center for the Study of Comparative Folklore and Mythology at the University of California, Los Angeles was authorized to grant the doctorate in folklore in 1980. There are several hundred students pursuing advanced degrees in folklore. And there are numerous professors trained in folklore and teaching still more students across the country. Though there is still a division between the anthropological and the literary in folklore studies, it is no longer the acute division that it once was. It is now more a filigree, a complex pattern of scholarly study, with the underlying historical division overlaid by the new framework of folklore studies.

Folklorists and anthropologists have, in recent years, become aware of the implications of classification for structuring the outcome of research. (See Gossen 1971, 1974; Goodenough 1956.) It has been suggested that the categories used for gathering and analyzing information tell as much about the researcher as about the people studied. (See Rabinow 1977, 1979.) Thus, it is appropriate to examine these two categories, the literary folklorists and the anthropological folklorist. Who uses these terms? And do the terms reflect the categories of the folk—in this case, the folklorists— or of the researcher?

These two categories, that of the anthropological folklorists and the literary folklorists, are recognized by folklorists themselves as an important and significant division in the discipline. McNeil (1980), in "The History of American Folklore Scholarship to 1908," mentioned the rivalry between the literary folklorists and the anthropological folklorists as the most persistent historical theme in the development of the discipline. Susan Dwyer-Shick (1979) traces the effects of this division on the organization of the American Folklore Society. Alan Dundes (1966a), in "The American Concept of Folklore," examines both the literary and anthropological orientations to folklore, and discusses how these have shaped the current state of the discipline. Dan Ben-Amos (1973) has identified the differing centers of activity for the literary and the anthropological folklorists, the former in the universities and the latter in the American Folklore Society. Clearly, the leading scholars in the history of American folkloristics use this classification of the literary folklorists and the anthropological folklorists. It is, as it were, a folk category of classification.

In a letter to Alfred Kroeber, Richard Dorson used a variation of the categories:

> Dear Professor Kroeber:
>   The first volume of Stith Thompson's expanded *Motif-Index of Folk Literature* is now published, and it occurred to me that you might be willing to review it for the Journal of American Folklore, to signalize the partnership of our Society between anthropologists and literary folklorists. It would be fitting for our foremost anthropologist to review the major work of our foremost literary folklorist.
>
>   (Kroeber Papers, Dorson to Kroeber, 5/28/1957)

And finally the emergence of a new identity is emphasized in a letter from Dorson to Archer Taylor: "Dundes goes from Kansas to Berkeley *as a folklorist*, in the anthropology department. It's not even official yet, I under-stand" (Taylor Collection, Dorson to Taylor, 12/10/1962; his emphasis).

In order to distinguish between the anthropological folklorist and the literary folklorist, it is perhaps more correct to refer to the period before the founding of the Ph.D. programs in folklore. A crucial factor, then, in the past division between the two groups had to do with an obvious and immediate distinction, their department of affiliation. Thus, the literary folklorists were usually located in departments of literature, and the an-thropological folklorists in the departments of anthropology. Indeed, this was the case with the literary folklorists who will be discussed in chapter 4. Francis James Child became the first professor of English at Harvard in 1876 (Hyder 1962, 28). George Lyman Kittredge succeeded Child as chair of modern languages in 1894–1895 (Hyder 1962, 41). Stith Thompson, who was to become the first professor of folklore and English in the country, maintained his primary identity as a professor of English. And Archer Taylor went from the German Department at Washington University in St. Louis (1915–1925) to the University of Chicago (1925–1939), and finally to the German Department at the University of California, Berkeley, in 1939, where he taught for eighteen years (Hand 1974, 4–6).

The anthropological folklorists who will be discussed in chapter 5 were often the same people responsible for founding the departments of an-thropology. Franz Boas established anthropology at Columbia University, and trained the other anthropologists who then fanned out across the country to found or to strengthen centers of study. Kroeber established anthropology at the University of California, Berkeley (1901); he was later assisted by another of Boas's students, Robert Lowie who joined the faculty in 1921. Speck went to the University of Pennsylvania initially to help and later to battle with Gordon. Herskovits went to Northwestern (1927). Bene-dict, Reichard, Parsons, and Bunzel worked closely with Boas at Columbia.

A clear exemplification of these two approaches, the literary and the anthropological, can be found in work of Francis James Child and of Franz Boas. Child spent much of his scholarly life collecting and annotating ballad texts. His years of work resulted in *The English and Scottish Popular Ballads* (1882–1898), a five volume work. Child examined the texts of *all* the ballads he was able to collect, and thoroughly annotated them. His was the literary approach, a concern with ballad as popular poetry. Ballads were best captured from time past, in manuscript texts, and not from the people themselves. As he said, "No Scottish ballads are superior in kind to those recited in the last century by Mrs. Brown of Falkland" (Child [1882] 1962, vii). For Child and for the literary folklorists, this was a legitimate enter-prise, to study folklore as a literary form *apart* from the people and their culture. A perusal of the table of contents of the first volume will illustrate this. It is a numbered listing of the ballads considered, fifty-three in all. For each of the ballads, Child endeavored to give every available version. Thus, for Lord Randal, there were fifteen versions printed. Child advised the reader, "To forestall a misunderstanding which has often occurred, I beg to say that every traditional version of a popular ballad is desired, no matter how many texts of the same may have been printed already" (Child [1882] 1962, ix).

In 1883–1884, Boas conducted the fieldwork which resulted in *The Central Eskimo*. To introduce his work, Boas said, "The following account of the Central Eskimos contains chiefly the results of the author's own observations and collections made during a journey to Cumberland Sound and Davis Strait" (Boas 1888, 409). Boas attempted to describe the *whole* life of the Eskimos of Baffinland. He described the "distribution of the tribes," the geographical conditions, the "trade between tribes," hunting and fishing, the material culture. Included in this description was a consideration of social and religious life, tales and traditions, science and arts. Boas's anthropological approach to folklore necessitated a consideration of the culture and the people.

The key distinction, then, between Child's approach to folklore and Boas's lay in their disciplinary bent. For Child, folklore was studied as the remnants of the unlettered portion of the European literary tradition. For Boas, folklore existed as a part of the culture and a reflection of the culture. This, in essence, was the line of division between the literary folklorists and the anthropological folklorists.

For both the literary folklorists and the anthropological folklorists the source of major intellectual influence can be traced to seminal figures and to centers of academe. Using the metaphor of diffusion theory, one can visualize the spread of the anthropological folklorists and of the literary folklorists like waves moving out from a center point. For the literary folklorists, the center of distribution was Harvard; for the anthropological folklorists, it was Columbia. But like diffusion theory, this is a metaphor of movement and not a representation of fact. One should not be surprised by irregularities in the pattern. When, for instance, a major literary folklorist like MacEdward Leach came to folklore through his study at the University of Illinois, the Johns Hopkins University, and the University of Pennsylvania, one must recognize that there were centers of influence for literary folklorists other than Harvard. The pattern is there, but the mistake would be in expecting it always to shape the course of folklore studies.

Thus, in distinguishing between the literary folklorists and the anthropological folklorists, the primary criterion is the department of affiliation. And from this—be it in literature or in anthropology—the scholar's identity lies. He/she has received training in a certain orientation to the material. For the literary folklorists, obviously the orientation is toward literary works and the unwritten tradition from which they derived. The focus has also been on the study of literary types or genres. Child and Kittredge studied the ballad; Thompson, the folktale; Taylor, the riddle and the proverb. In anthropology, the orientation of study was directed toward cultures without writing, and the emphasis was on fieldwork. Boas, in his own work and in training his students, stressed *collection* of every aspect of the life of the people. And *part* of the material collected was folklore. The emphasis for anthropological folklorists, then, was on folklore as part of the cultural whole, as a reflection of a way of life.

To simplify, it could be said that the literary folklorists looked at literary *forms* for folklore; and that the anthropological folklorists looked at the *life* of the people and saw folklore as part of it. In the beginning, there were the seeds of the present controversy: the literary folklorists were concerned with text; the anthropological folklorists, with context. This, like the metaphor of intellectual diffusion, is a condensation of a complexity. Still the threads of the current theoretical controversies are woven into the intellectual past. And when tugged a bit, these threads do show the tensions of time.

It could be said that a sense of history emerges from an identity, and that history is written only when there is a sense of the past. Thus, a discipline without a written history is a thing of new creation. American folklore, until the last decade and a half, has been such a discipline. Richard Reuss remarks on this, "Curiously, it has taken American folklorists a full three generations before any ground swell of interest in our professional folklore study antecedents has emerged" (Reuss 1973, 3).

In the afterword to the *Journal of the Folklore Institute* devoted to "American Folklore Historiography," Richard Dorson discussed a session on the methods and aims of the history of folkloristics: "I presented remarks on the writing of my history of *The British Folklorists,* after which Richard Reuss asked me why I, as an American folklorist, had deserted my own country to pursue a transatlantic trail" (Dorson 1973a, 125). His response to Reuss's question certainly conveyed his enthusiasm for his British research:

> The answer is that the English folklorists, whose works I stumbled on accidentally in the summer of 1948 on a chance visit to the Folklore Society library in London, immediately fired my imagination by the verve, the excitement, the intellectual rigor, the scope and sweep of their vast output of books, essays reviews, and editions. . . . Nothing comparable to the productions of Lang, Gomme, Hartland, Clodd, and Nutt and their associates and predecessors, exists in American folklore both in terms of their theoretical emphasis and of their intellectual interrelationship. The history of American folklore discloses no books of theory, no continuity, no consensus, no high order of polemics such as distinguished the British nineteenth-century folklorists, for there was not enough of a common platform to lead to disagreement.
>
> (Dorson 1973a, 125–26)

Dorson's evaluation of the history of American folklore scholarship illustrates a view that was prevalent for many years—that American folklorists should look to Europe for their models, be it in method, theory, or history. Further, his appraisal also brings to the fore a possible explanation for the paucity of research in this area. If American folklore scholarship is considered to lack continuity, theory, and vitality, why, indeed, should anyone attempt to write its history?

Obviously, there were those who disagreed with Dorson on this point. Reuss raised the issue of Dorson's neglect of his own folklore history. And Dan Ben-Amos suggested that there was a trend in American folklore scholarship. Dorson acknowledged this: "Yet, as Dan Ben-Amos whispered to me during the panel, there is a history of discontinuity as well as of continuity" (Dorson 1973a, 126). He continued:

> If no firm consecutive narrative can be constructed from the history of our subject in this country, episodic chapters, passing currents, and arresting personalities command our interest, and we live in the midst of a great upsurge of enthusiasm and achievement in our field. Just in my own lifetime I have witnessed, and participated in, the rise of the American Folklore Society from the doldrums of the 1940's when it seemed on the verge of dissolution to its present spectacular successes of four-day independent conferences.

> (Dorson 1973a, 126).

He remarked on the growth of the Folklore Institute at Indiana University, from a sparse half dozen students to "one hundred and fifty higher degree candidates in the past fifteen years" and on the development of a new undergraduate folklore major in 1970, at a time when all other new programs were being curtailed.

The contemporary situation in American folklore scholarship is one of vibrance and life. With the 1988 Centennial of the American Folklore Society, the discipline has gained a sense of its intellectual history and a feeling of independence as a community of scholars. This is certainly reflected in the recent research on the history of American folklore scholarship, and most specifically in the dissertations completed in the last decade.[5] As Dan Ben-Amos says, "If nobody else does so, at least students of folklore claim an intellectual and scholarly tradition for their discipline that sanctions its scientific identity and confirms its position in academe" (Ben-Amos 1973, 113–14).

But still with this vibrance, with this growth, and with this recognition of tradition, there remain the scars of the old division. There is a sensitivity— an almost defensive stance—on the part of some American folklorists. And this sensitivity or defensive posture will come forth when there is a perceived challenge to the legitimacy of folklore studies, to the respectability of the enterprise. Folklore is a young discipline, protective of its territory and defensive of its identity.

Now, after this perusal of the development of professions, the boundaries of the disciplinary matrix, and the categories of the literary and the anthropological folklorists, the past—when the field of folklore was carved out as an intellectual domain—beckons.

TWO

American Folklore Studies

Field and Scope

In the first volume of the *Journal of American Folklore*, the April to June issue of 1888, William Wells Newell briefly explained the founding of the American Folklore Society: "A proposal to establish a Folk-Lore Society in America was made in the form of a circular letter, dated at Cambridge, Mass., May 5, 1887, and subscribed with seventeen names." A second letter was sent in October with 104 signatures from supporters residing throughout the United States and Canada: "the number of signers having reached the necessary number, the American Folk-Lore Society was organized at Cambridge, January 4, 1888" (Newell 1888a, 3).

Crucial to the society, both in the initial organization and the direction in the first two decades, was the work of William Wells Newell (1839–1907). At the founding of the American Folklore Society, Newell was forty-nine years old and of independent means. Like other wealthy and well-educated men of his time, he chose the enterprise of science as his avocation.[1] This selfless dedication won praise from Boas years later: "He always seemed to me in a way like a representative of a time of greater devotion to ideals and a greater unselfishness than we are accustomed to find at the present time" (Boas Papers, Boas to Dixon, 2/1/1907). Newell threw himself whole-heartedly into securing what he referred to as "the scientific future of the Journal" (Boas Papers, Newell to Boas, 9/13/1888). His formal education had not prepared him for this field. After graduating second in his class at Harvard University in 1859, Newell entered Harvard Divinity School where he took his degree in 1863. He worked for a short time as Unitarian minister in Germantown, Pennsylvania, then as a tutor in philosophy at Harvard (1868–1870) (Robinson 1907, 59). Subsequently he opened a private school in New York, where he began his collection of children's games, which resulted in *Games and Songs of American Children* (Newell 1883; see Bell 1973, 7). In the early 1880s, Newell retired from teaching, toured Europe, and then settled in Cambridge to "the life of private scholarship" (Bell 1973, 7).

Newell was in a position to shape and direct the early development of the American Folklore Society. It was he who suggested the location for the first meeting of the society, who named the prospective editors, and who guided the plans for the journal. His tone of leadership and diplomacy are conveyed in his letters. On March 15, 1888, Newell wrote to Boas, "I agree heartily to your proposal in regard to division of the field, and empower you," then choosing a more egalitarian phrase, scratched out "empower you," and continued, "think you had better arrange with Mr. Dorsey for dividing the Indian tribes in any way you see fit" (Boas Papers, Newell to Boas, 3/15/1888). In planning the first meeting, Newell wrote to Boas, "I hope that you will go to Phila., at any cost of trouble. It is very desirable that the Journal should be represented by some editor other than myself. Being the first meeting, it is important to get things right" (Boas Papers, Newell to Boas, 11/22/1889). And in the same letter, he noted that Brinton and Matthews should be added to the editorial committee. "If then the Committee wish me to be general Editor, I am willing to be such; and I have done most of the work, and must take the responsibility, perhaps my name might appear separate as General Editor." Such was the case. Newell served as editor of the journal from 1888 to 1900, and as editor of the American Folklore Society memoir series from 1894 to 1906 (Robinson 1907, 59).

The first volume of the *Journal of American Folklore* opened with a statement by Newell, "On the Field and Work of a Journal of American Folk-Lore." Newell saw the "principal object" of the American Folklore Society linked to the publication of "a Journal, of a scientific character," which would provide:

1. For the collection of the fast-vanishing remains of Folk-Lore in America, namely:
    a. Relics of Old English Folk-Lore (ballads, tales, superstitions, dialect, etc.).
    b. Lore of Negroes in the Southern States of the Union.
    c. Lore of the Indian Tribes of North America (myths, tales, etc.).
    d. Lore of French Canada, Mexico, etc.
2. For the study of the general subject, and publication of the results of special studies in this department.

(Newell 1888a, 3)

Newell followed this outline of the orientation of the society with a discussion of each point. He stated his opinions clearly about what constituted a proper study of folklore. Newell's emphasis was primarily on collection and preservation of the lore which he viewed as fast-vanishing due to the forces of "uniformity of the modern world" (Newell 1888a, 4). Enough remained of old English lore to warrant collection, but the time for the richest harvest had passed. As for ballads, the collector should look to the Scottish and Irish ballad singers, though again the prime time for collecting had "almost passed in the 17th century." Prospects were better for nursery tales: "Fairy tales, beast fables, jests, by scores, were on the lips of mothers and nurses" (Newell 1888a, 4). And superstitious beliefs "which supply material to the psychologist" were abundant as were the minor elements of folklore. Newell included among the minor elements children's games, proverbs, riddles, "racy sayings," and peculiar expressions. And finally, he says, the folklorists should study the local dialects which are characteristic of "the older and more retired towns." The information thus gleaned could be useful to the historians of American life (Newell 1888a, 5). It is clear from Newell's discussion of what *remained* to be collected that he shared the nineteenth century attitude toward folklore as a survival from a previous age, something which was in the process of passing away in the modern world.

The second division for collection in Newell's outline was black folklore. "It is but within a few years that attention has been called to the existence among (American Negroes) of a great number of tales relating to animals. . . . The origin of these stories, many of which are common to a great part of the world, has not been determined" (Newell 1888a, 5). He also directed attention to the music, songs, and superstitions of the Afro-American.

Newell stressed the collection of the "traditions of the Indian tribes." This focus of study, he said, "will be generally regarded as the most promising and important part of the work to be accomplished" because these traditions were still part of "whole nations" (Newell 1888a, 5). This was living lore rather than "the relics of a crop once plentiful, but, unhappily, allowed to perish ungarnered." He was prescient in recognizing the scope of the studies to come: "Systems of myth, rituals, feasts, sacred customs, games, songs, tales, exist in such profusion that volumes would be required to contain the lore of each separate tribe" (Newell 1888a, 5).

The living lore of the American Indians would soon become an "essential part of history." Newell saw this life passing away: "For the sake of the Indians themselves, it is necessary that they should be allowed opportunities for civilization." And for the future, it was imperative that "a complete history should remain of what they have been" since their "wonderful life" would soon be no more, and their uniqueness would be absorbed by the modern world (Newell 1888a, 6).

In the initial planning for the first volume of the journal, Newell wrote to Boas about his idea for a "record of American Folk-Lore," with a parenthetical note that this would be "for Native Races only," and asked him "If such a heading . . . were introduced, would you take charge of it, and provide yourself with assistants as you may see fit?" (Boas Papers, 3/16/1888). In another letter, Newell wrote Boas, "I . . . think you had better arrange with Mr. Dorsey for dividing the Indian tribes . . . or delegate any part of the work to any one" (Boas Papers, 3/15/1888).

Newell's inclusion of the American Indians and their "living lore" in the initial statement "On the Field and Work of a Journal of American Folk-Lore" would require clarification in subsequent publications (Newell 1888b, 79–82; 1890). It would also provide the nexus for some disagreement about the American concept of folklore (Bell 1973; Dundes 1966a). Clearly the inclusion of the American Indian in folklore studies was an innovation of an American scholar. It showed Newell's creative approach to folklore studies. It set American folklore scholarship apart from European folklore scholarship, since in the European framework, the American Indian as "savage" would be studied by the ethnologist and not by the folklorist.

In addition to collecting, the second major purpose for the journal was to encourage "the study of the general subject." For Newell, this entailed the connection between folklore of the United States and that of other continents. The folklore of the British in America "can neither be understood nor collected without reference" to England. And English folklore, in turn, is part of a wider complex. This second major focus for the journal, the study of the general subject, was well within the framework of Newell's first focus, the collection of folklore in America. He was proposing to study the collection of folklore from other countries as a means of augmenting our understanding of American folklore. He was not proposing a general study of folkloristics. This distinction is important since Newell's "study of the general subject" would have different connotations for contemporary folklorists.

The field and scope of American folklore studies is pursued further in an anonymous contribution to "Notes and Queries," in volume 1 of the *Journal of American Folklore*. The author, known to be Newell, refers to the creation of the term folklore by Ambrose Merton in 1846 and the foundation of the English Folklore Society in 1878.[2] This was founded for "the preservation and publication" of British and foreign folklore (Newell 1888b, 79). The author notes, "The rules of this society have served as the model of those adopted by the American Folk-Lore Society, which must, therefore, in an especial sense, regard the British organization as its parent" (Newell 1888b, 79–80).

Dundes observes that this explicit statement of parentage in "Notes and Queries," this line of institutional kinship, as it were, from the English Folklore Society to the American Folklore Society marked American folklorists as "imitators rather than innovators" (Dundes 1966a, 238). Newell's opening statement "On the Field and Work of a Journal of American Folk-Lore" was followed by Thomas F. Crane's "The Diffusion of Popular Tales." Crane's model for the study of folktales was the European comparative method and he suggested that this be applied to American narratives (Crane 1888, 8–55).

This identification with Europe was carried further in "Notes and Queries" when the author reviewed the folklore societies and journals that existed on the continent. He included the French Société des Traditions Populaires, which published a monthly journal *Revue des traditions populaires*, and *Mélusine*, a monthly journal edited by Gaidoz and Rolland. Additionally, he discussed the Italian *Archivio per lo Studio delle Tradizioni Popolari*, edited by Pitré and Salamone-Marino and published four times a

year, as well as the Hungarian *Ethnologische Mittheilungen aus Ungarn,*
edited by Anton Hermann.

The author included the review of folklore journals and societies to stress
the point of a common bond between them. As Newell said in a letter to
Boas on this topic, "I think it will be necessary to make some brief record of
European research: both for our readers, and on account of the comity [*sic*]
of exchange, since the chief of these journals will notice us" (Boas Papers,
3/15/88). Though numerous subjects were included in the approaches to
folklore, the shared element was the focus on oral tradition. And this
verbal aspect distinguished folklore studies from literary studies. "Lore
must be understood as the complement of literature"; it is knowledge that
is transmitted verbally without the use of writing (Newell 1888b, 80).[3]

While the initial statements made by Newell in "Notes and Queries"
emphasized the link with European folklore studies, the following statement marked the innovative stance of American folklorists. Since lore
belongs to "a whole people" it is termed *folk* and, "it does not appear either
desirable or possible, in dealing with a primitive people, to include a part
and exclude another part of its traditions. In dealing, therefore, with the
Indian tribes of America, it is the intention of this journal to include the
entirety of their oral traditions" (Newell 1888b, 80–81).

Thus, the first volume of the *Journal of American Folklore* sets out with a
more inclusive concept of folklore than the European concept of the same
era. Whereas, according to European definition, folklore includes the study
of peasant populations and excludes primitive people, following the points
made in Newell's opening statement and in "Notes and Queries," American folklore would include the study of American Indian oral tradition in
its entirety. There would be no exclusion of either the Indian or of mythology as outside the scope of study.

Apparently this inclusive approach to the study of folklore brought forth
some debate. In volume 1, number 2 of the *Journal of American Folklore,*
Newell clarified his position:

> In the first number of this journal it was pointed out that it was the intention of
> the editors to include the mythology of the native races in the scope of their
> labors, an inclusion obviously wise and necessary. But, in making this state-
> ment, it was by no means intended to discuss the relation of the terms "folk-
> lore" and "mythology."
>
> (Newell 1888c, 163)

The author added that opinions differed as to whether or not these terms
could be differentiated and applied to separate groups of people. However,
for the purposes of the journal, mythology would refer to "the living
system of tales and beliefs which, in primitive peoples, serves to explain
existence"; and folklore would refer to the body of unwritten traditions of
civilized countries. "Had it not been out of regard to brevity, this publica-

tion might have been called the 'Journal of American Folk-Lore and My-thology' " (Newell 1888c, 163).

On March 24, 1890, in a paper delivered before the New York Academy of Sciences, Newell returned to his initial position and defined folklore as belonging to both folk culture and primitive culture. As he explained it, "It was soon evident that the oral traditions of Europe could not be treated by themselves without consideration of oral traditions in other parts of the globe" (Newell 1890, 134). It was discovered that the folklore of the European immigrants in the United States and the folklore of the "families of the purest English stock" shared aspects with "practices and beliefs . . . among savage tribes" (Newell 1890, 135).

Newell noted the controversy that arose over the inclusion of American Indian material within the domain of folklore studies: "There was some protest against these, inasmuch as the name *folk* belongs properly to races in which isolated tribes have been amalgamated into something resembling a nation. But this difficulty could not be allowed to prevent a convenient inclusion" (Newell 1890, 135).

Newell discussed the controversy with scholarly removal: "it was soon evident" that the customs and superstitions of the American Indian would be considered as folklore; and "there was some protest against this" inclusion. In fact, he was at the center of the dispute. It was Newell's initial concept of folklore presented in the first editorial statement of the *Journal of American Folklore* and in the first "Notes and Queries" that brought on the protests alluded to in the second volume of the journal. And in this second volume, Newell attempted to quell the storm and to quiet those of traditional European folklore persuasion: the peasants have folklore, the Indians have mythology.

But this was not Newell's conviction. And so in the 1890 address to the New York Academy of Sciences, he reaffirmed his initial position. Indeed, he said, folklore "came to be used, first, in a definite sense, as including tales, beliefs, and practices now retained among the unlettered peasantry of Europe; secondly, with a wider connotation, as embracing traditionary tales, customs, and usages of uncivilized races" (Newell 1890, 135).

Newell linked the second or "Wider connotation" of folklore with folklore's "broader meaning." And he saw this broader meaning as tying folklore to anthropology. To be sure, "the subject has two sides, the aesthetic or literary aspect, and the scientific aspect" but Newell's statement is more forceful on the latter connection: "In its broader meaning, therefore, folk-lore is a part of anthropology and ethnography, embracing the mental side of primitive life, with especial reference to the narratives in which beliefs and habits are related or accounted for" (Newell 1890, 135).

Apparently Newell was under some constraint to continue at least a topical division between folklore and mythology in the *Journal of American Folklore*. On October 15, 1890 (Boas Papers), Newell wrote to Boas, "The next number of the Journal is mainly in type," and he continued with a listing of suggested headings:

1. General—discussions on folk-lore, mythology, etc.
2. Folk-literature—tales, ballads, etc.
3. Superstitions, customs, etc.
4. Travels, ethnological material therewith connected
5. Mythology
6. Primitive religions.

Even though this division between folklore and mythology was continued in the journal, Newell had made his position clear concerning folklore and the study of folklore. And if one reads his statements carefully, there really should not be much to dispute. Yet, dispute there is. In "William Wells Newell and the Foundation of American Folklore Scholarship," Michael J. Bell takes issue with Alan Dundes's position as stated in "The American Concept of Folklore." Bell and Dundes refer to Newell's articles in the *Journal of American Folklore* and "The Study of Folklore" in the *Transactions of the New York Academy of Sciences*, the same articles discussed here.

Dundes stressed Newell's division of the field into folklore and mythology. And Dundes tied this to the European evolutionary framework and the European concept of folklore: "Thus by definition the American Indian, since he was not 'civilized' but 'savage,' in the then popular tripartite unilinear evolutionary scheme of savagery, barbarism, and civilization, could not have folklore" (Dundes 1966a, 228). Dundes notes that Newell solved this problem by using the designation "mythology" for American Indian materials. It was in 1890, Dundes adds, that Newell realized "the distinction was a false one" and adopted a more inclusive attitude toward folklore (Dundes 1966a, 228–29).

It should be noted that Dundes's review of Newell's concept of American folklore is somewhat condensed. As discussed above, Newell published three separate statements in 1888 about the scope and the field of folkore. In his first and his second statement, Newell stressed the need for collecting American Indian material (Newell 1888a; 1888b). It was in the third, "Folklore and Mythology," that Newell felt compelled to clarify his position and to distinguish between the primitive folk and the savage Indian. Thus Newell's inclusive attitude toward American folklore was present in his first statement in 1888, when he suggested that the "lore of the Indian tribes of North America (myths, tales, etc.)" be collected (Newell 1888a, 3). It was not in 1890, as Dundes states, that Newell realized the distinction between folklore and mythology was a false one. Rather it was in 1890 that Newell reasserted his initial position, the broad inclusive approach to American folklore.

Michael Bell, in his interpretation of Newell's concept of American folklore, stresses the continuity in Newell's thought. He sees no difference in intent between Newell's first and second statement about folklore, and the third statement where Newell differentiates between folklore and mythology. Referring to the statements in the first issue of the *Journal of American Folklore* (wherein Newell includes American Indian material in the study of folklore) and the statement in the second number of volume 1 (wherein Newell classifies American Indian material as mythology) Bell says,

> The variance between these two conceptualizations is, however, less real than it appears at first glance. The second definition may rightly be seen as a lemma that qualified but does not deny the validity of the first; rather than, as some scholars have felt, Dundes in particular, as a contradiction brought about by the presence of the Indian in America.

> (Bell 1973, 12)

Now, as Newell himself noted, his statement made in "Folklore and Mythology" was intended to quiet the debate that arose after his comments in the first issue of the *Journal of American Folklore*. It can be surmised from his 1890 address to the New York Academy of Sciences that Newell, in spite of the controversy, had consciously and publicly decided to use a "convenient inclusion" and discuss the folklore of savage people (Newell 1890, 135).

In stressing the continuity in his position, and in not adhering carefully to Newell's words, Bell has diluted Newell's major contribution to the concept of American folklore—that in spite of the debate which raged, Newell insisted on including the American Indian in folklore studies. This is a truly significant contribution and marks Newell as an innovative scholar.

To contemporary thought, it seems patently obvious: of course the American Indian has folklore. But at the end of the nineteenth century, when the statement was still on the wind that the only good Indian was a dead Indian, and the evolutionary framework still equated the Indian with the savage, and the peasant with the barbarian, Newell was making a revolutionary break. He was striking a new path for American folklore scholarship. Just as the presence of the American Indian distinguished the Americas from Europe, so the study of American Indian folklore distinguished American folklore scholarship from European folklore scholarship.

In "The American Concept of Folklore," Dundes inserted the following comment in parenthesis: "It might be noted in passing that the American folklorist's work with American Indian folklore has had important influences upon the direction of American folklore theory" (Dundes 1966a, 228). This point deserves more than parenthetical treatment. It is this unique approach to folklore, to the study of American Indian material, that sets American folklore studies apart from European studies. And it is this unique approach that shapes much of the history of the discipline of folklore in the United States.

Bell explains that Newell of necessity used the term mythology "because the term folklore did not suffice to describe a living system, not because the living system was not also folklore." Bell maintains that it was not a matter of the evolutionary framework—not a classification of "civilized man and savage Indian"—but rather the presence of "a living active tradition that exists without written record, and a popular tradition that coexists with a written tradition" (Bell 1973, 12). In this passage, Bell has taken the definitional dispute about folklore and mythology, savage and civilized, out of the nineteenth century intellectual milieu and placed it in the latter half of the twentieth century. Thus he focuses on the division between the non-literate and the literate: the non-literate people had mythology, the literate had folklore. At issue, according to his argument, is not the savage nature of the Indian and the civilized aspect of the folk.

Yet it was precisely the nineteenth-century evolutionary framework that shaped and infused the orientation to folklore. To quote a Scotsman who said it succinctly, "The student of folklore is thus led to examine the usages, myths, and ideas of savages, which are still retained, in rude enough shape, by the European peasantry" (Lang 1893, 11). Andrew Lang penned this in 1893 in *Custom and Myth,* a book he dedicated to E. B. Tylor.

Michael Bell has dismantled the nineteenth-century evolutionary ladder of savagery to barbarism to civilization, and substituted the twentieth-century two-step evolutionary framework from the non-literate to the literate. He has taken the definitional dispute out of the theoretical orientation of the time, and without examining the evolutionary mind-set, he has placed the definitional dispute in the same theoretical framework, masquerading in different terms. He states that "folklore did not suffice to describe a living system" and yet he fails to tie this in with the orientation toward folklore. Folklore could not be associated with a living system of belief *precisely because* folklore was viewed as dead or dying in the cultural evolutionary scheme. Mythology in this framework preceded folklore; it was the whole garment, while folklore was only the remnant.

THREE

The Schism in Folklore

The conflict between the anthropological folklorists and the literary folklorists came to the fore in the 1890s. At issue was the International Folk-Lore Congress, planned and organized by Fletcher S. Bassett, to be held in the Department of Literature of the 1893 World's Fair Auxiliary of the Columbian Exposition (McNeil 1980, 452; Congresses at the Columbian Exposition 1892, 247–48). The objections raised by William Wells Newell and Franz Boas stated explicitly that the scientific credibility of folklore studies would be threatened by this association with literature. This dispute between Bassett, as representative of the Chicago Folk-Lore Society, and Boas and Newell, as representatives of the American Folklore Society, was stilled in 1893. Yet the voices of dissension, those of the literary folklorists and the anthropological folklorists, resounded throughout the twentieth century. The two clashed on many fronts—within the American Folklore Society, in theoretical debates, and over the affiliation of folklore studies, be it with anthropology, with literature, or as an independent discipline. Here the concern is with the latter—the affiliation of folklore studies—and how Bassett, and Newell and Boas struggled to situate folklore studies in what they viewed to be the correct intellectual domain.

The Chicago Folklore Society was established, under the guidance of Fletcher S. Bassett (1847–1893), a retired naval officer, in December 1891, "for the purpose of collecting, preserving, studying and publishing traditional literature" (Bassett 1973, 5; see also Dorson 1973c, 182–84; McNeil 1985). While literary in their approach, the society represented their goals symbolically through the seal of *Akaninili*, the meal sprinkler of the Navajo Indians who was sent out as courier during the ceremonies of the Mountain Chant (Vance 1893, 594; Bassett 1973, 6). The motto of the society encircled this figure, "Whence these legends and traditions?"

The society emphasized gathering folklore, specifically the folklore "west of the Alleghenies." The Chicago Folklore Society was to provide a forum for regional folklore research (McNeil 1980, 445). *The Folk-Lorist*, journal of the Chicago Folk-Lore Society, did not, however, reflect this regional orientation. Articles were included that covered a wide range, both geographically and topically, such as Mrs. M. French Sheldon's "African Folk-Lore," Martha F. Seselberg's "Amazonian Beliefs, Traditions and Superstitions," Rev. W. E. Griffis's "Japan, Tar Baby," and Helen M. Wheeler's "Penobscot

Idea of the Origin of Maize." Regional folklore was limited to Wheeler's and Bassett's article entitled "Illinois Folk-Lore." Had the Chicago Folk-Lore Society and *The Folk-Lorist* endured longer (it lasted from 1892 until 1893), it is possible that the regional emphasis would have become apparent.

In his work with both the Chicago Folk-Lore Society and the International Folk-Lore Congress, Bassett was attempting to counter the sway of the anthropological folklorists and to lay the foundation for an independent discipline of folklore (McNeil 1980, 445; 1985, 7; Bassett 1898, 18; 1973, 5). Bassett had full hopes "that colleges and universities, which foster other branches of Science and literature," would follow the example set in Helsingfors, where Kaarle Krohn was professor of folklore.

Bassett saw great potential in the study of folklore. According to him, it had the power of correcting and organizing the differing approaches to the study of man. As he stated, "Into this chaos of widely-differing conclusions about the habits of action, thought, and feelings of man, came the new science Folk-Lore, to correct by the data of experimental comparison, these erroneous ideas" (Bassett 1898, 18). Though Bassett did not explain what comprised "the data of experimental comparison," in his work, *Sea Phantoms: Or Legends and Superstitions of Sea and of Sailors* (1892b), the comparative element was present in the collection of legends and superstitions concerning the sea from literary works, diaries and ship's logs, and from customs recorded about people "in all lands and at all times."

Bassett eschewed adherence to a single theoretical orientation. As he said, "In attempting to solve the many problems presented in the various parts of [*Sea Phantoms*], I have endeavored to avoid a bias toward any theories" (Bassett 1892b, 6). The maritime superstitions were "the results of widely differing causes," and thus no single explanation would suffice. Though Bassett acknowledged that "most myths of antiquity originated from speculations about natural phenomena," still there were other influences on modern superstitions that needed recognition. The reference to the origin of myths and superstitions from the forces of nature was an acknowledgment of the nature allegorical approach, a popular orientation to the study of folklore in the nineteenth century.[1] Bassett was also restrained in reference to the cultural evolutionary approach. "Folk-Lore," he said, "is not merely a study of the survival of decay." Rather than using a single theory, or expecting to find a single truth, Bassett saw in folklore "the demonstrator of the possible and probable in history, the repository of historical truths otherwise lost, the preserver of the literature of the people and the touchstone of many of the sciences" (Bassett 1898, 18 19). In other words, for Bassett, folklore preserved the past, not just as a remnant or a survival, but as a body of history and of literature.

Agreeing with Sir Laurence Gomme, Bassett viewed folklore as useful to many disciplines, to the study of geology, botany, literature, history, and mythology (Bassett (1898, 18). But this very interdisciplinary element posed a threat to folklore. As Bassett said, there were "those zealous scholars who claim that Folk-Lore is but a part of some other science," that it forms "only a proper dependency of some other kingdom of thought" (Bassett 1898, 21). Folklore might draw from other fields, Bassett cautioned, but it was unique since "it differs from them all" (Bassett 1898, 22). He quoted "one of the greatest authorities," whom he unfortunately did not name, as advocating "a Folk-Lore Section of the British Association; 'I think the time has come for this. Anthropology has long since been recognized there; Folk-Lore should also, now be recognized, and independently.'" Bassett envisioned folklore as independent of, and intermediate between, literature and science: "As literature itself is a science correllated [sic] to others, Folk-Lore is at once a part of literature and of science, but ought to be preserved apart from any other study, and not merged into or made a portion of any other science" (Bassett 1898, 22).

Encompassing in his embrace, Bassett invited all who were interested in folklore to join the Chicago Folk-Lore Society. As Wayland Hand remarked, "Every level of Chicago life was represented in the membership: industrial and business, intellectual and religious, military and naval, social and political, literary and art life" (Hand 1943, 168). All were made welcome, and this included the amateur.

The conflict between the Chicago Folk-Lore Society and the American Folklore Society emerged in 1892. Bassett laid plans for the International Folk-Lore Congress to be held as part of the World's Fair Auxiliary of the Columbian Exposition. First Bassett prepared a "Preliminary Address of the Committee on a Folk-Lore Congress," and sent it to all people active in folklore studies (Bassett 1892a, 249–50). Appeals were made to folklore societies, with advice that they appoint "Committees of Cooperation." He also invited the participation of organizations sharing an interest in folklore: "Oriental and Linguistic Societies, Ethnographical and Anthropological Societies, Indian, Egyptian, and Sinologue Societies, and the Gypsy Society." As planned by Bassett, the Folklore Congress was to cover four main divisions: (1) myths and traditional beliefs, (2) oral literature and folk music, (3) customs, institutions, and ritual, and (4) artistic, emblematic, and economic folklore. For each of these divisions, Bassett listed possible topics that might be addressed. But he saw this as a guide, as merely suggestions for papers. As he wrote, "The Committee will welcome suggestions in this matter, while believing that the arrangement proposed may be satisfactory in the main" (Bassett 1892a, 250).

Fletcher Bassett sent his letter of invitation to the American Folklore Society. The editors of the *Journal of American Folklore* printed the invitation but deleted the accompanying list of the Advisory Council, which included the following members: Charles C. Baldwin, Franz Boas, Henry Carrington Bolton, Daniel G. Brinton, Thomas F. Crane, Stewart Culin, James Denas, J. Owen Dorsey, Alice Cunningham Fletcher, J. Walter Fewkes, Alcee Fortier, Horatio Hale, Charles Godfrey Leland, and Otis T. Mason (Officers of the American Folk-Lore Society 1892, 352). As they remarked,

In this list are mentioned several present and past officers of the American Folk-Lore Society; but as the names of these officers have been added without their consent or authority, and as they have not expressed approval of the plan of the Congress, it must not be supposed that the presence of their names on the roll commits them to any responsibility.

(Conclusion 1892, 252)

The Council of the American Folklore Society, while "returning thanks for the invitation, deemed it inexpedient officially to cooperate" in Bassett's Folk-Lore Congress. The reason was stated explicitly: "The Congress is classed among the literary congresses. . . . The American Folk-Lore Society has always considered folk-lore to belong to anthropological science" (Congresses at the Columbian Exposition 1892, 248).

The American Folklore Society resolved to recommend to the World's Fair Congress Auxiliary that a section on folklore be included in the Congress of Anthropology (Congresses 1892, 248). Clearly this was a reaction to Fletcher Bassett's International Folk-Lore Congress, located as it was in the Department of Literature. One can almost hear the scurrying behind the scenes to formulate an alternate plan for a folklore congress. Yet when Newell reports on "Folk-Lore at the Columbian Exposition," it is as a simple statement of fact:

In the congresses of The World's Columbian Exposition, folk-lore is likely to have a double representation. In the first place, a *separate* Folk-Lore Congress has been provided for, to be held, in connection with the Department of Literature, in the month of July. . . . In the second place, a Congress of Anthropology will be held, in which folk-lore will *naturally* find a place.

(Newell 1892, 239; emphasis added)

In 1893, Lee Vance commented on these two folklore congresses, "one in connection with the Department of Literature; and the other . . . with the Congress of Anthropology." He concluded that "the proper place of the 'science of folk-lore' remains to be settled" (Vance 1893, 598).

Thus, while Bassett organized a whole congress on the subject of folklore, Newell and other members of the American Folklore Society were anxious that folklore be included as a *part* of the anthropology congress. Newell commented on this. He acknowledged a link between folklore and literature, "the connection between early written literature and oral popular tradition naturally would belong to the history of literature" (Newell 1892, 239). At the same time, folklore as the study "of primitive customs, and their modern survival among civilized peoples" falls in the realm of anthropology. "It might, therefore, from some points of view, seem a matter of indifference as to whether a congress concerned with folk-lore should be referred to the department of literature or to that of science" (Newell 1892, 239). For Newell, however, the matter was not one of indifference. He viewed the association of folklore with literature as a threat to the scientific credibility of folklore studies. He referred to the "extravagant pretensions and loose theorizing" in the studies of popular tradition and mythology (Newell 1892, 239–40). When folklore is removed from the scientific framework of anthropology, these wild embellishments occur. And the result is a tarnished image: " 'Folk-Lore' is a useful word, but also one which is exposed to discredit" (Newell 1892, 239).

The way was clear for Newell: "In order to secure respect and usefulness for [folklore] studies, they must be under a strict scientific direction, and so controlled as to proceed in the modest and guarded method of all truly scientific research" (Newell 1892, 240). Folklore was not to be "a separate science." The term was to refer to "a body of material," and this material was to be studied "as a part of anthropological science." In short, Newell said, "the word 'folk-lore' itself is not of that abstract character which can properly be used as the title of a science" (Newell 1892, 240).

To retain the regard of the scientific community, Newell counseled folklore societies to "refrain from undue self-assertion" (Newell 1892, 240). If the folklore societies directed their investigations toward completing the record, a gathering of scientific information, then their contribution was noteworthy. However, if these societies aimed at "undue self-assertion," if they attempted "to establish a separate field independent of anthropologi-cal research," then they were no longer serving a worthy purpose (Newell 1892, 240). For Newell, work in folklore was to be directed toward "promot-ing the general cause of anthropological investigation."

Newell concluded his remarks on "Folk-Lore at the Columbian Exposi-tion" by noting that the members of the Council of the American Folklore Society "officially join in a general Anthropological Congress. . . . If the Congress of Anthropology can be made educational, by setting an example of true scientific spirit and method, a good work will be accomplished for American anthropology" (Newell 1892, 240). As a result, a Committee of the World's Congress Auxiliary on the International Congress of An-thropology was formed to organize and to direct the Congress of An-thropology. The executive committee consisted of Daniel G. Brinton, president; Franz Boas, secretary; C. Staniland Wake and Edward E. Ayer, as members of the World's Congress Auxiliary Committee (Congresses 1893, 67).

The April–June 1893 issue of the *Journal of American Folklore* carried a report on the "Congresses at the Columbian Exposition." The Folk-Lore Congress planned by Bassett published a selected listing of the more than seventy papers to be delivered during the week of July 10, 1893. The authors were eminent, the titles, varied. They included Professor G. Mas-pero (Paris, France), "Certain Modern Egyptian Superstitions Coming from Antiquity"; Horatio Hale (Clinton, Ontario), "The True Hiawatha"; Surgeon Washington Matthews (Fort Wingate, New Mexico), "Navajo Songs and Prayers, as Recorded by the Edison Phonograph, with Sacred, Agricultural,

Building, War, Gambling, and Love Songs"; Dr. Stanislaus Prato (Sessa Aurunca, Italy), "The Symbolism of the Vase in Mythology, Ideography, Language, Hagiography, Literature, and Folk-Lore." It should be noted that Washington Matthews was the only representative from the Bureau of American Ethnology who participated in the Folk-Lore Congress. He was a friend of Fletcher Bassett and also the vice-president of the Chicago Folklore Society (McNeil 1980, 330).

This announcement of Bassett's Folk-Lore Congress in the *Journal of American Folklore*, appearing as it did with the impressive list of authors and titles, was followed by a call for papers for the Congress of Anthropology which would meet the week of August 28, 1893. "It is requested that the title and abstract of any paper to be offered to the Congress be forwarded as early as possible to the Secretary of the Local Committee with a statement of the time required for its reading" (Conclusion 1893, 159).

The Congress of Anthropology was to be divided into five sections with the following people in charge of the program arrangements:

> *Physical Anthropology:* Franz Boas, Department of Ethnology, World's Columbian Exposition, Chicago, Illinois.
>
> *Archaeology:* W. H. Holmes, Bureau of Ethnology, Washington, D.C.
>
> *Ethnology:* Otis T. Mason, U.S. National Museum, Washington, D.C., and Stewart Culin, Department of Ethnology, World's Columbian Exposition, Chicago, Ill.
>
> *Folk-Lore and Religions:* W. W. Newell, Cambridge, Mass., and Cyrus Adler, U.S. National Museum, Washington, D.C.
>
> *Linguistics:* D. G. Brinton, Media, Pa.
>
> (Conclusion 1893, 159)

Brinton, as president of the section, was to open the first session with an address (Boas Papers, Brinton to Boas, 7/20/1893), which was to be followed by a discussion from 10:00 A.M. to 1:00 P.M. on myth and ritual, and papers from 2:00 to 4:00 P.M. The second day of the meeting was to be devoted to a discussion of methods in the study of religion; and the third, to an address by Alder, as well as to other papers, and a museum visit (Boas Papers, Newell to Boas, 9/21/1893).

Despite the work of the distinguished Program Committee, the Anthropological Congress was not a success. A cryptic entry in "Notes and Queries," says, "In the end, the plan of this Congress was so far altered that the arrangement in separate sections was abandoned. . . . The Congress devoted to Folk-lore but one afternoon, on August 29, given to the Collection of Games in the Anthropological Building, and one morning, August 31, when a certain number of papers were presented." The plans for the fruitful exchange of scientific ideas did not materialize: "The attendance at the Congress, as at most of the scientific congresses, was limited but the occasion was found pleasant by those who took part" (Officers 1893, 228).

The proceedings of the Anthropology Congress were published in 1894.

No mention was made of the disappointing results of the congress—the rearrangement of sections and the sparse attendance. Indeed, from a reading of the *Memoirs of the International Congress of Anthropology*, with the preface by C. Staniland Wake (1894) and the thirty-five papers by distinguished scholars, one is left with the impression that the Anthropology Congress was well organized and well received. Undoubtedly, the *Memoirs* reflect the way in which the congress was intended to proceed.

In contrast, the International Folk-Lore Congress, organized by Bassett, was a success. There were "twelve formal sessions extending over eight days—July 10 to July 17." The paper that drew the most enthusiastic response was delivered by Lieutenant H. L. Scott of Fort Riley, Kansas, on "The Sign Language of the Indians." The headlines in the *Chicago Tribune* reported "IN A SIGN LANGUAGE FOUR SIOUX INDIANS CONVERSE WITHOUT THE USE OF WORDS" (McNeil 1985, 14). As an additional attraction, the participants were the "guests of Col. W. F. Cody at his *Wild West Show*." A folksong concert was so popular that arrangements were made to present the show simultaneously in the Hall of Columbus and the Hall of Washington (Bassett and Starr 1898, 10–14).

In his opening remarks to the congress, Fletcher S. Bassett explained his reason for calling the meeting the Third International Congress, and proclaiming it the first American International Folk-Lore Congress. The congress, Bassett said, was international in scope and drew scholars from a "wide geographical range" (Bassett 1898, 17). Indeed, as he pointed out, in the first Folk-Lore Congress held in Paris in 1889, Germany, Norway, Russia, Austria, Spain, and Portugal were not represented. And in the second Congress held in 1891, in London, several countries did not attend. "Now," Bassett noted, "for the first time, the co-operation of all has been asked, and representatives from all parts of the world have contributed papers, and some have travelled great distances, to be with us" (Bassett 1898, 17). For this reason, Bassett viewed this 1893 Congress as the "first great International Folk-Lore Congress."

Bassett regretted that the official International Council of the International Folk-Lore Congress had not "fully participated in this Congress" (Bassett 1898, 17). He did not mention the manner in which they had failed to participate, though one might suspect that the council did not approve of Fletcher Bassett's assuming the organizational control, and indeed, proclaiming and convening the International Folk-Lore Congress. He pointedly remarked that "the council of the oldest American society should, from local feelings of jealousy, hold aloof from it" (Bassett 1898, 17). This is an allusion to the decision made by the leaders of the American Folklore Society not to participate in this congress. And Bassett's mention of this in these opening remarks clearly showed that he wanted to make public the slights he had felt from the international and national folklore community.

For Newell and Boas, the compelling thrust for folklore studies was toward professionalism. They saw as a potential danger both Bassett's

International Folklore Congress and the problematic contributions of amateur folklorists. The American Folklore Society, under the leadership of Newell and Boas, closed ranks against Bassett's Chicago Folklore Society. An editorial policy was formulated by Newell and Boas that would minimize the effect of the amateur folklorists. On December 10, 1890 (Boas Papers), Newell wrote to Boas concerning the credentials of a certain person who wished to join the American Folklore Society, but who seemed to Newell to be less than a desirable member. He queried Boas, "You know more about his scientific status than I do; what is your opinion?" Newell expressed the wish "to see our membership more select," a goal that could only be attained through an elective society. Five months later, Newell acknowledged that local amateurs would no doubt continue to participate in the activities of the American Folklore Society (Boas Papers, Newell to Boas, May 9, 1890).

Still, Newell stipulated, the society should adopt increasingly rigorous standards of scholarship. These he stated clearly in the *Journal of American Folklore*. He eschewed "philosophic speculation" about the origin of myths and customs; and he encouraged collection by stating that, "it cannot be too strongly urged that the present need of the study of the religions of primitive races is not theoretic discussion, but practical research; not comparison, but collection" (Newell 1888c, 162). This collection of "the mythology of native races" should be approached not "as curious fancies or absurd superstitions, but as living beliefs" (Newell 1888c, 162). Newell's emphasis was on folklore in context, as living traditions. This was the anthropologist in Newell. In his opening editorial statement for the first volume of the *Journal of American Folklore*, Newell clearly emphasized his predilection for the *oral* nature of living folklore by pointing out that the literary versions were inferior and not genuine. As an example, he referred to the "inferior rhymes of literary origin" which had replaced the old ballads. Still, Newell opined, "genuine ballads" could be found in the colonies where they had "been transmitted from generation to generation by oral tradition" (Newell 1888a, 4).

Clearly, then, Newell's editorial preferences were directed toward the presentation of folklore as a living system of oral traditions. He was straightforward about this, as he was about his disdain for speculative work on the meaning or origin of folklore. He disapproved of the "attention . . . given to the supposed origin of certain widely diffused systems of myth and custom" (Newell 1888a, 7).

As Newell remarked, "the editors are agreed" about the focus of the articles which "should be free from controversial references, treated solely with a view to the elucidation of the theme in hand" (Newell 1888a, 7). And, more specifically, the authors "should follow the narrow path of historical criticism, rather than diverge into the broad fields of philosophic speculation." If the authors follow these stipulations, "the editors will endeavor to keep the readers of this journal informed of such views of this sort as seem to possess sufficient scientific status to make them worth recording" (Newell 1888a, 7).

Newell adhered to what he termed "scientific standards of research, and facilitated the efforts of fieldworkers when possible. On one occasion he wrote to Boas asking him to obtain "a graphophone for Alice Bacon who is gathering negro folk-songs at Hampton Institute." Miss Bacon intended to bring the wax cylinders to the American Folklore Society meeting, and Newell added, "I think that would have an excellent effect toward exhibiting the scientific energy of our Society" (Boas Papers, Newell to Boas, 12/9/1898). In his editorial tasks as well, he always used the criterion of science to guide him. Referring to a folktale Boas had collected which had obscene content, Newell wrote Boas, "I suppose . . . that you think the passage in question is all right in Latin. I can't say that I enjoy these features of tales; but I suppose that science requires their noting" (Boas Papers, Newell to Boas, 3/2/1897).[2]

Franz Boas concurred with Newell's strictures on "amateur" contributions to the *Journal of American Folklore* and to the American Folklore Society as well. Boas was working with direction and purpose toward making anthropology a professional discipline. For Boas, as for Newell, the study of folklore was part of anthropology. It was a serious and integral part of his own work, of his students' work, and of his vision for the development of anthropology in the United States.

Writing about "The Foundation of a National Anthropological Society," Boas restated the concerns that he and Newell had shared about the American Folklore Society more than a decade earlier.

> A difficult problem often arises among those societies which are most successful in popularizing the subject matter of their science, because the lay members largely outnumber the scientific contributors. Whenever this is the case there is a tendency towards lowering the scientific value of discussion. . . . The greater the public interest in a science, the less technical knowledge it appears to require, the greater is the danger that meetings may assume the character of popular lectures.   (Boas 1902a, 805)

Newell and Boas had acted with swiftness and with urgency to counter, indeed, to undermine Bassett's plans for developing folklore. Bassett's clarion call—for folklore apart from anthropology, for folklore as an independent discipline, and for the inclusion of all, even the amateur—sounded alarm in the American Folklore Society. Newell and Boas lived to regret the clash. Bassett did not. In 1893, shortly after the close of the International Folk-Lore Congress of the World's Fair Columbian Exposition, Fletcher S. Bassett died of a heart attack. Boas wrote to Newell on February 24, 1894, "Do you know if the report of the death of Lieut. Bassett is correct? Somebody, I have forgotten who, told me about it a few weeks ago" (Boas Papers, Boas to Newell, 2/24/1894). Boas added that, prior to hearing of Bassett's death, he had intended to become acquainted with the members of the Chicago Folk-Lore Society. This effort he would delay for a respectful period of time with the hopes, as he said, that "I shall be able to bring about an understanding between the Society here and the American Society" (Boas Papers, Boas to Newell, 2/24/1894). Newell replied to Boas that he had not heard of Bassett's death, but that he was sure "that a little attention and a few words to some of the more influential members of the Chicago Folk-Lore Society, at this time, would induce the Society to cast its lot with us, sooner, or later" (Boas Papers, Newell to Boas, 5/2/1894). And he added, "I can hardly think that the gentlemen engaged in that work will be contented to go on as at present." This attempt at reconciliation was not motivated out of concern for the Chicago Folk-Lore Society, or for the interests of folklore studies in general. Rather, it was tied to a serious and constant consideration—how to increase the membership in the American Folklore Society. (See also Dwyer-Shick 1979, 33–48.)

Newell planned to make efforts at reconciliation with the Chicago Folklore Society, and he encouraged Boas to do the same: "I hope to be able to remove any feeling on the part of his friends by attention to his widow who is in my neighborhood" (Boas Papers, Newell to Boas, 2/27/1896). He continued: "I think that with the best intention something of a mistake was made by us in that direction. I have not, and never had any feelings against them; but if I had the thing to do over again, I would have attended their Congress in spite of their way of doing things" (Boas Papers, Newell to Boas, 2/27/1896).

The editor of the *Journal of American Folklore* was in a crucial position to maintain the early editorial policy—one directed toward increasing professionalism and anthropological affiliation of folklore studies. And it is in this position, the editorship of the *Journal of American Folklore*, that much of the drama of the literary-anthropological split was enacted. The framework for this tension can be glimpsed in Dwyer-Shick's sketch of the editorship from 1888 to 1940: "From the founding of the *Journal of American Folklore* in 1888 through 1940 there were only five individuals . . . who served as its Editor. . . . Except for the first Editor, William Wells Newell (1888–1900), the others were all anthropologists" (Dwyer-Shick 1979, 8). Alexander F. Chamberlain (1901–1907), who succeeded Newell, had been a student of Boas at Clark University.[3] Franz Boas was editor from 1908 to 1924, and was succeeded by two more of his former students: Ruth F. Benedict (1925–1939) and Gladys Reichard (1940).

Though Dwyer-Shick does not classify Newell as an anthropologist, he was adamant in his view that folklore should be part of anthropology, and that its scientific credibility was threatened by a close association with a literary organization. Indeed, he characterized his own work as directed toward building "up the Society in such manner as to make it a power in advancing ethnology and anthropology" (Boas Papers, Newell to Boas, 1/29/1906). Thus, the following can be added to Dwyer-Shick's sketch of the editorship of the *Journal of American Folklore*: from 1888 to 1940, the articles included in this journal were selected and shaped by one of the five editors, all of whom were anthropological in their orientation to folklore.

Clearly, up to 1940, the *Journal of American Folklore* was heavily influenced by Boas and his students. Of the first fifty-two years of the journal's existence, Boas served as editor for sixteen. His close friend and associate, W. W. Newell, who served thirteen years, was the only editor who was not one of Boas's students. The other three editors had been strongly influenced by Boas's training, and were respectful of his views. The Boasian influence even extended to the location for the editorial office. From 1908, when Boas became editor, until 1941, when Gladys Reichard ended her year as editor, the editorial office for the *Journal of American Folklore* was at Columbia University in New York City (Dwyer-Shick 1979, 8).

The control of the *Journal of American Folklore* by anthropological folklorists was cause of concern to those who were not in the Boasian circle. On January 3, 1898, Daniel Brinton wrote to Boas pertaining to the content of the journal articles, "I am inclined to think that our Society ought to keep closer to Folk-Lore, pure & simple, than it has done. There is enough of it if we seek it." Brinton's objection was linked to the debate as to what constituted folklore: "Comparative mythology & religion are not folklore. There are avenues for the publication of these elements of Ethnology" (Boas Papers, Brinton to Boas, 1/3/1898). Brinton assured Boas that, "in the same manner I have opposed the introduction of Folk-Lore in the Anthropologic Section of the Academy of Nat. Sciences of Phila."

Newell had at least attempted to present a range of material in the journal, both anthropological and non-anthropological. As he wrote to Boas on February 9, 1889, "To carry out the publication scheme, I would print two volumes annually: one of Indian Lore, one of English, French, etc, as long as the material held out" (Boas Papers, Newell to Boas, 2/6/1889). However, the articles by "the Indian men," as the anthropological folklorists were called (Boas Papers, Newell to Boas, 3/26/1889), far outnumbered those of the literary folklorists. This was a reflection of the interests and efforts of both Newell and Boas as is shown in their early correspondence:

> Certainly you should have an article in the next number, I think of at least 10 pages, as your journey will afford an interesting field. . . . Mr. Horatio Hale will contribute the first of a series of articles on Huron Folk-lore; and Mr. DeCost Smith has sent me an article on Witchcraft of the Modern Iroquois. So much for Indian lore.
>
> (Boas Papers, Newell to Boas, 8/7/1888)

In 1898, when the first volume of the *American Anthropologist* appeared, there were suggestions that the *Journal of American Folklore*, already anthropological in orientation, should merge with the new journal. Newell, fatigued from his ten years of ceaseless work on the *Journal of American*

Folklore, wrote Boas, "As to the proposed amalgamation with the American Anthropologist, my point is that after next year I wish to be free from the charge of editing the Journal. If another editor can be found, well and good." However, Newell was not altogether sanguine about the demise of the journal. "I am glad to find that there is a disposition to maintain the Journal, and I shall be pleased to have some arrangement made. The Society is not very strong; the Journal just about pays for itself" (Boas Papers, Newell to Boas, 10/13/1898).

This talk of merging the *Journal of American Folklore* with the *American Anthropologist* continued for another decade. As Boas wrote to Tozzer in January 31, 1907, "You may be aware that about two or three years ago we talked seriously about the desirability of combining the Folk-Lore Journal with the American Anthropologist, but after a good deal of discussion, we all agreed that this step would not be desirable." Boas said this discussion was reached because "the constituency" of the *Journal of American Folklore* differed "a good deal" from that of the *American Anthropologist*, and could not be transferred successfully. Further, Boas remarked, there was "ample folklore material" for the *Journal of American Folklore*, and there was not adequate space for its publication in the *American Anthropologist* (Boas Papers, Boas to Tozzer, 1/31/1907).

In 1907, after Newell's death, the first concerted attempts were made to strike a balance between the anthropological and the literary. Roland B. Dixon wrote to Boas,

> You have doubtless heard the sad news before this, of Newell's sudden death on Monday. I had seen him Saturday, and although he had a cold, he seemed to be quite his usual self. He went to Wayland as usual for Sunday, to his sister's, and was found dead Monday morning, in his bed. I have called a Council meeting today to pass formal resolutions for insertion in the Journal, which Chamberlain is holding up for the purpose.
>
> (Boas Papers, Dixon to Boas, 1/23/1907)

Boas responded to Dixon, "Your letter informing me of Newell's death was a great shock to me. Mr. Newell was a man who won the admiration and respect of every one who came in contact with him, and I feel that his death is a severe loss to all of us" (Boas Papers, Boas to Dixon, 2/1/1907).

At the memorial service held for Newell in Cambridge on March 10, 1907, Boas read a eulogy. He spoke of Newell as "a man of literary inclinations [who] came to be a power in the field of anthropology. . . . Thus it came to pass that he set anthropologists thinking in new lines, that he added new recruits to our ranks and that he pressed one of us after another into his service." Boas concluded his eulogy, "It is left to us to see that his work may live; and our task has been made easy by him, for those ideas for which he stood have taken firm hold. May his memory help us to follow in his steps" (Boas Papers, Newell Memorial, 3/10/1907).

However, plans had been set in motion scarcely a week after Newell's death to chart a different course for the society and the journal, to diverge from the path struck by Newell. In fact, there had been talk of replacing Newell even prior to his death. Kroeber wrote to Dixon about a conversation he had had with Tozzer:

> I had a talk with him while in Cambridge as to the necessity of someone looking after the Society in all ways, on the side of the organization and membership as well as editorially, both with a view to supplementing Newell's often unsystematic work and with the idea of taking it up when he should no longer be able to serve.

(Kroeber Papers, Kroeber to Dixon, 1/30/1907)

Kroeber concurred with Dixon that "Cambridge is the most desirable place in which to run the Society." Further, Kroeber saw "the present occasion" of Newell's death as "an admirable one" for giving Tozzer "a hand in the Journal" as well as in the society, since Newell had served as assistant editor as well as secretary.

On January 28, 1907, Tozzer, in his new capacity as secretary pro tem, wrote to Boas, "With the very greatest respect to the memory of Mr. Newell, it seems to me as if the affairs of the Society and, to a greater degree, those of the Journal were getting very much into a rut." Tozzer continued, "The Society has among its members about all the Anthropologists of the country and there is little hope of growth in that direction." He echoed Brinton's 1898 remarks, "If the Journal is to be simply a medium for presenting the Folk-Lore of the American Indians, why should it not be combined or attached to the American Anthropologist? What is the need of a separate publication?" Tozzer suggested instead that "the range of the Journal . . . be extended." He further stated that "this expansion would be on the literary side of Folk-Lore, growth in this direction would seem possible." Tozzer suggested trying "to reawaken the interest of such men as Professor Kittredge who was a founder of the society but who has long ceased to have any hand in the government or the policy of the association." He indicated that each issue of the journal should contain at least one article on a "general phase of Folk-Lore," as well as "a contribution in relation of Folk-Lore and the literatures of the world."

> If the Journal is to live as a separate publication, it must find a place for itself and this place is not, it seems to me strictly among the Anthropologists who have their own Journal but in a field of wider interest including to be sure the Anthropologists and those interested in Folk-Lore as showing the growth and development of literature.

(Boas Papers, Tozzer to Boas, 1/28/1907)

Responding to Tozzer's letter, Boas noted that Newell "as well as many of us have been dissatisfied with the condition of the Journal." Part of the difficulties with the journal, as Boas saw it, had to do with the policies of

Chamberlain who was "always looking for the curious, not for the ordinary material." Boas added, "last Christmas we were discussing the possibility of taking the management of the articles of the journal away from Dr. Chamberlain, and of letting him keep merely the bibliographical portion." Boas did not, however, agree with Tozzer concerning the ambitious expansion of the literary material: "It is my own opinion that it is of doubtful advisability to try to make a strong development of the literary side of European folklore in America, while it would be quite appropriate to develop the study of negro folk-lore." Boas was convinced that the orientation of the European folklorists differed substantively from that of the anthropological folklorists:

> The groups of people interested in the study of European folk-lore differ so much in their general points of view and in their other interests from our people, that the "Folk-Lore Journal" might become very heterogeneous unless we happen to interest strongly a number of men who are at the same time imbued with anthropological spirit.
>
> (Boas Papers, Boas to Tozzer, 1/31/1907)

Boas suggested that Tozzer "talk over the matter with Professor Kittredge" to get his advice.

At the 1908 Chicago meeting of the American Folklore Society, Chamberlain was replaced as editor of the journal. To soften his demotion, he was appointed bibliographic editor. And as Tozzer wrote to him, "We are assuming that the bibliographical side of the work is the one which appeals most strongly to you" (Boas Papers, Tozzer to Chamberlain, 1/7/1908). The Council appointed Boas editor, since he was "in intimate communication with the workers in folk-lore." Kittredge was recruited "to father the literary side of the subject."[4]

Tozzer sent a form letter to all the secretaries of the American Folklore Society that explained the change of editorship. He noted that the addition of Boas and Kittredge as editors, with Chamberlain in charge of bibliographic materials, was intended to strengthen the journal and to make it of interest to a broader audience. He restated that "it is our endeavor to give more prominence to the literary side of folk-lore in the Journal so that the interest will not be confined strictly to the aboriginal side" (Boas Papers, Tozzer to Secretaries of AFS, 1/10/1908). Tozzer ended the letter graciously, noting that "we are beginning to reap the results of Mr. Newell's constant devotion and energies."

Just as Newell was wearied after ten years as editor of the *Journal of American Folklore,* so was Boas. On October 17, 1918, he wrote Tozzer, "I feel . . . on the whole strongly inclined to give up the matter, and perhaps it might be as well for the Folk-Lore Society to have a change of editors" (Boas Papers, Boas to Tozzer, 10/17/1918). Tozzer wrote an urgent reply, typed in red for emphasis (10/23/1918), "You *must not do this.* The Society would die." Apparently Boas was persuaded: he remained editor until 1924.

Another of Tozzer's concerns was increasing the membership of the society. For the twentieth annual meeting of the American Folklore Society, held in Baltimore, Maryland, Tozzer presented a detailed report on the state of the society which indicated a decrease in membership (Dwyer-Shick 1979, 36; Tozzer 1909, 85–86). This he attributed to a lack of concerted effort toward recruitment of new members. The declining membership and the anthropological orientation of the journal and of the society were proof to Tozzer of the need to redirect the society.

Two years after taking over as secretary of the American Folklore Society, Tozzer gave a positive review of the *Journal of American Folklore* in his Annual Report: "Thanks to the efforts made by Professor G. L. Kittredge and others, a considerable amount of material relating to European folklore has been offered for publication in the Journal, and it is the hope of the Editor that this department of the Journal may be considerably strengthened in coming years" (Tozzer 1909, 88). Though there are no reports in the *Journal of American Folklore* relating to the Committee on Membership which was formed following Tozzer's recommendation (Dwyer-Shick 1979, 37), it is doubtful that the committee had much effect. As Dwyer-Shick reports, "there was no appreciable increase in the total membership of the Society until the end of the next decade, about the beginning of the 1920s" (Dwyer-Shick 1979, 37).

On a lesser, but still important scale, the division between the anthropological folklorists and the literary folklorists featured in the selection of the president of the American Folklore Society, and in the choice for the location of the annual meetings. Though attempts had been made to elect presidents from "the side of literature" (Boas Papers, Tozzer to Boas, 12/17/1908; Boas to Tozzer, 12/17/1908), still an imbalance had existed since the founding of the Society. In a period of twenty-six years—from 1888 to 1914—there had been only six men of a literary orientation to the study of folklore who served in the office of president.[5] Dwyer-Shick lists them as Francis James Child (1888, 1889), Alcee Fortier (1894), Henry Wood (1898), George Lyman Kittredge (1904), Henry M. Belden (1910, 1911), and John Lomax (1912, 1913) (Dwyer-Schick 1979, 61). Child, Belden, and Lomax served two-year terms. Thus, for nine years of this twenty-six year period the president of the American Folklore Society had been an individual with a literary orientation to folklore studies. For the remaining seventeen years, the office of president had been filled by an individual with an anthropological orientation to folklore studies.

This was a source of concern to members of the society. So in 1914, at the twenty-sixth annual meeting of the American Folklore Society, held in Philadelphia, Pennsylvania, a resolution was adopted by the council to effect an "annual alternation of Presidents without re-election, the alternating to be as far as possible between the literary and the anthropological aspects of folk-lore" (Twenty-sixth annual meeting 1915, 101; Dwyer-Shick 1979, 49). Dwyer-Shick remarked, "And yet, this was *not* what did in fact take place" (1979, 60). Actually, the situation remained precisely as it was prior to the 1914 resolution. From 1914 to 1940, a period of twenty-six years, there were three men and one woman elected as president who were of a literary orientation. These were Aurelio M. Espinosa (1923, 1924), Louise Pound (1925, 1926), Archer Taylor (1935, 1936), and Stith Thompson (1937, 1938, 1939) (Dwyer-Shick 1979, 60). From this list, it is apparent that these four presidents served a total of nine years. For the remaining seventeen years, the office of president was occupied by a person with an anthropological orientation to folklore.

The imbalance between the anthropological folklorists and the literary folklorists, while officially recognized by the 1914 resolution, was by no means rectified. This issue was the nexus in the selection of the president of the American Folklore Society in 1925. Unable to attend the thirty-sixth annual meeting of the society, Franz Boas wrote to Elsie Clews Parsons requesting that she see to several matters of importance. He mentioned the invitation from the University of Chicago to meet with the Modern Language Association the following year (Boas Papers, Boas to Parsons, 12/29/1924). Boas noted that the American Folklore Society had benefited from the 1924 joint membership agreement with the Modern Language Association whereby one could join both organizations for a single payment of six dollars (Dwyer-Shick 1979, 51): "We have received more than sixty new members . . . while they have received hardly any from us. . . ." The imbalance in the joint membership continued. By 1928, 115 of the 341 members of the society had joined through the joint agreement (Dwyer-Shick 1979, 53; Fortieth annual meeting 1929, 197), while the Modern Language Association had gained only a few members. Boas made the following suggestion to Parsons:

> I think it would be a good plan to elect one of the Modern Language people, perhaps Miss Pound of Nebraska, president, and to meet with the Modern Language people and try at the same time to arrange the time so that members may also attend the Anthropological Association meeting.
>
> (Boas Papers, Boas to Parsons, 12/29/1924)

Louise Pound was elected president of the American Folklore Society in 1925; and re-elected in 1926. Since she had not attended the thirty-sixth annual meeting, she was informed of her new position by letter which also informed her of the location for the next annual meeting:

> It was voted to hold a double meeting next Christmas, one meeting with the Modern Language Association in Chicago, and a second one in New Haven in connection with the American Anthropological Association and following an invitation to meet at the formal opening of the new Peabody Museum in New Haven.
>
> (UPFFA, Boas to Pound, 1/12/1925)

Even though it was politic to meet with the Modern Language Association for the annual meeting, the American Folklore Society was loath to give up an annual meeting with the American Anthropological Association. As Dwyer-Shick remarks, "the Thirty-Seventh Annual Meeting was held in two different cities, at two different times, *and* with two different professional organizations" (1979, 56). These bifurcated meetings, in effect, symbolized the divided loyalties of the American Folklore Society. Like Dr. Doolittle's two-headed llama, the American Folklore Society was pushed and pulled in two different directions at once. And yet, one direction had the stronger pull: the American Folklore Society held its business meeting in New Haven, at the time of the joint meeting with the American Anthropological Association.

Wayland Hand remarked that the American Folklore Society used to be "a poor step-sister" to the American Anthropological Association. He recalled the "petty annoyances" that existed for the folklorists in this affiliation. For annual meeting accommodations, the American Folklore Society was always given "the rinky-dink rooms." "Once when we met with the American Anthropological Association in New York—I don't remember what year, but it was in New York—we were given an old run-down hotel about 15 miles from the other hotels and meetings."[6]

Even the fiftieth anniversary celebration for the founding of the American Folklore Society was held as part of the joint meeting with the American Anthropological Association. Stith Thompson, who was president of the American Folklore Society in 1937, remarked that "the Society had reached a low ebb" so he organized a special program to mark the fiftieth year. The American Folklore Society had "a full day of programs and a special dinner in the evening." And as he said, the dinner "was well attended not only by members of the Anthropological Association but by a good many of the folklorists who came in from outside" (Thompson 1956, 156). Thompson continued, "Franz Boas spoke on the history of the society for its first fifty years, and I gave my presidential address, which was a look into the future" (1956, 157). This was a balanced program for the American Folklore Society. Boas, as an anthropological folklorist, spoke of the society's past; and Thompson, as a literary folklorist, looked to the future. In three years' time, this balance between the anthropological and the literary would be fixed in policy for the American Folklore Society.

Up to this time, the joint annual meetings of the American Folklore Society and the American Anthropological Association were an established pattern. From the founding of the American Anthropological Association in 1901 until the year 1941, all but four meetings of the American Folklore Society were held in conjunction with the American Anthropological Association.[7] As Dwyer-Shick and Dorson noted, the American Folklore Society planned meetings for one day of the three or four day meeting of the American Anthropological Association, during which time, papers were read. Additional time was allotted for meetings of the council and of the society (Dwyer-Shick 1979, 63; Dorson 1971a, 12).

Unlike the articulated attempt to regulate the selection of the president—to alternate between literary and anthropological folklorists—the scheduling of the annual meeting with the American Anthropological Association followed an informal procedure. It was never explicitly stated as policy that the American Folklore Society would meet on an annual basis with the American Anthropological Association. Yet it was always assumed that this would be the case. (See also Dwyer-Shick 1979, 62–66.) As the program chairperson for the American Anthropological Association said, "It has always been customary for the American Folk-Lore Society to meet with us" (UPFFA, Setzler to Herzog, 9/30/1940). This scheduling of the American Folklore Society meeting with the American Anthropological Association was cause for resentment. Herzog wrote to Hallowell on the subject, "The non-primitive group are dissatisfied. . . . One man writes whether it will be possible to hold the primitive and non-primitive groups together" and mentioned that "the latter always suffer since our meetings are always together with the AAA, not the MLA" (UPFFA, Herzog to Hallowell, 11/10/1940).

Stith Thompson in his memoirs entitled "Folklorist's Progress," recalled the situation:

> At that time [1936] the Folklore Society always met with the American Anthropological Association and occupied only one of the sessions of their program. . . . While it was good to have the interest of the American Anthropological Association, this arrangement brought it about that all that group of folklorists who were not anthropologists but who approached their subject from the point of view of English or one of the literatures usually stayed away.
>
> (Thompson 1956, 140)

The fifty-second annual meeting of the American Folklore Society, held in Philadelphia, Pennsylvania on December 27–30, 1940, proved to be a pivotal point for the society. Stith Thompson recalled that "at Chicago the year before a committee had been appointed to try to analyze the ills of the Society and to suggest ways in which it might be improved. It was generally agreed that the editorship of the *Journal of American Folklore* should move from Columbia University, where it had been for so many years" (Thompson 1956, 168–69).

On February 24, 1940, the Council of the American Folklore Society called a meeting "to discuss current affairs of the society connected with the change of editorship and the publication of the Journal" (UPFFA, Herzog, 2/1940). As mentioned, in 1940 Gladys Reichard was editor of the *Journal of American Folklore,* and the editorial office was located at Columbia University. The change of editorship to which Herzog was referring would result in the appointment of the first editor who was not a student or close colleague of Boas. And this would be the *first* editor with a literary orientation to folklore studies. Archer Taylor, professor of German literature at the University of California, Berkeley, would serve as editor for the *Journal of American Folklore* for 1941. And he would move the editorial office from its location of thirty-three years at Columbia University, New York, to the University of California, Berkeley. Clearly, there were changes afoot, and these were set in motion at this meeting.

However, this change of location was not accomplished without a struggle. Parsons wrote to Herskovits on November 17, 1940,

> Suggestions: For administration, representatives as far as possible from all centers interested in folk lore; but the editorship of the Journal to remain in the hands of a folklorist who is also an experienced anthropologist. Assistant editors representing all fields to be consulted or asked to edit contributions within their field.
>
> (Parsons Papers, Parsons to Herskovits, 11/17/1940)

Still, the consensus of opinion was, as Herzog said, "that the Journal and the society were directed for too long by people in New York City" (UPFFA, Herzog to Herskovits, 11/18/1940). And, in a letter to Stith Thompson, Herzog remarked, "I do not feel that a journal like the folklore journal needs to be tied all the time to New York or to the East" (UPFFA, Herzog to Thompson, 3/3/1940).

Still another result of the special council meeting that was convened in February 1940 was the Committee on Policy. A. Irving Hallowell, as president of the American Folklore Society, appointed Ralph Boggs, Ann H. Gayton, Elsie Clews Parsons, Archer Taylor, Stith Thompson, and Leslie A. White as members of this committee. Melville J. Herskovits was appointed chairman of the Committee on Policy (UPFFA, Herskovits to Parsons, 11/15/1940). The committee was to draft a series of recommendations which would be considered by the council at its next regular meeting, during the fifty-second annual meeting.

The report of the Committee on Policy was presented at the annual meeting, and was also published in volume 54 of the *Journal of American Folklore*. The committee was straightforward and succinct in identifying the main problem of the American Folklore Society: "It is clear that the major difficulty facing the Society arises from a failure to assess the importance of the fact that, by its very nature, the Society and its *Journal* are peripheral to two major concerns—those of anthropologists and those of persons in the humanities" (Fifty-second annual meeting 1941, 76). The committee suggested that, in the future, "the Society should recognize more explicitly than in the past the importance of this fact" and should emphasize the points of convergence between the two fields. The committee made thirteen specific recommendations. Eight of these were concerned with organizational aspects of the society. Four were directed toward changes in the journal. And the final recommendation dealt with cost-reduction for the journal.

These recommendations of the Committee on Policy were approved by the Council of the American Folklore Society on December 30, 1940, signed by the members of the committee on January 9, 1941, and printed in the January–June 1941 issue of the journal. They, therefore, had the official approval of the society, and they laid the foundation for a major reorientation—if not reorganization—of the American Folklore Society.

The first two recommendations concerned the nomination of the president and the vice-president. Recommendation number one was a restatement of the 1914 resolution which provided for the annual alternation of the president from the literary and anthropological circles (Twenty-sixth annual meeting 1915, 101). The 1940 recommendation read, in part, "the Nominating Committee shall be instructed to select a President each year from a field differing from that of the incumbent" (Fifty-second annual meeting 1941, 76). Recommendation number two requested that the Nominating Committee choose candidates for the vice-presidency on an annual basis, and that the choice be guided by the needs of the society at that time. The Committee on Policy drew attention once again to their major concern: "It is recommended, however, that in selecting the President and Vic-President [*sic*], every effort be made to see that the fields of anthropology and the humanities are equally represented" (Fifty-second annual meeting 1941, 76).

Recommendation number three addressed the choice of location for the annual meeting. It was suggested that the place of the meeting be chosen with the thought of all the members in mind. Thus, a balance should be achieved between meetings held jointly with the Modern Language Association and the American Anthropological Association. The Committee was not proposing "a rigid policy of alternation," but they noted

> that the tradition of meeting exclusively with the American Anthropological Association, except when the Modern Language Association happens to meet in the same city as the American Anthropological Association, tends to discourage the attendance at the annual meetings of the Folklore Society of those whose major interest lies in the humanities.

> (Fifty-second annual meeting 1941, 76–77)

The fourth recommendation concerned the appointment and the length of tenure of the editor. It was suggested that the editor be nominated and elected on an annual basis; and that no editor should occupy this position for more than five consecutive years. Recommendation number eight provided for the annual nomination and election of the associate editors. And one associate editor would be designated as book review editor of the journal.

The fifth recommendation established the Committee on Membership as a standing committee, and suggested a policy for concentrated recruitment of new members, that is, that the committee would focus intensely on one geographical region per year.

In the sixth recommendation, it was suggested that a new committee be formed to work toward closer cooperation with other folklore organizations, "and also to devise ways and means of integrating the interests of amateur collectors with the work of the Society" (Fifty-second annual meeting 1941, 77).

The Committee on Policy noted that the *Journal of American Folklore* "is recognized by all as paramount." The four recommendations concerning the journal were formulated to help "guide the new Editor," and to record the society's sincere intention "to widen the appeal of the approach toward folklore to be taken by our *Journal*." To this end, the ninth recommendation was for the discontinuance of single topic issues. Number ten suggested that more space be allotted for short articles, and "that efforts be made to obtain theoretical papers to balance the collections of raw data" (Fifty-second annual meeting 1941, 77). Number eleven suggested that information helpful to amateurs be provided in the journal. To this end, discussion of collecting techniques, presentation of sample questionnaires, and a consideration of methodology should be included. Recommendation number twelve suggested a return to an earlier feature of the journal, a review of the contents in other folklore and related journals.

These recommendations were taken seriously by the society. As noted, the editor who was chosen after the approval of these recommendations was Archer Taylor, a literary folklorist. And following recommendation number five, a Standing Committee on Membership was formed. A. Irving Hallowell, as president of the society, appointed Elsie Clews Parsons and Cora DuBois. Subsequently, Stith Thompson and Joseph Campbell, who were councilors of the society, were added to the membership committee to represent the literary side of folklore studies (UPFFA, Herzog, 2/1940; Fifty-first annual meeting 1940, 194).

Undoubtedly, in its first year, the Standing Committee on Membership worked with commitment to increase the membership of the society. But it was really in its second year, when Verne F. Ray replaced Cora DuBois as chairman, that a systematic attempt was made to implement the recommendations of the Committee on Policy. As Ray wrote to Hallowell, who was president of the society, "I believe that results can be achieved if, and only if the recommendations of the Committee on Policy be strictly followed" (UPFFA, Ray to Hallowell, 12/22/1941). If these recommendations were followed, Ray was confident that there would not only be an increase in membership, but that many new members with literary interests would join the society.

Ray emphasized that a regular publication schedule for the journal was imperative in order to increase membership: "a membership appeal is pretty weak unless tangible evidence of one's selling points can be presented to the prospect" (UPFFA, Ray to Hallowell, 12/22/1941). And Ray had some suggestions for making the product more appealing.

> In particular I would like to see the cover conform more closely to modern journal practice. I believe that amateurs, in particular, would be more receptive to the Journal if it bore a more attractive cover and a livelier format. The scholar and editor know that the quality of content is the proper criterion of a journal but secretary and treasurer know that subscribers consider appearance also.
>
> (UPFFA, Ray to Hallowell, 12/22/1941)

In the review of the recommendations made by the Committee on Policy, and the recapitulation of these points by Ray, it is striking to note how the orientation of the society and the journal had changed. During the early years of the society, Boas and Newell had carefully steered a course close to the anthropological interests in folklore. In fact, they viewed an identification with the literary interests in folklore studies as perilous to professional recognition. The policy of the editors of the *Journal of American Folklore* was explicitly stated: articles should be scientific in nature; and literary articles that met scientific standards could be included. The participation of amateur folklorists in the activities of the society, while tolerated, was not entirely welcomed. And the American Folklore Society sought to set itself apart from the Chicago Folklore Society, and from other local societies in the early years.

Newell and Boas were primarily concerned with establishing folklore studies as a professional—but not independent—enterprise. Folklore was to nest under the wing of anthropology, protected by the scientific respectability of the anthropological discipline. But the division between the anthropological folklorists and the literary folklorists was always present. Sometimes the points of disagreement appeared as innocuous recollections of past injustices—as in Thompson's memoirs where he noted the slight dealt the literary folklorists by the perpetual joint meeting with the American Anthropological Association. And at times the disagreement yielded a society resolution—as in 1914 when the council of the society voted to alternate presidents between the literary and the anthropological interests in the society.

Finally, in 1940, the Committee on Policy made a series of recommendations that were predicated on a recognition of the division within folklore studies. As the committee stated it, the society and the journal were "peripheral to two major concerns," those of anthropologists and those of people in the humanities (Fifty-second annual meeting 1941, 76). According to the Committee on Policy, the viability and success of the society and the journal required a conscious effort to draw these two concerns together; and to make the business of the society, and the publications of the journal relevant to individuals of both concerns.

To this end, there was a concerted attempt to draw new members from literary circles. And members with a literary interest in folklore studies could be assured that the society would meet with the Modern Language Association with some regularity, and that the president of the society and the editor would alternate between an anthropological folklorist and a literary folklorist. So in organizational structure, the society and the journal were directed toward the inclusion—not the exclusion—of folklorists with a literary interest in folklore studies. This was a complete reversal of Boas's and Newell's earlier orientation.

Further, in order to increase membership and bring money to the coffers, the journal had to appeal to a larger audience, and this audience was composed of amateurs with an interest in folklore. So, whereas Boas and Newell eschewed the participation of amateurs in the affairs of the society, in 1940 the Committee on Policy encouraged their participation. And in 1941, the chairman of the Committee on Membership even suggested that the cover of the journal be made livelier and more appealing to draw the amateur folklorists into the society.

The policy of the American Folklore Society and the *Journal of American Folklore* took a pendulum swing from an exclusively anthropological orientation to folklore, to a conscious attempt to include the literary folklorists in the activities and publications of the society; from a movement toward professionalism, to an active recruitment of amateurs.

F O U R

The Literary Folklorists

While the struggle for hegemony went on in the American Folklore Society, the literary folklorists were intently pursuing their academic work. And in many instances, they were penning the future classics of folkloristics. The power and control that were exercised by the anthropological folklorists were expressed in organizational terms. Succeeding with their game strategy for control of the American Folklore Society, the anthropological folklorists claimed the turf, at least until 1940.

But from the halls of academe, another scene unfolded. The action began at Harvard University, where Child started work on the ballad and Kittredge continued it. From this common source, the halls of Harvard and the tutelage of Child and Kittredge, the literary folklorists fanned out across the country. At Texas, Colorado, Maine, and Indiana, the young Stith Thompson pursued his work on the folktale. At Berkeley, Walter Morris Hart devoted himself to the ballad. Archer Taylor, who specialized in the proverb, came to Berkeley after his years at Washington University in St. Louis and the University of Chicago. At Los Angeles, Hustvedt continued the work of his mentors in ballad scholarship. He was joined by Wayland Hand who focused on folk beliefs, folk medicine, and legends.

Dan Ben-Amos has remarked on these differing centers of control for the anthropological folklorists and the literary folklorists: "While the anthropological approach remained dominant in the American Folklore Society itself for many years, it was the literary approach, heralded by Bassett and the Chicago Folklore Society, that was the dominant force at the universities" (Ben-Amos 1973, 123). To understand the extent to which literary folklorists in certain university departments directed the course of academic folklore studies, one must note the academic genealogy and the major works of several leading scholars. To do this, one should start with the source, Harvard University, and the scholar, Francis James Child.

Francis James Child (1825–1896) was a Chaucerian scholar who is remembered primarily for the ballads he canonized (Ben-Amos 1973, 122). In 1857–1858, he published eight volumes of *English and Scottish Ballads* which were included in the series British Poets. This work was to become a lifelong concern, or as Child represented it, one of his religions. In a letter dated "Sunday Afternoon, April 24, 1887," and written to a young lady of whom he was very fond, Child said, "Love of roses is another religion. . . .

45

Do you mean to be shut out of the other superstitions? I have very few: love of women, roses, Shakspere, my friends, wild flowers, trees, violin music, voila!" (Child 1920, 55).[1]

Child's work on the ballad followed his two years of study in Germany. In 1849, he went to the University of Berlin to hear Jacob and Wilhelm Grimm lecture; he also attended the University of Gottingen. Child himself remarked that the time in Berlin was a formative influence on his life (Bynum 1974, 24). His student and successor in ballad scholarship at Harvard, George Lyman Kittredge, said Child's "own greatest contribution to learning, The English and Scottish Popular Ballads, may even, in a very real sense, be regarded as the fruit of these years in Germany" (Kittredge 1898, xxv). Kittredge recalled an element in the decor of Child's study that testified to the lasting impact of Jacob and Wilhelm Grimm. Over the fireplace, Child had placed a picture of the Grimm brothers, and it remained there throughout his life.

Child himself was displeased with the eight volumes of the *English and Scottish Ballads*. In a letter dated March 26, 1872, written to the great Danish folklorist, Svend Grundtvig, Child alluded to these eight volumes as "a sort of *job*—forming part of one of those senseless huge collections of *British Poets*" (Hustvedt 1930, 246).[2] Child told Grundtvig of his "intention of making some day a different and less hasty work" (Hustvedt 1930, 246). Indeed, as Kittredge related, Child determined to compile a corpus that would "include every obtainable version of every extant English and Scottish ballad, with the fullest possible discussion of related songs or stories in the 'popular' literature of all nations" (Kittredge 1898, xxvii). And, Kittredge tells us, "to this enterprise he resolved, if need were, to devote the rest of his life."

This is precisely what Child did. An account of this dedication runs through *A Scholar's Letters to a Young Lady*. On June 13, 1888, he wrote, "I am just now kept with very sharp nerves by the necessity of printing up my book which ought to be done leisurely. I have the literature of the past two or three years to run through, but must print very soon" (Child 1920, 67). In a letter dated May 27, 1890, Child told of the assistance given him by his dear friend, James Russell Lowell. The latter wrote to Lord Rosebury on Child's behalf, and requested permission to consult a valuable manuscript collection of ballads (Child 1920, 101–02).

Much time was spent endeavoring to obtain access to unpublished manuscripts of ballad collections. As Child wrote to Grundtvig, "There are . . . several manuscripts in existence which have never been printed and which I should wish by all means to get hold of: such as Herd's and Mrs. Brown's MSS., used by Jamieson and others, and a Glenriddel MS. referred to by Walter Scott" (Hustvedt 1930, 248).[3]

Great effort was made to obtain permission to examine one particular manuscript, the Percy Manuscript, at Ecton Hall. But the bishop's descendants who had possession of the manuscript would allow no one to see it.

Finally after eight years, the Percy Manuscript was published (Kittredge 1898, xxvii). And gradually, over the years, other manuscript collections became accessible. On August 8, 1890, Child wrote to his friend about the acquisition of one very important manuscript, "For a good many days I have not had a breathing-spell in consequence of my getting the things from Abbotsford, which have upset work which I supposed to be done, and so coming into embarrassment with my printers . . ." (Child 1920, 102–03).[4]

The first volume of *The English and Scottish Popular Ballads* was published in 1882, and the remaining nine volumes appeared in the years following, until the last volume was published posthumously in 1898. Before its completion, the work began to wear on Child. On December 6, 1890, he wrote, "I am rid of a seventh ballad book and well into an eighth. I do not care now except to finish them, for the romantic things are all done" (Child 1920, 103). And a year later, on December 25, 1891, he wrote again, "I see my way to the end, and all I care about now is to have things in such shape that, in case of accident, the book might be complete" (Child 1920, 116). In 1893, he was still writing about finishing his ballad work, "I am getting slowly through with the last parcel of ballads (not the last number of the book, there will be one more of indexes, etc.) and shall be very glad to have it off my hands, for now it is only a necessity to me and no interest. There are other things which I should like to do" (Child 1920, 138). Yet his work on the ballad continued. In a letter dated "Monday Evening, 23rd December, 1895, he wrote "I am thoroughly weary of ballads . . . and feel no more interest in the business" (Child 1920, 147).

The work on the final volume of *The English and Scottish Popular Ballad* continued after his death. He died on September 11, 1896, after a month's illness. All of volume 10 was completed save for the introduction and the bibliography, which was soon completed by Kittredge who remarked: "The introduction, however, no other scholar had the hardihood to undertake. A few pages of manuscript,—the last thing written by his pen,—almost illegible, were found among his papers" (Kittredge 1898, xxix). In place of the introduction, Kittredge wrote on Francis James Child's ballad studies and the excellence of his teaching at Harvard.

Child had completed his life's task; he had published his ten volumes of *The English and Scottish Popular Ballads*. During his years of research, Child was haunted by one prospect. As he wrote to Grundtvig in January 24, 1880, "I have often been afraid of dying before 1879 ended. I want to live long enough to put the world in possession of all the English ballads, and find it necessary to say to myself that this is the only matter of essential importance" (Hustvedt 1930, 283).

Child's corpus on the ballad has left a classic in folklore scholarship. The work is so crucial for ballad studies that folklorists cite the number of the "Child Ballad" as their point of reference. Throughout the course of his research, Child himself was consciously selecting ballad texts that would represent the purest form, the classic ballads. His orientation to the material was that of a scholar steeped in literature. He mistrusted oral versions and preferred manuscript sources.[5]

Child viewed the English and Scottish ballads "as sealed or dried up forever" (Hustvedt 1930, 248).[6] Education—or what Child had referred to in his writings as Book-Culture—had spelled doom for this form of oral literature (Michael 1960, 33). Child, with a survivalist orientation, expected folklore to endure on the fringes of society, in nooks and crannies where time had passed the people by. As he remarked to his students, "the less book education [there is], the more hope, with persons of native intelligence, of a memory well stored with traditional treasures" (Michael 1960, 33).[7] Thus Child anticipated that some ballads "must linger" on the Shetland Islands (Howe and Cottrell 1952, 44).

In 1873, he spent eight weeks in England and Scotland collecting ballads in manuscript form and from oral sources. He returned to this area in 1877. And on January 29, he wrote to Grundtvig, "I have now got all the manuscripts that are to be had, and I am trying to collect ballads that are left in Aberdeenshire, but I have no reason to wait longer" (Hustvedt 1930, 271). Clearly, Child viewed collecting from oral sources as a salvage operation: he was collecting the ballads that were *left* in Aberdeenshire.

Still, Child's study of the ballad should not be reduced simply to a survivalist orientation. He had an aesthetic about the ballad that was linked to the force and beauty of life. In his letter to James Russell Lowell about the possibility of ballads existing on the Shetland Islands, he said, "There *must* be ballads there:—how else have the people held out against poverty, cold & darkness?" (Howe and Cottrell 1952, 45). The aesthetic sense guided him in determining what was or was not to be considered a popular ballad. Certainly, the broadside did not fit this category.

> The vulgar ballads of our day, the "broadsides" which were printed in such large numbers in England and elsewhere in the sixteenth century or later, belong to a different genus; they are products of a low kind of *art*, and most of them are, from a literary point of view, thoroughly despicable and worthless.
>
> (Hart 1906, 757).

Though Child did prefer working from old manuscripts and held in low esteem the material he collected in the field (Michael 1960, 71), still he encouraged his students to collect ballads. As he said,

> If popular ballads are not *soon* collected, they will perish for ever from popular remembrance; and secondly . . . ballads which have never been found in England, but which are the delight and glory of other nations, may chance at any time to be encountered in the recollection of some utterly "uneducated" poor old woman.
>
> (Michael 1960, 33)[8]

Child's students did continue collecting and studying ballads. One such student was George Lyman Kittredge who returned to Harvard as an instructor of English in 1888, when Francis James Child was working on *The English and Scottish Popular Ballads* (Birdsall 1973, 57). Kittredge worked closely with Child on this project; and, as noted, completed the work on volume 10 after Child's death.

In addition to work on the ballad, Kittredge wrote scholarly articles on a variety of subjects. As his biographer noted, "Kittredge's first learned article" (Hyder 1962, 33), appearing in 1885, showed both his interest in folklore and in classical studies: "Arm-Pitting among the Greeks," published in the *American Journal of Philology*, appeared while Kittredge was still an instructor of Latin at Phillips Exeter Academy in Exeter, New Hampshire. Kittredge discussed the practice of mutilation of the dead; Greek murderers would sever the arms of their victims and fasten them to the body under the armpits, thereby making it impossible for the avenging spirit to harm the murderer (Kittredge 1885).[9]

Kittredge's range of scholarly interest can be exemplified by the topics of his publications in the year 1904. Kittredge edited works on the ballad, the sonnets of Shakespeare, Virgil's *Aeneid*, and a volume for the Albion Series of Anglo-Saxon and Middle English Poetry. The work on the ballad was the Student's Cambridge Edition of Francis James Child's *English and Scottish Popular Ballads*, a one volume work that was edited by Kittredge and Helen Child Sargent, Child's daughter. Kittredge's book on the farmer's almanac, first published in 1904, was reprinted by Harvard University Press in 1920. The complete title was *The Old Farmer and His Almanack: Being Some Observations on Life and Manners in New England a Hundred Years Ago Suggested by Reading the Earlier Numbers of Mr. Robert B. Thomas's FARMER'S ALMANACK, Together with Extracts Curious, Instructive, and Entertaining, as well as a Variety of Miscellaneous Matter.*

Kittredge viewed himself as part of the community of folklore scholars. He corresponded with others working in folklore, with Andrew Lang and with Franz Boas.[10] Responding to an invitation of his former student, John A. Lomax, Kittredge lectured at the University of Texas, Austin, on April 3 and 4, 1913. He spoke on "The Study of Folk-Lore: Its Meaning and Value" at the third annual meeting of the Texas Folklore Society. Indeed, according to Lomax, it was Kittredge's suggestion that was instrumental in the founding of this society (Hyder 1962, 117). And Kittredge wrote the preface to the first volume published by the Texas Folklore Society (1916), a volume that was edited by Stith Thompson, a former student of Kittredge (Hyder 1962, 198, n7).

In 1904, while he was president of the Modern Language Association and serving the fourth year of his seven year term as president of the Colonial Society of Massachusetts (Thorpe 1948, 39, n10), Kittredge was elected president of the American Folklore Society. In 1911, Kittredge became first vice-president of the society, a position he retained until 1918. This latter appointment was part of Tozzer's plan to enlist the aid of the literary folklorists in broadening the base of support for the society. Kittredge was recruited to the position of assistant editor of the *Journal of American Folklore* for the same reason. As Dixon said, "We want to get Kittredge if possible to be one of the Associate Editors, and see if we can't get through him some material of the sort we used to have, which would enlist the interests of a wider circle, than the almost exclusively Indian material" (Boas Papers, Dixon to Boas, 11/18/1907).

Accepting the position, Kittredge was emphatic that he control the section of the journal under his supervision. His comments in letters were terse and cryptic. In 1912, he wrote to Boas to complain that a ballad article published in the journal had not been reviewed by him for publication: "If I am to be held *in any manner* responsible for the editing of the Journal, it is desirable (even requisite) that such articles as this should at least be *seen* by me before they are published. Put yourself in my place, and you will agree with me, I am sure" (Boas Papers, Kittredge to Boas, 10/29/1912). In another communication, Kittredge circled a sentence in Boas's letter that related a comment by a member of the Romance Department at Columbia University concerning the quality of the work of a literary folklorist, and he scrawled at the bottom of the letter, "Whoever said this knows nothing about folklore, however much of a pundit he may be in other respects" (Boas Papers, Kittredge to Boas, 10/3/1912).

While active in the American Folklore Society, Kittredge was never a controlling force in the society. His crucial role in folklore studies was not within the organizational framework, but rather in his capacity as a professor at Harvard. A list of the courses he taught illustrates not only the range of his expertise, but also the areas that his students would pursue in later years. During alternate years, from 1889 to 1896, he taught Icelandic and Old Norse. Beginning in 1890, and continuing for more than twenty years, Kittredge taught a course in the Department of German on Germanic mythology. From 1892 on, Kittredge taught a graduate course on English metrical romances. He taught a course on *Beowulf,* and he was renowned for his course on Shakespeare. From 1903, on alternate years, Kittredge and Fred Norris Robinson jointly taught a course on Germanic and Celtic religions.[11]

Just as Kittredge continued the work begun by Child on *The English and Scottish Popular Ballad,* so he also carried on with the ballad course taught by Child. In 1894–1895 and 1895–1896, Francis James Child had lectured on "The English and Scottish Popular Ballad" at Harvard. George Lyman Kittredge continued the instruction of this course, teaching it on alternate years beginning in 1897 (Ben-Amos 1976, x).

Kittredge was scornful of the American emphasis on pedagogy. In response to an educator's written request to audit his class, Kittredge replied:

Of course you may attend as many exercises in English 2 as you wish. However, you must not expect to get enlightenment from me on "methods of teaching.". . . . I believe that it is possible for any normal person to learn anything; but I am very skeptical of anybody's ability to *teach*: that is, in the sense in which this verb is commonly understood by American students of "education."

(Hyder 1962, 47–48)[12]

In another instance, a specialist in education asked Kittredge about the length of time he spent in preparing his lectures. At first, Kittredge refused to answer, saying it was his trade secret. And finally, he responded, "Just a lifetime—can't you see that?" (Brown 1948, 65–69).

Kittredge, his methods of instruction, and his eccentric behavior formed the nucleus for the legends of "Kitty." His biographer, Clyde Kenneth Hyder, paints a generous picture of Kittredge, reporting only the stories that reflected well on his image as a revered and esteemed professor. Stith Thompson was more honest in his appraisal of Kittredge, "I have seen him do inexcusable things in his Shakespeare class to humiliate students. . . . Kittredge always patronized his students, even the most advanced" (Thompson 1956, 58). Still, Thompson remembered Kittredge as "one of the greatest teachers" he had ever known (Upadhyaya 1968, 109). Kittredge offered Thompson kindness and encouragement with his dissertation, telling him that he might "come over to see him at any time without appointment" (Thompson 1956, 58). On one occasion, Kittredge asked to keep his dissertation. When he returned it to Thompson, he had rewritten two pages in long-hand. Thompson remarked, "I still have this long-hand pencil document among my precious possessions" (Upadhyaya 1968, 110).

Thompson recalled Kittredge's method of instruction for his graduate seminars in Shakespeare and medieval romance. He would lecture and give assigned readings during the first semester. Yet, in order to take the class, the students "had to agree to come to his house every Wednesday evening during the second semester and read the papers which we had prepared." Thompson continued:

I think one of the pleasant things that most of us remember about those Harvard days was the meeting together in this informal way in Professor Kittredge's study on these Wednesday nights. He would have his birch fire going and have excellent cigars and even cigarettes, as he said, "for the weaker sisters." The paper would be read and discussed somewhat languidly, and then Professor Kittredge himself would talk about it for perhaps half an hour.

(Thompson 1956, 58–59)

Historians of folklore studies are agreed, the courses taught by Child and Kittredge at Harvard were crucial for the development of folklore scholarship. Esther Birdsall, in her article "Some Notes on the Role of George Lyman Kittredge in American Folklore Studies," says, "The influence of this course on American folklore activities cannot be overestimated" (Birdsall 1973, 58). And D. K. Wilgus, in *Anglo-American Folksong Scholarship since*

1898, remarks that Child and Kittredge had made Harvard the unofficial center of folksong study at the beginning of the century. "The direct and indirect influence of Harvard University produced results which, when archives and theses are eventually surveyed, will be truly staggering" (Wilgus 1959, 174). Ben-Amos notes that most contemporary university courses in folklore "are related directly and indirectly to [Child's] teaching at Harvard at the end of the nineteenth century, and the courses offered by his disciple, George Lyman Kittredge" (Ben-Amos 1973, 122).

As is so often the case with great teachers, the contributions of Child and Kittredge to the field of folklore can be measured by the accomplishments of their students. To be sure, their scholarly works remain. But in terms of the development of folklore studies, it was the students, who left their classrooms and took their knowledge of folklore with them to other academic centers, who were to be the creators of the new discipline of folklore. The students of Child and Kittredge went from Harvard to the University of California, Berkeley; to the University of California, Los Angeles; to Ohio State University, Columbus; to the University of Texas, Austin; and to Indiana University, Bloomington. They continued the work of their mentors in the courses they taught at these institutions and the research they pursued. One must also acknowledge that these universities are among the leading centers in academic folklore research today.

Walter Morris Hart, who as an undergraduate had been a student of Francis B. Gummere (Thompson 1956, 49), was one of Kittredge's early students. Hart went to the University of California, Berkeley where he taught a course on the English and Scottish ballad, Middle English language, and the epic (Thompson 1956, 49; Ben-Amos 1976, x). He continued his research on the relationship between the ballad and epic poetry.

Hart trained two outstanding folklore scholars, Stith Thompson and Sigurd Bernhard Hustvedt. Of his teaching, Thompson recalled that Hart followed Gummere's and Kittredge's communal theory of ballad origin—the idea that the ballad was created through the inspiration or spirit of the group.[13] Thompson said, "I am certain that we were given the true doctrine." And he continued, "Although I have come to disagree with his conclusions, the methods of stylistic analysis which he used for these ballads and epics, was [*sic*] so excellent that I still know of no better model to give my own students" (Thompson 1956, 49). Hart encouraged both Hustvedt and Thompson to continue their graduate work at Harvard under Kittredge's instruction. The two, who had first met in Hart's ballad class at Berkeley, roomed together in College House on Harvard Square and attended folklore classes together (Thompson 1956, 54).

Sigurd Bernhard Hustvedt completed his master's thesis under Hart in 1912. It was entitled "The Popular Ballad in English and Danish." At Harvard, Hustvedt continued his ballad studies under Kittredge's direction from 1912 to 1915. He became a Professor of English at the University of California, Los Angeles, where he remained until 1949 (Bynum 1974, 15).

Hustvedt continued his research on ballad scholarship, producing the classic *Ballad Books and Ballad Men* (1930) and offering his first course in English ballads in 1933 (Wilgus 1976, xiii).

As Bynum notes in his article, "Child's Legacy Enlarged: Oral Literary Studies at Harvard Since 1856," Archer Taylor and Stith Thompson are "generally regarded as the founders of modern folklore scholarship" in the United States (Bynum 1974, 16). They first met at Harvard in 1912, and continued a professional relationship for the rest of their lives. In a humorous and touching aside, Bynum says, they vied "amicably with each other throughout their lives as to which of them would live longest and do most for folklore studies." Bynum added "At this writing both are still living and their contest is undecided." And then in a footnote, Bynum says, "Between the writing and publication of this paper, Archer Taylor died, 30 September 1973" (Bynum 1974, 16).

Archer Taylor (1890–1973) completed his undergraduate studies in humanities at Swarthmore in 1909, and his masters in German at the University of Pennsylvania in 1910. He became an instructor in German at Pennsylvania State College from 1910 to 1912; and then he returned to the student life at Harvard University from 1912 to 1915. He studied German literature with Kuno Francke and Albrecht Walz, and German philology with Hans Carl Gunther von Jagemann. Taylor also studied Old Norse under Fred Norris Robinson, and he worked with George Lyman Kittredge in ballad studies. Taylor formed important and lasting friendships with student colleagues. In addition to Stith Thompson, he met Taylor Starck in Germanic Studies; Sigurd Hustvedt and Arthur G. Brodeur in English and Germanic Philology.

After Taylor completed his dissertation on the Wolfdietrich epics in 1915, he accepted a teaching position at Washington University, which he held from 1915 until 1925. During these years, he worked as editor for the humanistic series of the "Washington University Studies." It was while Taylor was at Washington University that he began his work on the proverb. His colleague in the German Department, Richard Jente, later edited the fifteenth-century corpus of Dutch and Low German proverbs, *Proverbia Communia* (Hand 1974, 5).

Taylor went to the University of Chicago in 1925 where he taught courses in literature, folklore, and bibliography. As the chairman of the Department of Germanic Languages, Taylor introduced folklore as one of the five fields of specialization for doctoral study, to be included with philology, older German literature, modern German literature, and Scandinavian languages and literatures (Hand 1974, 5). The Chicago years were important for Taylor. He published his classic work *The Proverb* in 1931. He worked with Tom Peete Cross in Celtic Studies, and William A. Nitze in Arthurian Studies.

Taylor arrived in Berkeley in 1939, and for the next eighteen years he taught in the German Department. He offered an upper-division "Introduction to Folk-Lore" which was listed in the 1939–1940 General Catalogue of the University of California as follows:

125. Introduction to Folk-Lore (3) II, MWF, 3 Taylor. Prerequisite: senior standing (for major students in anthropology, junior standing) and the ability to read one foreign language. A survey of the materials of popular tradition, the folk song, the folk tale, the proverb, the riddle, and other forms. The methods and results of investigation in this field will be presented.

(U. C. 1939, 266)

Taylor also taught a graduate course on "The Tale" which was described as "a survey of the types of popular narratives and of the theories of the origin and dissemination of tales" (University of California 1939, 267). There was also a course given on the German ballad and lyric poetry and the German folk song.

Taylor continued his work in ballad studies, the folktales, proverbs, and riddles. He wrote *A Bibliography of Riddles* (1939), and *English Riddles in Oral Tradition* (1961). He also edited the riddles in *The Frank C. Brown Collection of North Carolina Folklore* (1952) (Hand 1974, 6).

Archer Taylor served as president of the American Folklore Society (1936–1937) and editor of the *Journal of American Folklore* (1941–1942). He was one of the founders of the *California Folklore Quarterly*. His achievements were recognized both in the United States and abroad. He was a fellow of the American Philosophical Society, the Medieval Academy of America, the American Folklore Society, and the Newberry Library in Chicago; he was a member of the Folklore of Ireland Society, the Folklore Society in London, the Finnish Literary Society, the Société Finno-Ougrienne, the Schweizerische Gesellschaft für Volkskunde, the Norsk Videnskabasselskab, Gustav Adolfs Akademie for Folklivsforskining, and the Asociación folklórica argentina (Hand 1974, 8). He is honored even now with the annual Archer Taylor Memorial Lecture given at the California Folklore Society meetings.

Among the students of Archer Taylor were two whose work was crucial for the development of folklore: Ralph Steele Boggs and Wayland Debs Hand. Boggs went to the University of North Carolina as a professor of English, where he founded the folklore program (Boggs 1981). Hand, after completing his Ph.D. dissertation on "The Schnaderhupfel: An Alpine Folk Lyric" (1936), taught one year at the University of Minnesota (1936–1937). He then went to the University of California, Los Angeles (1937), and in 1940, he began teaching a course in German folklore (Wilgus 1967, xiii). Along with Hustvedt, he developed the interdisciplinary program in folklore (Wilgus 1967, xiii–xiv). In 1961, the Center for the Study of Comparative Folklore and Mythology was established, with Hand as the director until his retirement in 1974.

Wayland Hand was editor of volumes 6 (1961) and 7 (1964) of *The Frank C. Brown Collection of North Carolina Folklore*. In 1966, these volumes, subtitled *Popular Beliefs and Superstitions from North Carolina*, were awarded the Giuseppe Pitre Folklore Prize, the first American works to be so honored (Wilgus 1967, xiii). Hand provided annotations with material from Canada and the United States. As he explained, this required recording 25,000 items on individual slips of paper, and eventually reducing them to 8,520 items (Hand 1961, ix). Hand noted that the work on the Frank C. Brown Collection would provide "the cornerstone" for the "Dictionary of American Popular Beliefs and Superstitions" (Hand 1964b, xviii). In 1944, Hand had begun gathering material for this dictionary (Hand 1980, xxiii). The files resulting from Hand's collection and from bibliographic research, including the work on the Frank C. Brown Collection, contain approximately 675,000 primary entries and 815,000 cross references. These are located at the Center for the Study of Comparative Folklore and Mythology at the University of California, Los Angeles. In 1985, Wayland Hand and Frances Cattermole-Tally began editing these files for a projected work, entitled *Encyclopaedia of American Popular Beliefs and Superstitions*, which will be a major reference source in this area of folklore.

Among other works by Wayland Hand are the following: *A Dictionary of Words and Idioms Associated with Judas Iscariot* (1942), which was awarded the Chicago Folklore Prize; *American Folk Legend, a Symposium* (1971); *American Folk Medicine, a Symposium* (1976); *Magical Medicine, the Folkloric Component of Medicine in the Folk Belief, Custom, and Ritual of the Peoples of Europe and America* (1980); *Popular Beliefs and Superstitions: A Compendium of American Folklore from the Ohio Collection of Newbell Niles Puckett* (1981). Also active in professional organizations, Hand was editor of the *Journal of American Folklore* from 1947 to 1951; president of the American Folklore Society from 1957 to 1958; and in 1960, he was chosen as a fellow of the society.

Stith Thompson (1885–1976) first became interested in folklore during his undergraduate study at the University of Wisconsin, where he wrote his thesis "The Return of the Dead in Folk Literature" (1909), under the supervision of Arthur Beatty. Thompson did his master's work in English at the University of California, Berkeley, from 1911 to 1912. He took Walter Morris Hart's course in Middle English language, and his seminar on the English and Scottish ballad. He wrote his master's thesis on "The Idea of the Soul in Teutonic Popular Ballads and Literature" (1912).

An award of the Bonnheim Research Fellowship made it possible for Thompson to continue his graduate work at Harvard (1912–1913). In his memoir, *Folklorist's Progress*, Stith Thompson recalled one particular class meeting of Kittredge's "Medieval Romance":

One morning he opened his discussion a propos of nothing with the following: "Gentlemen, I received today a letter from Dr. Pliny Earle Goddard, the California anthropologist who is now in Saskatchewan among the Chipewyan

Indians. He had been collecting tales and he sent me two which he suspects may be of European origin. Now I should like to read one of these tales to you. It is called 'The Blue Band'."

(Thompson 1956, 59)

Kittredge read the tale, and then remarked that he had been working on this narrative recently. He suggested that its center of distribution "seems quite certainly to be Rumania"; and he had located one version in Norway. Though he had never found a version from France, he suspected that perhaps the French influence would be important in Saskatchewan. He hypothesized that the Chipewyan had learned the tale from Scandinavians. And he continued, "But I should really like to know. It would be an excellent task for someone to investigate just what the American Indians have done with stories which they borrowed from the Europeans" (Thompson 1956, 59).

In this way, by hearing a chance comment made by Kittredge in his class on medieval romance, Stith Thompson determined not only the subject of his doctoral dissertation, but the topic for a lifetime of work—folktales among the North American Indians. Stith Thompson recalled how this decision was reached, "The next day I had a talk with him and it was agreed that I should try my hand at this study. I was to begin with a small group of northeast Indians, the Micmac, Maliseet and Abanaki group" (Thompson 1956, 60).

At the time of his research, neither he nor Kittredge were aware of the work that had been done in Finland on the types of the folktale by Antti Aarne. This tale-type index of European narratives would have greatly facilitated Thompson's research. Years later, in 1920, Thompson looked through the new books in the Widener Library at Cambridge. He found Antti Aarne's *Verzeichnis der Märchentypen* (The Types of the Folktale). "How much would I have not given to have this when I was working on my own thesis! It had appeared in 1910 but apparently had not yet come to the attention of American scholars" (Thompson 1956, 81). It was so important for Thompson's research that he "made a longhand abstract of the whole thing" (Thompson 1956, 81). Thompson more than compensated for his initial bibliographic omission when, in later years, he revised *The Types of the Folktale*, and his name was joined with Aarne in hyphenated—even abbreviated—form as an indication of a folktale classification, the Aarne-Thompson or AT tale-type number.

After the completion of his work at Harvard, Thompson went to the University of Texas, Austin, as an English professor (1914–1918). He taught courses in English composition and literature. By serendipity, Thompson made contact with another of Kittredge's students who was living in Austin. When he first arrived, he engaged two rooms in a house. He recalled, "I had no idea who my landlord was but it turned out to be John A. Lomax, whose work as a collector of cowboy songs I already knew from Harvard days" (Thompson 1956, 66). Alan Lomax was born in the house that winter while Thompson was staying there. Through Lomax's invitation, Thompson attended the 1915 meeting of the Texas Folklore Society. He was elected secretary-treasurer; and he worked actively with the society during his remaining years in Texas (Thompson 1956, 69).

In 1921, Thompson was invited to Indiana University by his friend, John Rea. He made the trip to Bloomington and decided to take the position there. As he remarked, "I had a theory that no one should stay longer than four years at any university and get into a rut. At Bloomington I was to stay thirty-four" (Thompson 1956, 85).[14] Thompson taught courses in English composition, literature, and twentieth century poetry (Thompson 1956, 139). He developed a seminar on literary origins. He also taught a course on the ballad and on medieval romance (Thompson 1956, 89).

In an interview conducted when he was 83, Thompson talked of his professional self-view, "It must be remembered of course that I am primarily an English teacher and that folklore has always been an avocation" (Upadhyaya 1968, 110). Folklore, he said, was "a side issue" (Upadhyaya 1968, 117). His primary identification and his foremost concern in teaching was with English composition and literature. "When I came to Indiana University in 1921, it was not as a folklorist, but to supervise freshmen composition, which I did for the next fifteen years, until 1936" (Upadhyaya 1968, 111). And he added that it was only after he had been at Indiana for two years that he "had time to think about doing any work in folklore." Then, in 1923, he was given permission to teach a new graduate seminar on any topic of his choice. He offered "The Folktale and Allied Forms."[15] This developed into his favorite course which he continued to teach throughout the years.

For his research on American Indian narratives, Thompson developed a method to call these tales to mind: he made "abstracts and notes covering thousands of cards, mostly four by six slips" (Thompson 1956, 62). This was the beginning of his interest in the basic elements, or motifs, that combine to form a narrative. When he looked over these notes, he

> realized that no one had ever arranged such motifs in any logical order. . . . I can well remember the day when I said to myself that the study of these American Indian motifs must wait until I could have a chance to elaborate a classification on which to base the study. I thought it might take six months to classify such motifs as I already had.
>
> (Thompson 1956, 89)

It was to take forty years to complete the project (Upadhyaya 1968, 111). And the scope of the undertaking was to expand. In the summer of 1924, Thompson showed his work to Archer Taylor, who "immediately saw the significance" of what he was doing (Thompson 1956, 89). Taylor convinced Thompson to broaden the scope of the classification. Rather than just covering the material that Thompson had in his notes, Taylor suggested the inclusion of "great areas of traditional literature that I had not thought of working on—the great mythologies, the mediaeval romances, the ballads, the oriental tale collections. . ." (Thompson 1956, 91). Thompson and Taylor did agree, however, that the original work on the motif classification should be finished. And Thompson completed this four-hundred page manuscript in 1924.

Archer Taylor was traveling to Finland in the summer of 1924 to visit with Kaarle Krohn, the great scholar of the folktale. Taylor carried along Thompson's manuscript to show to Krohn. The latter read it, and was very impressed with Thompson's plan for a motif-index. Taylor wrote to Thompson, conveying this encouraging news, but adding that Krohn had a request to make of Thompson. Kaarle Krohn's ablest student, Antti Aarne, had died suddenly, and his planned revision of *The Types of the Folktale* had not been effected (Upadhyaya 1968, 111–12). Krohn thought that Thompson would be the appropriate person to undertake this revision. "One has only to realize how basic this list had been in the study of the international folktale to know how important the invitation was to me" (Thompson 1956, 93). He accepted, and his work on the motif index overlapped with his revision of Aarne's *The Types of the Folktale*.

In 1926–1927, Thompson traveled to Europe and to Scandinavia to work on the revision of the Antti Aarne *Verzeichnis der Märchentypen*. Together, Kaarle Krohn and Stith Thompson worked on the plans for the revised tale-type index. "We agreed that the original index-numbers were not to be disturbed but I was left with a great deal of discretion as to just how I should revise the work" (Thompson 1956, 96). This work was published by the Folklore Fellows Communication in 1928 as *The Types of the Folktale: Antti Aarne's "Verzeichnis der Märchentypen," Translated and Enlarged*. Seven years later, at the 1935 Congress for the Study of the Folktale, in Lund, Sweden, a session was devoted to the revision of the index. It was suggested that the tales of the Mediterranean, the Near East, and India should be included (Thompson 1956, 132). This second revision appeared in 1961 as *The Types of the Folktale: A Classification and Bibliography: Antti Aarne's "Verzeichnis der Märchentypen," Translated and Enlarged*.

For *Tales of the North American Indians* (1929), Thompson selected narratives that would represent most of the motifs characteristic of the Indians' tales. "For every type of tale among the Indians, some ninety-six, I tried to choose the best-told of the versions. Then at the proper place I made a note of any motifs that I cared to discuss" (Thompson 1956, 93). In his review, Franz Boas found "the value of the book for the student of American folklore . . . in the very full comparative notes." These, he said, "will be an indispensable source for anyone who wishes to study the distribution of incidents of North American folklore" since Thompson had collected and expanded on all of the available concordances (Boas 1930, 223–24).

An account of the unending work on the *Motif-Index of Folk Literature* runs through Thompson's memoir, *Folklorist's Progress*. In April 1928, Thompson noted that he had completed the preliminary arrangement of the index into the twenty-three chapters and he was ready to begin the sorting of the slips of paper. "By the end of the School year in June of 1929 I had finished the F chapter." "By the beginning of 1930 I finished the H chapter and during the following spring completed J." And in the fall of 1930, he "finished K chapter of the Index" and had completed the fourth volume (Thompson 1956, 107–11). In 1935, Thompson recalled, "I was racing against time so as to finish the last stroke on the Motif-Index by my fiftieth birthday. Early in March, about three or four days before that eventful moment, I was able to say that the whole job was now complete" (Thompson 1956, 126). He had finished the six volumes of the *Motif-Index of Folk Literature*.

In his life's work on the folktale, Thompson remained true to the responsibility passed on to him by Kaarle Krohn. In 1927, when Thompson was completing his revision of *The Types of the Folktale* and preparing to return to the United States, Krohn talked with Thompson about his plans for the future. Thompson recalled, "He gave me to understand that he was counting on me strongly to carry on the work in folktale scholarship not only in another country but also in a new age" (Upadhyaya 1968, 114). The next day Krohn recalled his own visit in 1883 to Reinhold Kohler, the Ducal Librarian in Weimar, the renowned folktale scholar of the nineteenth century. Kohler told Krohn, "Dr. Krohn, I am now an old man. I have spent many years working on the folktale but now I can do very little more. It is to you that I look for carrying on these researches in your generation." Krohn turned to him and said, "I hope you remember what I said to you yesterday" (Thompson 1956, 105). So, in truth, the line of expertise on folktale scholarship passed from Reinhold Kohler to Kaarle Krohn to Stith Thompson.

With his research on American Indian narratives, Thompson provided a link between the literary folklorists and the anthropological folklorists. While conducting research on European tales among the American Indians, Thompson spent much time at the Peabody Museum Library. Here, as he said, he made his "first contact with anthropologists"; he met Roland B. Dixon and Alfred M. Tozzer. Thompson noted, "Dixon gave me real help toward my thesis and some suggestions toward anthropological methods" (Thompson 1956, 62). When *Tales of the North American Indians* appeared in 1929, Thompson gained recognition from anthropologists. As he said, "This work strengthened my ties with the anthropology teachers over the country and became a standard part of all of the anthropology libraries" (Thompson 1956, 109).

In "Recollections of an Itinerant Folklorist," which was an address delivered to the Texas Folklore Society on May 20, 1956, Stith Thompson gave an appraisal of his work in folklore. He said he had spent his time working on indexes and classifications in order to facilitate the process of archiving material (Thompson 1957, 120). "I am quite unblushing in admitting that I have never collected any folklore myself. I have been out with collectors, for I like to go along and see them gather material. But I recognize that collecting has its own techniques and I know that I would bungle things very badly" (Thompson 1957, 121). As a contrast to his approach, Thompson spoke of Vance Randolph, who was "a great collector. . . . But he was honest enough to say when he received my *Motif-Index* that he would never try to annotate his stories. 'I should have made an unholy mess of it . . . if I had tried that' " (Thompson 1957, 121).

Like Stith Thompson, Francis Lee Utley (1907–1974) did his undergraduate work at the University of Wisconsin where he received his bachelor of arts degree in 1929. He went on to Harvard, completing his master's degree in 1934, and his doctorate in 1936. Utley took a position as Professor of English at Ohio State Univeristy in 1935 and remained there for the next thirty-nine years. Through his research and publications, he established an international reputation (Finnie 1975, 127). His interests in folklore and medieval literature were manifested in the courses he taught and the library he amassed, twenty-one thousand volumes which were bequeathed to Ohio State University.

Utley's success in establishing folklore studies at Ohio State University was recognized by his colleagues when they voted to confer upon him the title created specifically for him, Professor of English and Folklore (Finnie 1975, 128). Yet this success did not come easily. As Utley himself remarked, he had to jump "countless hurdles" before he could establish "one introductory course in folklore. . . . At one time, indeed, I estimated that I had fourteen ex-students teaching the subject in American colleges before I had one course at my own institution" (Utley 1970, 111). Utley did, however, succeed in bringing folklore instruction to Ohio State University. He established the folklore program and the Folklore Archives (Finnie 1975, 127). In addition to "Introduction to Folklore," Utley taught a seminar on "Arthurian Literature and International Folklore."

Utley was an outstanding teacher, one who conveyed the enthusiasm he felt for the material. W. Bruce Finnie recalled that "to hear Professor Utley read and discuss the ending of Chaucer's masterwork [*Troilus and Criseyde*] was an emotional as well as an intellectual experience" (Finnie 1975, 128). Utley took pride in the accomplishments of his students. He named James Tidwell, Edson Richmond, D. K. Wilgus, and Bruce Rosenberg as those who had "gone on to do systematic research and teaching in the field" (Utley 1970, 111).

Utley published extensively on medieval literature and folklore. In *The Crooked Rib* (1944), he examined medieval attitudes toward women. He contributed to biblical studies with his work on the Bible and folklore, and the flood narrative, and to Chaucerian study. The bibliograhy of Utley's writings includes over two hundred entries (Amsler 1975).

In addition to his expertise as a literary folklorist, Utley also had a secure grasp on anthropological folklore. In his outstanding article, "The Migration of Folktales: Four Channels to the Americas" (1974), Utley exhibited a control of the literature—folkloristic, linguistic, and anthropological—that was truly formidable. Utley examined the possible routes of diffusion of the folktale: (1) from Northeast Asia across the Bering Strait, (2) from Southeast Asia across the Pacific Islands, (3) from Europe across the North Atlantic, and (4) from Africa across the South Atlantic. As Dundes remarked in his commentary on the article,

> Utley's survey is truly a tour de force. The scholarship pertinent to each of the four proposed channels is simply immense, and yet Utley moves with apparent ease from Polynesian to African sources. One wonders how many anthropologists could return the favor by surveying the intricacies of medieval-literature scholarship!

> (Dundes 1974, 16)

There are others whose contributions were vital and lasting. Fred Norris Robinson, a student of Child and Kittredge, received his Ph.D. from Harvard in 1894. Following the advice of his mentors, he went to Freiburg, Germany to specialize in Celtic Studies. The two Harvard professors were hoping to groom Robinson to fill the void in this field at their university. Their plan succeeded. Robinson returned to Harvard in 1896, and remained until 1939. Stith Thompson spoke of Fred Norris Robinson with esteem: "He carried on to us the tradition of the Harvard of Francis James Child, the great ballad scholar. He had studied Irish and the other Celtic languages in Europe and had come back and, almost singlehanded introduced Celtic studies into America" (Thompson 1956, 55).

John A. Lomax (1867–1948) was the enthusiastic folksong collector. When he was a small boy, he began collecting cowboy songs, and when he left his family farm to attend Granbury College, "he carried a small roll of cowboy songs, tied with a cotton string" (Michael 1960, 11). Lomax was still interested in cowboys and their music when he was a student at Harvard University. In 1906, for his class in American literature, Lomax asked Professor Wendell's permission to write a paper on cowboy songs. Wendell directed him to Kittredge. And under Kittredge's tutelage, Lomax began collecting songs seriously (Michael 1960, 11). Kittredge helped his student obtain three summer fellowships from Harvard for fieldwork (McNeil 1980, 551).

John Lomax received his M.A. from Harvard in 1907. (He had already received the same degree from the University of Texas in 1906.) He returned to Texas where, along with T. W. Payne, he founded the Texas Folklore Society in 1909 (Michael 1960, 11–12). He was president of the American Folklore Society from 1912 to 1913, and Honorary Curator of the Folk Song Library in 1934. Throughout his life, he continued to collect folksongs. His work stands as a tribute to what a true fieldworker and dedicated person can do. He was innovative in his collecting methods. Among other approaches, he used newspaper appeals which yielded quantities of ballads. He also found success by attending auctions and bidding on old trunks that contained copies of ballad texts (Michael 1960, 22–23). But nothing, Lomax emphasized, replaced personal contact with the people to whom the songs belonged.[16]

Milman Parry was another outstanding student of Kittredge. Parry's work on the Yugoslavian epics stirred the academic world. He brought forward the suggestion that the *Illiad* and the *Odyssey* had been created by oral tradition. He studied the Yugoslav singers of tales in order to ascertain how such a rich epic tradition could be recorded in memory and passed orally (Bynum 1974, 29). For fifteen months in 1934 and 1935, Parry collected Yugoslavian epics throughout the Slavic-speaking regions of the western Balkans. He used aluminum discs, a new recording technique. This extensive epic collection is preserved in the Milman Parry Collection of Oral Literature at Harvard University. There are over 12,500 individual texts and 3,000 recorded twelve inch aluminum discs. (See also Bynum 1974, 29; Lord 1960, 279, n2.)

Parry returned from Yugoslavia in 1935, with plans for a major work on epic singers. He died after he had written the first few pages (Lord 1960, 279, n1).[17] Parry's student, Albert Lord, continued the work. In 1937, Lord went to Albania under the auspices of the Society of Fellows at Harvard to collect epic poetry. He traveled to Yugoslavia in 1950 and 1951, and to Bulgaria in 1958 (Lord 1960, ii).

In 1960, Lord published his book on epic singers, a consideration of "the manner in which they learn, and transmit their epics." It was entitled *The Singer of Tales,* the same title that his mentor, Parry, had intended to use for his work. The opening lines show the orientation of both Parry and Lord: "This book is about Homer. He is our singer of tales." Lord continued, "Among the singers of modern times there is none equal to Homer, but he who approaches the master most closely in our experience of epic song is Avdo Mededovic of . . . Yugoslavia. He is our present-day Balkan Singer of Tales" (Lord 1960, i).

According to oral formulaic theory, epic poetry is created through the use of oral formulas, "groups of words" that are used following "the same metrical conditions to express a given essential idea" (Lord 1960, 30). As Lord explained, the singer learned his art from others, and also learned oral formulaic patterns. Thus, the formula "mounting the horse" appeared in the repertoire of many epic singers.

> "By Allah," he said, he mounted the white horse.
> "By Allah," he said, he mounted the brown horse.
> "By Allah," he said, he mounted the animal.
> And he said this, he mounted the brown horse.
> And he said this, he mounted the animal.

> (Lord 1960, 48)

The songs were built around certain traditional themes, which were formulated through "a grouping of ideas" (Lord 1960, 69). Lord gave an example of the theme of the council in the "Song of Bagdad." The sultan received a letter from his field commander who had been laying siege to Bagdad for twenty years without success. He called his councilors together and asked their advice. He received good advice from one, and evil advice from the other. "And the theme is concluded with the writing of an imperial letter to Bosnia and dispatch of the messenger" (Lord 1960, 68). Through the use of themes and oral formulas, the singer of tales created their epics.

Three leading folklorists, MacEdward Leach, Louise Pound, and Aurelio Espinosa, did not follow the pattern of the foregoing scholars who came to folklore through the influence of Child and Kittredge. MacEdward Leach (1896–1967) became interested in folklore through his work in Middle English literature, which he studied at the University of Illinois (B.A. 1916; M.A. 1917). During the First World War, he taught at the Johns Hopkins University, and then returned to graduate study at the University of Pennsylvania where he received his doctorate in 1930. Here he was influenced by Cornelius Weygandt and Frank Speck, with whom he later did field-work in the Delmarva Peninsula (Greenway 1968, 105).

Leach was trained as a philologist and a medievalist as is illustrated by his *Paris and Vienne* and the homage volume for Albert Baugh (Utley in Greenway 1968, 119). Through his early work in medieval literature, he was drawn to ballad studies. Leach recalled his first course in the ballad, which he took at the University of Illinois.

> [My professor] had the mistaken idea that ballads were something you dance to. . . . After an afternoon of class work we were taken out behind the auditorium on the greensward. And, this teacher had the idea that you didn't dance folk dances with your shoes on, and so we all had to peel off our shoes and stockings, boys and girls, singing "Lord Randall" and "My son Edward."
>
> (Glassie in Greenway 1968, 107)[18]

Leach's publications in this field include *The Ballad Book* (1955), *The Critics of the Ballad* (1961), co-edited with Tristan P. Coffin, and *Folk Ballads and Songs of the Lower Labrador Coast* (1965).

MacEdward Leach dedicated himself to folkore studies, both in academe and in the professional societies. He sustained the American Folklore Society through its years of insecurity. Richard Dorson remarked, "For many years he was in effect the Society" (Dorson in Greenway 1968, 103).[19] As William Fenton expressed it, "His central purpose in life seemed to be to improve folklore as a field" (Fenton in Greenway 1968, 105). And for this, he used his energy and his good humor. MacEdward Leach recalled the surreptitious manner in which folklore courses were introduced into the curriculum at the University of Pennsylvania. This was done, Leach said, "by devious methods of one sort or other."

> We had a man there years ago who taught a course called "Epic and the Short Story." He died prematurely and I inherited the course and gradually eased it away from epic and from short story into general folklore and folktale. The

English department didn't know that I was teaching folklore and folktale; they thought I was still teaching "Epic and the Short Story."

(Glassie in Greenway 1968, 107)

Still another course fell to MacEdward Leach, this one on the ballad as poetry. "But gradually the course edged away toward what a ballad is, namely, a folksong" (Glassie in Greenway 1968, 108). He continued to teach the course "Early English Literature" (MacFadden in Greenway 1968, 116), and the "Arthurian Legend" which was the last course he taught before his retirement (Johnson in Greenway 1968, 113).

In his tribute to MacEdward Leach, Wayland Hand wrote, "Great as was his work as a field collector and scholar in folklore, MacEdward Leach will be remembered as one of the most successful teachers of folklore in the country" (Hand 1968, 43–44). Among his students are the following: Tristram P. Coffin, G. Malcolm Laws, Edith S. Krappe, Horace P. Beck, William E. Simeone, John Greenway, David Fowler, Ellen Stekert, Kenneth S. Goldstein, Roger Abrahams, and Archie Green (Hand 1968, 44). His students recalled Leach's ability to hold a class, both through his erudition and his charisma. Helen Sewell Johnson said that he had a "vast experiencing power" (Sewell in Greenway 1968, 112).

Louise Pound (1872–1958) was a native of Lincoln, Nebraska, and it was here that she stayed, save for summer study at the University of Chicago (1897, 1898), and a year at Heidelburg where she took her doctorate (1900). Pound entered the University of Nebraska as a student in 1886; she remained there as a professor until her retirement in 1945.

Benjamin Botkin, a student of Louise Pound, said, "She was equally at home in the fields of American literature, linguistics, folklore, and folksong" (Botkin 1959, 201). She worked actively with the American Dialect Society, serving as vice-president (1927–1937) and president (1938–1944). She viewed dialect studies as a branch of folkore. Pound also worked with the American Folklore Society, as president (1925–1927) and councilor in the years following. She was advisory editor of *Folk-Say* (1929–1930) and of the *Southern Folklore Quarterly* (1939–1958). In 1924, the Texas Folklore Society made her a life member (Botkin 1959, 201).

Pound's interest in folklore grew out of her Nebraskan heritage. This is reflected in *Nebraska Folklore* (1959), a book of collected papers published posthumously by the University of Nebraska Press. Botkin said of her, "She was a staunch opponent of mystical and romantic theories of the 'folk mind' and communal origins" (Botkin 1959, 201). She directed her *Poetic Origins and the Ballad* (1921) "to the systematic and documented refutation" of these theories.

Botkin remembered her, above all, as a teacher. "With her, teaching was a way of life that became a part of the lives of her graduate students, who treasure her memory as a guide, philosopher, and friend" (Botkin 1959, 202). In response to a reporter's question on the eve of her retirement,

Louise Pound said, "I believe the pleasantest thing that has happened to me is that I've had a number of books dedicated to me (Botkin 1959, 202).

Aurelio Macedonio Espinosa (1880–1958) came to folklore on his own, through his interest in the Hispanic culture of the Southwest. He did his undergraduate and master's work at the University of Colorado (B.A. 1902, M.A. 1904), and took a position as professor of modern languages at the University of New Mexico. Espinosa received his doctorate from the University of Chicago in romance languages and literatures, with a minor in Indo-European philology (Espinosa, J. M. 1985, 14). He completed his Ph.D. in 1910. His dissertation, "Studies in New-Mexican Spanish," appeared in three parts between 1909 and 1914 in the *Révue de Dialectologie Romane*. In 1910, he took a position at Stanford University where he remained for the rest of his life (Espinosa, J. M. 1978, 222–23). Espinosa organized a graduate program and directed fifty master's theses and twelve doctoral dissertations, many of which focused on folklore and dialectology (Espinosa, J. M. 1985, 15).

Espinosa's interest in collecting a wide range of folklore is reflected in a letter he wrote to Boas in 1913:

> I just returned a few days ago from the southern part of California and I find that the field in Cal. is as abundant & valuable as in N. Mex. I found ten versions of five old Spanish ballads, a large collection of nursery rhymes, some 50 riddles, proverbs, and 100 versos, various other popular songs & modern ballads, some old prayers, and several short stories, one long folktale . . . and other material.
>
> (Boas Papers, Espinosa to Boas, 9/3/1913)[20]

Espinosa collected folktales and ballads in the Southwest; and then, sponsored by Elsie Clews Parsons, he carried his work to Spain in 1920. In 1923–1926, he published the results of this work in the three volume *Cuentos populares españoles* (Espinosa, J. M. 1978, 223; Fife 1960, 98). Augmenting his work in Spanish folktales was his research in Spanish ballads, called *romances tradicionales* or *corridos* (Espinosa 1985). He also researched proverbs, folk theatre, folk drama, and children's games.

Espinosa was active in folklore societies. He served as president of the American Folklore Society in 1924–1925, and as associate editor of the *Journal of American Folklore* for a number of years beginning in 1914. He was associate editor of *Western Folklore* from 1947 to 1953, and consulting editor of the *New Mexico Quarterly* from 1930 to 1936, and helped with the establishment of the New Mexico Folklore Society in 1931 (Espinosa, J. M. 1985, 16–17).

In focusing on the growth within academia—the passing on of the scholarly tradition from Child to Kittredge to their students—it should not be assumed that all of the important contributions of the literary folklorists have been presented. There are those individuals who carried on their research outside of academia but whose work had an impact on the development of folklore studies. Dan Ben-Amos emphasizes this point: "The struggle over the control of the centers of scholarly activities should not overshadow the role of the individual in the advancement of the discipline" (Ben-Amos 1973, 123). One such individual was Alexander Haggerty Krappe (1894–1947). His early schooling was in England, Holland, and Germany where he studied romance languages and medieval history. Krappe did his undergraduate work at the University of Berlin, received his masters at the University of Iowa (1917), and his doctorate at the University of Chicago (1919). Krappe was devoted to folklore scholarship; he looked to folklore to reconstruct the history of humankind. Krappe's orientation to folklore was literary. Yet he viewed folklore as a science, because the inductive method was used. Krappe's theoretical outlook was conservative nineteenth century; he ignored much of anthropological theory. From his rigid European perspective, Krappe denied that American folklore existed.

A large factor in his peripheral position in American folklore studies had to do with his irascible personality. Though a brilliant scholar—able to write with facility in English, French, and German—and author of *The Science of Folklore*, Krappe was not successful in holding any of his numerous academic appointments long. He was outspoken, flamboyant, and abrasive.[21]

There are many other literary folklorists who merit attention, and whose lives and works are woven into the fabric of American folkloristics. But following the pattern which has been selected in this chapter, the focus has been on the literary folklorists in their position within academia. In truth, these scholars often attained positions of power and control. This was certainly the case with Child, Kittredge, Thompson, Taylor, Hand, Leach, and Utley. As leaders in their fields of literature and folklore, and as respected members of their departments, these men were in a position to encourage young students and to train them. In effect, then, they created a following, a body of students who continued to research, to elaborate, and to add to the concerns and ideas of their mentors.

It is important to recognize that there are differing arenas of activity within American folkloristics. In the previous chapter, the jockeying for power—especially editorial power—within the American Folklore Society was examined. And it was concluded that until 1940, the anthropological folklorists maintained control over the major activities of the society and the publications of the journal. In this chapter, the formation of a school of literary folklorists who developed and perpetuated an academic tradition was discussed. Hence there was the activity in the organizational arena, which encompassed the struggle for power in the American Folklore Society, and the activity in the academic arena, which perpetuated a scholarly tradition of folkloristic study.

If one considers the organizational and the academic arenas as two legitimate circles in which American folkloristics developed, then the complexity of the past is recognized and the tendency to iron out the wrinkles of this complexity in favor of a single-line progression of power is avoided. It is simply not the case, as Michael Bell claims, that the demise of the Chicago Folklore Society "eliminated the sole forum in the United States for the concept of folklore as a form of literature and effectively halted for some forty years the widespread promulgation of this concept by American folklorists" (Bell 1973, 20). It is true that the demise of the Chicago Folklore Society was the end of an organizational forum for literary folklorists, but, as noted in this chapter, the literary folklorists did not remain silent for forty years. They were active as teachers and as scholars in academia.

FIVE

The Anthropological Folklorists

George Foster, a student of Alfred Kroeber, commented on his early training in anthropology, "In those days, we all did folklore."[1] And Melville Jacobs made a similar comment, "Indeed, only a few students returned [from the field] without folklore in some form" (Jacobs 1959b, 122). In the first three decades of this century, the assumption was made that students of anthropology would collect folklore as part of their training in linguistics and ethnology. In addition they would receive training in physical anthropology and archaeology. This inclusive approach was part of Boas's grand scheme for the development of academic anthropology in the twentieth century. Folklore was, in effect, an area of study within anthropology. Important though it was, still it was to remain just that—part of the larger whole.

In addition to its position as a subfield of anthropology, there was another consideration that provided impetus for the study of folklore. This had to do with the need for a publication outlet. On December 15, 1902, Franz Boas wrote to Kroeber,

> My dear Kroeber,
>   My only reasons for preferring the Folk-Lore Society are that the author is in a better position to control the form of the publication, and the publication will be so much more prompt than in the Bureau.
>
>   (Kroeber Papers, Boas to Kroeber, 12/15/1902)

Boas's strategy was politically astute. It was also necessary. Newell, in his review of Boas's 1895 *Indianische Sagen von der Nord-Pacifischen Kuste Amerikas*, told of the difficulties Boas had in finding a publisher for his work. Failing in the United States, he tried publishers in Holland. Then he turned to Germany: "in the end the matter was issued in parts by the Berlin Society. Had the Memoirs of the American Folk-Lore Society been in existence when the arrangement was made no doubt a place might have been found in that series" (Newell 1896, 78–79). According to Newell this circumstance was not unique to Boas, but occurred frequently.

With Boas and his students as editors, the *Journal of American Folklore* became a major concern of anthropologists. Since publication of the dissertation was a requirement for the Ph.D. at Columbia (Willis 1973, 317), many of Boas's students published their entire dissertations in the journal. The first footnote to Goldenweiser's "Totemism, an Analytical Study," reads, "Dissertation submitted in partial fulfillment of the requirements for the degree of Doctor of Philosophy in the Faculty of Philosophy, Columbia University" (Goldenweiser 1910, 179, n1). Save for four pages of book reviews, this comprised the entire issue of the *Journal of American Folklore*.

The journal remained a sympathetic forum for anthropological folklorists. As William Fenton recalled,

In the 1930's young ethnologists in the Boas tradition were advised on receiving their doctorates to join the American Anthropological Association and the American Folklore Society, because the JOURNAL OF AMERICAN FOLKLORE carried material of interest to those working in the oral tradition, and it was a good place to publish.

(Fenton in Greenway 1968, 104)

Boas's careful planning and jockeying for power must be viewed as part of the realities of the time. In "The Development of American Anthropology 1879–1920: From Bureau of American Ethnology to Franz Boas," Darnell points to "the localism of mid-nineteenth century American anthropology" which was centered in Washington, D.C., Cambridge, and Philadelphia (Darnell 1969, 140). She remarks that Boas "deliberately built up a counter power-bloc to the Bureau, in large part through the American Folklore Society and the American Ethnological Society" (Darnell 1969, 875). This was part of the same battle that Boas waged against the Washington anthropologists and their plans for the founding of the American Anthropological Association.[2]

Boas was important to the development of American anthropology in many ways. In addition to his critical influence on the organizational framework—the development of university programs, museum programs, and societies—he also helped shape anthropological and folkloristic studies through his work as a scholar and a teacher. Melville Jacobs in his appraisal of Boas's contribution to folklore, remarked.

Among those who worked in non-European folklore, Boas was foremost in collecting and encouraging the gathering of folktales; in setting up rigorous oritoria for the ways in which they should be obtained; in their use to show diffusion; and in noting the elements of social organization and culture they contained.

(Jacobs 1959b, 119)

Franz Boas (1858–1942) came to anthropology through his training in physics and the same route brought him to the United States from Germany. In 1881 Boas received his doctorate at Kiel in the subjects of geography, physics, and philosophy. As Boas recalled, his objectives changed during his university training: the natural sciences lead him to geography.

> In the course of time I became convinced that a materialistic point of view, for a physicist a very real one, was untenable. This gave me a new point of view and I recognized the importance of studying the interaction between the organic and inorganic, above all the relation between the life of a people and their physical environment.
>
> (Boas Papers, Boas to Jacobi, 4/10/1882)

From this perspective, Boas developed his projected plans for his "life's work." "In order to solve such a question I must at least have a general knowledge of physiology, psychology, and sociology which up to now I do not possess and must acquire" (Boas Papers, Boas to Jacobi, 4/10/1882).

Boas was writing to his Uncle Abraham Jacobi in the United States who was attempting to obtain a fellowship for him at Johns Hopkins University (Boas Papers, Boas to Jacobi, 4/12/1882, 11/26/1882).

> The chief point is that even in Baltimore I wanted to prepare myself to go out now on scientific expeditions, to see, to learn, and to accomplish something. . . . My greatest desire is directed to the American polar region. . . . I am completely at home in the literature of this region. . . . Furthermore I am learning everything that is needed for scientific trips, and finally and most important I am learning the Eskimo language.
>
> (Boas Papers, Boas to Jacobi, 11/26/1882)

And he concluded, "If I should really succeed in getting there my chief field of work would be the wandering of the Eskimos."

Boas put together his own course of study and obtained funding for his trip from a German newspaper and from the German Polar Commission (Boas Papers, Boas to Jacobi, 2/8/1883, 5/2/1883). Boas's contract with the *Berliner Tageblatt* brought him instant attention. In characteristic modesty, he remarked to his uncle, "Through my activities I have become fairly well known in Germany, but this 'fame' (as the newspapers say) is very unpleasant coming before I have achieved anything" (Boas Papers, Boas to Jacobi, 5/2/1883). Boas closed his letter to his uncle, "I hope that a happy fate will lead me from the North to you, and let me obtain a permanent position." This desire to come to the United States was linked to his romantic attachment to Marie Krackowizer and to the hope of being able to pursue his career unencumbered by the restraints of the anti-Semitism of Germany (Boas Papers, Boas to Jacobi, 1/2/1882; Rukyser Materials, Boas's autobiographical statement, 9/1915; see also Cole 1983, 13–17).

Boas's work in anthropology received the enthusiastic support of E. B. Tylor, who wrote,

You must allow me to say from conversation with you & reading your writings that I have seldom known anyone better qualified for all-around work in Anthropology. If we are to get the native religions & other ideas of the North-West thoroughly investigated, I think you are the anthropologist to carry through this task.

(Boas Papers, Tylor to Boas, 12/9/1889)

Both Tylor and Boas were convinced that a great deal of American Indian culture was the result of Asiatic influence. As Tylor wrote to Boas, "It seems to me very likely that you may trace an Asiatic-American connexion [*sic*] by transmission of folk-tales" (Boas Papers, Tylor to Boas, 10/9/1890). Under Tylor's sponsorship, Boas began his study of the Northwest Coast.

In his work on folklore, Boas was concerned with an accurate recording of the texts; and an analysis of the texts either for linguistic purposes or for reconstruction of cultural history through distribution. In 1896, while conducting fieldwork among the Tsimshian, Bella Coola, Tlingit, and Bella Bella on Vancouver Island, he wrote in his diary of the emergence of a new idea through his work in folklore: "This mass of stories is gradually beginning to bear fruit because I can now discover certain traits characteristic of the different groups of people. I think I am on the right track in considering mythology a useful tool for differentiating and judging the relationship of tribes" (Rohner 1966, 159).[3]

As in all of his work, Boas was intensive, never superficial; he was rigorous, never careless. The narratives he collected were carefully recorded in the native language with literal translations and free translations. His collection techniques were a model for proper field recording. While he insisted that *all* material be recorded, Boas acquiesced to the restraints of publication in the United States and translated obscene portions of Eskimo narratives into Greek or Latin. Even with the translations, there were objections. Boas's Tsimshian texts were investigated on a charge of using the mail for obscene purposes (Darnell 1969, 34).[4]

In his research and writing, Boas focused on folklore, especially oral narratives. This was apparent in his earliest publications. In 1884, he published "Sedna und die religiosen Herbstfeste"; and in 1885, "Die Sagen der Baffin-Land-Eskimos." In 1887, Boas published an article on the religion and beliefs of the Central Eskimo, "Die religiosen Vorstellungen und einige Gebrauche der zentralen Eskimos"; another on "Poetry and Music of some North American Tribes"; and a third on "The Serpent among the North-West American Indians."[5]

Boas's publications in folklore continued throughout his life. Some of his more outstanding works are the following: *Chinook Texts* (1894), *Tsimshian Mythology* (1916), *Kutenai Tales* (1917), and *Kwakiutl Culture as Reflected in Mythology* (1935). An examination of *Kutenai Tales* will illustrate Boas's thoroughness in the presentation of narrative texts. As Melville Jacobs noted, this work illustrated Boas's concern for making original texts available for both folklore and linguistic study (Jacobs 1959b, 120). In the first section of the book, Boas published the tales collected by Alexander F. Chamberlain in 1891. In the second section, he presented the tales which he himself had collected in the summer of 1914. In the third section, he gave abstracts of all known Kutenai tales, and provided comparative notes for similar tales from other North American Indian groups. The book ends with a Kutenai-English and English-Kutenai vocabulary, with each item carefully keyed to its location in the text (Boas 1917b).

As Melville Jacobs represented his work, "Boas' thinking on folklore method and theory was virtually complete by the first World War, and its major exemplification appeared in 1916 in the prodigious *Tshimshian Mythology*" (Jacobs 1959b, 1920). And Stanley Walens appraised Boas's collected works on the Kwakiutl as "one of the monuments of American cultural anthropology, the achievement of a half-century of diligent research and careful scholarship" (Walens 1981, 7). Boas presented "the underlying thought" of his approach to the study of narratives in the preface to *Kwakiutl Culture as Reflected in Mythology*. Boas maintained that through an examination of the cultural life as portrayed in tales it would be possible to present "a picture of their way of thinking and feeling that renders their ideas as free from the bias of the European observer as is possible" (Boas 1935, v). The narratives provided a candid, unedited view of self.

In *Kwakiutl Culture as Reflected in Mythology*, Boas attempted to write an ethnography using narratives as a source of cultural information. The book is divided into the following categories: material culture; personal and family life; tribal organization; emotional life and ethics; ceremonial objects and ceremonial procedure; ceremonials and relation to supernatural power; magical power and objects; numbers; the world; supernatural beings; animals, plants, etc.; origin of local features (Boas 1935, ix-xii). For Boas, drawing ethnographic information from narrative texts was not an idle exercise. It was an attempt to provide an account of a culture whose traditional way of life had been destroyed. In his restudy of Boas's Kwakiutl material, Walens found Boas "so diligent in recording every possible aspect of a topic that in some ways every given section of his ethnographies is a microcosmic" representation of Kwakiutl custom and belief (Walens 1981, 8).

In 1896, Franz Boas was appointed Lecturer in Anthropology at Columbia University. He offered a course in American Indian languages. A young student of literature, Alfred Louis Kroeber, enrolled in this course, along with two other students. Boas "had his students come each Tuesday evening to his home on 82nd Street . . . where, at the dining table lighted by a fringe-shaded lamp, he held his class" (Kroeber, T. 1970, 46). Kroeber recalled this course, "We spent about two months each on Chinook, Eskimo, Klamath, and Salish, analyzing texts, and finding grammar"

(Kroeber, T. 1970, 47). Of Boas's method of instruction, Kroeber said, it was wholly inductive. "He set before students an interlinear text and proceeded to analyze it, developing the structure of the language as he proceeded" (Kroeber, T. 1943b, 14). His students found this approach both novel and stimulating.

Boas brought an informant to class, an Eskimo woman who was originally from Labrador. Kroeber worked with her and phonetically transcribed her dialect. It was this type of intense, linguistic work to which Margaret Mead referred when she said, "We heard stories of how, in earlier years, he [Boas] would assign a topic to be reported on within a couple of weeks in a language the student did not read. The generation of our elders—Kroeber, Lowie, Goldenweiser, Radin, Sapir . . . had had a hard time." Mead concluded, "But he treated us rather like grandchildren, and we called him 'Papa Franz' " (Mead 1972, 141).

In addition to American Indian languages, Boas taught a course on anthropological theory, which he called "Statistical Theory" (Steward 1961, 1041), and a course on physical anthropology (Kroeber, T. 1970, 47).[6] When Kroeber took this course, it was held in the American Museum of Natural History where Boas had all the necessary implements for anthropometry, including skulls and the skeletons. As Margaret Mead recalled, "With the exception of an occasional course taught by an outsider from another institution, Boas taught everything" (Mead 1972, 140).

Margaret Mead also recalled Boas's manner of instruction. "His lectures were polished and clear. Occasionally he would look around and ask a rhetorical question which no one would venture to answer" (Mead 1972, 121). He retained "a strong German accent" and would "give references in German, as an afterthought in English" (Hays 1971, 175). Mead remarked that Boas's course on methods—the same course that Steward referred to as "Statistical Theory"—was formative for herself and for Ruth Benedict. In her article "Apprenticeship under Boas," Mead includes excerpts from her own lecture notes and from Benedict's, to illustrate the kinds of ideas presented by Boas, the careful instruction given on a wide range of concerns. All this was given with the stipulation, as Mead's notes read from a lecture on Cassirer delivered by Boas on March 17, 1925, "to be very critical and skeptical."

Boas expected his students to be self-motivated. He provided support and encouragement, and schooled them in critical thinking, but they were expected to develop their area of interest. Ruth Bunzel wrote to Margaret Mead in 1959 of her memories of Boas, "You know how he always refused to give reading lists, hated examinations, scorned erudition for its own sake. One learned what one needed when one needed it. It was the sense of problem that was important. He always advised students to spend less time reading and more time thinking" (Mead 1959b, 34). And Melville Herskovits recalled that "dissertation topics were brought to Boas for his approval, not suggested by him." The student had the freedom to choose the topic and methods of study, "only results were presented for appraisal" (Herskovits 1953, 23).

At times, however, Boas offered the direction that created a career. In her letter to Margaret Mead, Ruth Bunzel recalled,

> You want to know how I came to write *The Pueblo Potter* and became an anthropologist. It is really a story about Boas and the things he believed in. It began in the spring of 1924. I had been working for Professor Boas for two years as secretary and editorial assistant and was becoming increasingly involved with anthropology, but without any formal training whatsoever. That summer Boas was going to Europe and Ruth Benedict was going to Zuni to collect mythology. I thought that if I could see an anthropologist at work at the most crucial and mysterious part of his study, and perhaps try a bit on my own, I would know whether or not I wanted to be and could be an anthropologist. So I thought that I would take my vacation time and . . . meet Ruth Benedict in Zuni. My plan was not too ambitious—I was a good stenographer and I would take down folk tales and interviews in shorthand, and do all our typing. Ruth Benedict seemed pleased with the suggestion so I took it to Boas.
>
> Boas heard me out, snorted in his inimitable fashion and said, "Why do you want to waste your time typing?" (He always thought typing a "waste of time.") "Why don't you work on a problem of your own?" I said that I didn't think I was equipped to do a "problem of my own," but he paid me no mind and went on. "You are interested in art. Why don't you do a problem in art? I have always wanted someone to work on the relation of the artist to his work."
>
> (Mead 1959b, 33–34)

Bunzel's portrait of Boas shows him as the supportive, encouraging teacher he was to so many students. Noteworthy in this instance was Bunzel's relationship to Boas: she was his secretary and editorial assistant with no formal training in anthropology. Boas recognized her talent and intelligence for anthropological work. And that, for him, was enough. This was not so for Elsie Clews Parsons who was "outraged" and "threatened to withdraw her support of the mythology project were I permitted to go" (Mead 1959b, 34). But Boas supported Bunzel. "Intelligence and will were what counted."

Bunzel went to Zuni to study aesthetics in pottery. After she completed her work at Zuni she moved on to other pueblos. She commented, "I was too ignorant at the time to know that I was pioneering; that I was on the frontier of a whole new field of anthropology" that this was the first approach to the study of "the individual in culture" (Mead 1959b, 34). *The Pueblo Potter* was written during the following winter on week-ends between her regular job. She planned another fieldtrip to Zuni for the following summer. "Elsie Parsons sponsored this trip. A gallant lady, she acknowledged in her own gracious fashion that Boas had been right" (Mead 1959b, 35).

A list of Boas's students reads like a roster of the important names in anthropology and folklore: Alfred Louis Kroeber, William Jones, Louis J. Frachtenberg, Edward Sapir, George A. Dorsey, L. Farrand, Pliny Earle Goddard, James A. Mason, Frank Speck, Robert H. Lowie, Paul Radin, Fay-Cooper Cole, Martha Warren Beckwith, Ruth Fulton Benedict, Melville J. Herskovits, Gladys A. Reichard, Ruth L. Bunzel, G. Wagner, M. J. Andrade, T. Adamson, Gene Weltfish, E. Deloria, A. Phinney, Alexander Chamberlain, Frederica de Laguna, Zora Neale Hurston, Laura Watson Benedict, and Melville Jacobs (Jacobs 1959b, 122).

In his appraisal of Franz Boas, Alexander Lesser says, he produced two generations of anthropologists "and his students went on to build departments at other major institutions" (Lesser 1981, 2–3). One such student was Alfred Louis Kroeber (1876–1960). Kroeber received his B.A. (1896) and his M.A. (1897) at Columbia University in English. While completing his master's degree, Kroeber began taking Boas's course on North American Indian languages. He worked with six Smith Sound Eskimo who had been brought to the Natural History Museum by Robert E. Peary (Rowe 1962, 395; Kroeber 1956, 153). In a letter dated December 10, 1897, Boas told Kroeber how to find his way to the house where the Eskimos lived:

My dear Mr. Kroeber,
I went up to see the Eskimos last night, and everything is ready for you to continue your work. . . . They are located on Feather-Bed Lane, which you reach by taking the cars to Washington Bridge, crossing Washington Bridge, and then taking the street to the north. . . . You will come to a parting of the roads, and there you will see to the right, a small brownish frame house. The Eskimos live in this house. . . .
Please let me know what arrangements you have made. I think I shall be able to go out with you once a week or so, and we will make some appointment for a time to discuss the material that you are going to obtain.

(UC Archives, Boas to Kroeber, 12/10/1897)

This work led to his first publications in folklore, which appeared in the *Journal of American Folklore* in 1899: "Animal Tales of the Eskimo" and "Tales of the Smith Sound Eskimo."

In 1899, Kroeber conducted fieldwork among the Arapaho in Oklahoma (Kroeber 1956, 153; Rowe 1962, 395). His work was sponsored by the American Museum of Natural History with funds provided by Mrs. Morris K. Jesup (Rowe 1962, 395). This was followed in 1900 by work with the Arapaho in Wyoming; and in 1901, with work among the Gros Ventre and Assinibone.

In the spring of 1901, Kroeber completed his graduate work with a dissertation on the decorative symbolism of the Arapaho (Rowe 1962, 395). He was awarded the first Ph.D. in anthropology at Columbia University (Thoresen 1973, 42). Boas, who had just returned from Europe, wrote to him that his dissertation had been well-received. "Bastian asked me very particularly to tell you that he thought your paper a very important one and that he is expecting very good things from you" (Kroeber Papers, Boas to Kroeber, 10/19/1901). Boas said that Von den Steinen liked Kroeber's discussion on the development of art, but agreed with Boas that Kroeber had carried the conclusions too far.

The same year he received his degree, Kroeber, with the support of Zelia Nuttall and Frederick Ward Putnam, was successful in his search for a position. The job offer came in the form of a telegram from Phoebe Apperson Hearst: "The position here permanent. Hope this message will reach you in good time" (Kroeber Papers, Hearst to Kroeber, 7/29/1901; Thoresen 1975, 264.) Kroeber responded with the following telegram:

> Thanks for kind telegram. I accept. I have offer from Berlin Museum for four months. . . . To conclude unfinished researches among Arapaho Tribe which I began two years ago should therefore like to come California after delay four months, but will come at once if thought essential by you or President Wheeler.

> (Kroeber Papers, Kroeber to Hearst, 7/22/1901)

Four years later, Kroeber reflected on his decision and on his struggle to establish a department of anthropology, "I took California [because it offered] greater independence and a larger chance for activity. . . . But the kingdom must come soon or it will no longer find me waiting for it" (Kroeber Papers, 2/23/1905).

With his acceptance of the position, Kroeber became the instructor at the nascent Department and Museum of Anthropology at the University of California (Thoresen 1975a, 266). As Thoresen says, "This offer needs to be placed in some perspective. Kroeber in 1901 was young, educated, genial, promising, ambitious, and otherwise irrelevant." And, Thoresen adds, "There was no department of anthropology in California" (Thoresen 1975a, 265). Thoresen's sketch of Kroeber as a young man in 1901, certainly differs from Eric Wolf's recollection of Kroeber's importance in the 1940s. "For anthropologists of my generation, Kroeber was the living embodiment of American anthropology. His books and his words accompanied us through graduate school, and he appeared in our professional lives again and again" (Wolf 1981, 36). Wolf met him in later years, and recalled him as "personable and delightful, a benign, Apollonian, Olympian figure." "But," he adds, "there were many people who lived in terror of him" (Wolf 1981, 37).

Clearly, Kroeber had built a reputation for himself in forty years. He had also established the study of anthropology on the West Coast, and had directed the study of ethnology in California. Still, he started on a small scale, with one course on North American ethnology first offered in January 1902, for two hours credit to six students (Buzaljko 1982, 9; Rowe 1962, 397).[7] Among the students in this course was Samuel A. Barrett who continued to study with Kroeber. In 1903, Kroeber wrote a letter to the chairman of the Committee on Scholarship, saying, "Mr. Barrett has fol-

lowed three courses in Anthropology with me and has shown himself a
faithful and thorough student" (Kroeber Papers, Kroeber to Wickson,
5/24/1903). Barrett transferred to Columbia for a year of study with Boas,
Farrand, Bandelier, and Laufer (1907–1908). (See also National Research
Council 1940, 10; Peri and Wharton 1965a,b,c.) In his work in folklore,
material culture, and ritual, Barrett carried on the tradition of his mentors.[8]

Originally, Kroeber had been hired to direct the organization of the
museum and to collect specimens, and not to offer courses. Putnam, when
he heard that Kroeber was going to teach a course, reminded him that "the
primary object is investigation and the accumulation of material" (Kroeber
Papers, Putnam to Kroeber, 12/9/1901; Thoresen 1975, 266). And Boas
cautioned him,

> If you were to work out a course of systematic anthropological instruction, you
> would have to give up for years all research work, and even then your success
> would depend entirely upon the degree of co-operation that you could get
> from other men in the university. All you can hope to do is really to pave the
> way for systematic instruction.
>
> (Kroeber Papers, Boas to Kroeber, 5/20/1902)

Kroeber's correspondence with Frederick Ward Putnam, Phoebe Apperson
Hearst, and Franz Boas concerning this initial course on North American
ethnology clearly marks this as a sensitive issue (Kroeber Papers, Kroeber
to Putnam, 12/1901; Kroeber to Hearst, 12/27/1901; Kroeber to Boas, 1902).

Kroeber was apparently successful in assuaging Putnam. A few years
after this flurried exchange of correspondence concerning the course of
instruction in the Department of Anthropology, Kroeber published an
article in the *American Anthropologist* entitled "Recent Progress in Anthropology at the University of California." After a brief review of the
founding of the department, he stressed that "the primary object of the
department is research and the increase of knowledge" (Kroeber 1906c,
484). He linked this directly to the founding of the museum. This was, in
essence, a paraphrase of Putnam's remark in his 1901 letter to Kroeber
(Kroeber Papers, Putnam to Kroeber, 12/9/1901).

Kroeber did continue offering courses. On May 19, 1903, he wrote to
Boas,

> We shall have six courses in Anthropology next year, though none of them I
> regret to say will run beyond two hours a week for half a year. I gave three in
> the first half year and Merriam and Goddard three in the second. For the year
> after I have a scheme for more elaborate and thorough work, to talk over with
> Professor Putnam when he visits us this summer.
>
> (Kroeber Papers, Kroeber to Boas, 5/1903)

In 1905–1906, Goddard began teaching "Religious Practices and Beliefs of
Non-Literary Peoples" and continued teaching it through 1908–1909. This
was described as "A study of the religious practices connected with the

birth, development, death, and burial of the individual, and at the more general ceremonies performed at the change of seasons. . . . Especial attention is given myths which explain origins and creation, and beliefs concerning the human soul."[9]

Kroeber added his course on "Comparative Mythology" in 1906–1907, described as "Lectures on typical mythologies of civilized and uncivilized races of the Old and New World." In 1907–1908, the course title was changed to "Studies in Comparative Mythology," and the course description was expanded:

> A research course dealing with certain problems of comparative mythology, such as the question of the linguistic development or transmission of similar traditions among distinct peoples, and the variations undergone in different periods and regions by the same myths. 3 hrs., throughout the year. Prerequisite: Anthropology 14, or equivalent.

The prerequisite was "Comparative History of Mythology and Philosophical Speculation."

Waterman introduced a course called "Primitive Religions" in 1910–1911, which focused on "Conspicuous elements in primitive religions, and survivals of these among historic peoples." This course was taught by Wallis in 1915–1916, but the theoretical orientation had changed: "Magic and religion; the function of religion in social life. New religions, messianic manifestations, religious experience of the individual. Ceremony and ritual; prayer and offering; ethics; the sacred and the supernatural."

When Lowie joined the department in 1920, he taught "Primitive Religion" with a focus on "examples of the beliefs and ritual of primitive peoples." He examined "the relations of myth and ritual; the functions of ceremonialism; the relations of magic and religion; [and] taboo." And he compared the "theories of Tylor, Lang, Schmidt, Marrett, Goldenweiser, [and] Durkheim."

John Rowe lists Kroeber's first interests in anthropology as linguistics, ethnology, and folklore (Rowe 1962, 398). The interest in the latter was evidenced in Kroeber's early publications in folklore, in the courses he developed in the Department of Anthropology, and in the topics of graduate research pursued under his sponsorship. The first master's degree in anthropology was awarded to Louisa McDermott in 1904; her thesis topic was on the ethnography and folklore of the Flathead (Salish) of Montana. In 1908, Samuel A. Barrett earned the first Ph.D. with his dissertation on Pomo basketry (Rowe 1962, 397).

In the early years, Kroeber provided the link for the American Folklore Society with the far western state of California. He was appointed to a three-year term as councilor to the American Folklore Society. In the letter of appointment, Newell said, "You are one of the very few representatives of the Society on the Pacific Coast. Can you suggest any plans for extension of membership in that quarter?" (Kroeber Papers, Newell to Kroeber,

1/23/1901). In the two letters that followed, Newell suggested the formation of a local organization that would encourage the development of folklore studies in California (Kroeber Papers, Newell to Kroeber, 8/24/1901; 9/2/1901). In the letter dated September 2, 1901, Newell appended a handwritten note at the bottom of the page:

Members in California
Los Angeles
1. Charles F. Lummis
2. Dr. J. A. Munk, Pasadena
3. A. C. Vromen
4. Mrs. A. Fenges, Mare Island
5. Also Dr. G. P. Bradley

(Kroeber Papers, Newell to Kroeber, 9/2/1901)

In addition to these individual members, Newell included the libraries of Los Angeles, Sacramento, and the Mechanics Institute of San Francisco as subscribing members.

Kroeber took Newell's suggestion to heart. In 1905, he was a charter member in the Berkeley Folklore Club. And later the same year, he helped organize the California Branch of the American Folklore Society (Thoresen 1973, 42). The purpose of this latter organization was to study the folklore of California (Darnell 1969, 399).

Kroeber reported on the progress of both the California Branch of the American Folklore Society and the Berkeley Folklore Club in a note published in the *American Anthropologist*. At the seventh meeting of the California Branch of the American Folklore Society which "was held in South Hall, University of California, Berkeley, on Tuesday, March 20, 1906, at 8 P.M.," two new members were elected to the society, and "Professor Vernon L. Kellogg of Stanford gave an address, illustrated with lantern slides, on 'In Samoa' " (Kroeber 1906a, 435). At the next meeting, the California Branch of the American Folklore Society and the Berkeley Folklore Club agreed to investigate "the feasibility of making a special study of the folk-lore of Berkeley and vicinity" (Kroeber 1906a, 435).

From the viewpoint of the American Folklore Society, there were problems with the quality and the intent of the California Branch of the American Folklore Society. As Putnam reported in a letter to Newell, "Kroeber resorted to lantern slide lectures to arouse interest" (Darnell 1969, 399).[10] As the branch society grew, so did the feeling of independence. This regional organization did not identify with the national organization or with the journal (Darnell 1969, 400; Boas Papers, Kroeber to Boas, 1/14/1908). This was carried to such an extent that the California branch "nearly became an independent folklore society" (Kroeber Papers, Dixon to Kroeber, 1/22/1910; Darnell 1969, 400).

There was resentment in the national organization about this. As Tozzer wrote to Boas,

I have long felt that the California Branch and Kroeber especially seem to think that we cannot exist without their aid. As a matter of fact they have been a drag upon our resources ever since they joined the Society. Kroeber has always been the one to dictate to us rather than receive our views first.

(Boas Papers, Tozzer to Boas, 3/2/1908)

Tozzer suggested that the "scrappy contributions from California" be placed at the end of the journal under a separate heading. Boas wrote to Kroeber on October 6, 1908, that the California Branch of the American Folklore Society would soon have to be self-supporting. Boas also took issue with Kroeber about the need to "expand and go on expanding without improving our scientific methods" (Darnell 1969, 400). As Darnell notes, "Amateur contributions, at least to the anthropological segment of the *Journal* were virtually eliminated by Boas' editorial policies." Kroeber "favored a more inclusive policy." In spite of these problems, Kroeber maintained a secure position in the American Folklore Society. In 1906, he served as president of the society. He was the first of Boas's students to receive this high degree of professional recognition (Thoresen 1973, 42).

Timothy Thoresen in his work on Kroeber marks 1909 as the year when Kroeber's interests changed from folklore to archaeology and California linguistics (Thoresen 1973, 42). This change of emphasis is apparent in the course catalogue for the Department of Anthropology at the Unviersity of California. In 1910–1911, Kroeber's course, "Studies in Comparative Mythology," was not listed. It was taught once again in 1912–1913, and omitted from the catalogue after that. In Kroeber's correspondence still another change of emphasis is apparent between 1914 and 1915, when the topic of discussion shifted to social organization. It was decades later, after his retirement, that Kroeber returned to his old folklore texts in an attempt to prepare them for publication.

In 1921, Robert H. Lowie, joined Kroeber at the University of California, Berkeley, where he remained until his retirement in 1950. Lowie received his B.A. at the City College of New York in 1901. He entered Columbia University in 1904, where he studied with Boas. As he said, "I decided to study under Boas because his record appealed to me, because I felt that *he* could give me scientific method better than others in the field open to me" (Lowie Papers, Lowie to Radin, 10/2/1920). In an autobiographical statement, Lowie remarked, "In anthropology I took Professor Boas's seminars, linguistic and ethnographic courses, as well as a dreaded course in theory of statistics, in which one year I had as my only fellow students two members of the faculty" (Lowie Papers, Lowie to Liveright, 12/6/1919). While still a graduate student, Lowie worked in the anthropological division under Clark Wissler's direction at the American Museum of Natural History. He was asked by Wissler to undertake fieldwork with the Lenhi Shoshone of Idaho in 1906. "I seized this opportunity to meet 'savage man' in the flesh and derived a host of new impressions, both through ethnographical experience and my first contact with the life of the frontier." In 1907, Lowie worked among the Assinibone, Blackfoot, and Crow (Kroeber 1957, 142; 1958, 1–2). He continued his work with the Crow, focusing on social organization and religious practices. One year later, to reach the Chipeways, he undertook what he called the most interesting journey "from a traveler's point of view," "I descended the Athabaska River in the Hudson Bay Company's open scows, running rapids, eating dried moose meat, and hobnobbing with mixed breeds and Indians, not to forget the altogether peculiar type of Hudson Bay Company officials" (Lowie Papers, Lowie to Liveright, 12/6/1919). In 1908, Lowie completed his Ph.D. dissertation, entitled "The Test Theme in North American Literature." From 1912 to 1915, he continued his work with the Plains Indians. Working with ten tribes on the Great Plains, he published eighteen monographs with the American Museum (Kroeber 1958, 2).

Paul Radin praised Lowie as "one of the best ethnographers of his day" who "studied every aspect of culture . . . in detail. . . . His Crow work and his investigation of the Plains societies are in a class by themselves. The latter study, for its completeness, its clear-cut recognition of the problems involved and its admirable solution, has never been excelled" (Radin 1958, 360–61).

Lowie's early publications, both articles and book reviews, show his interest in folklore. In 1908, two articles appeared in the *Journal of American Folklore*: "Catchwords for Mythological Motives" and his dissertation, "The Test-Theme in North American Mythology." In 1909, he coauthored "Shoshone and Comanche Tales," wrote "Additional Catchwords," "Hero-Trickster Discussion," and a review of George Lawrence Gomme's *Folklore as a Historical Science*, all appearing in the *Journal of American Folklore*. Lowie's involvement in folklore resulted in his election to the presidency of the American Folklore Society in 1916 and 1917.

Of Lowie's work, Erminie Voegelin remarked, "More, perhaps, than any other anthropologist of his generation, Lowie concerned himself throughout his lifetime with American Indian folklore" (Voegelin 1958, 149). From her memories as his student, she recalled that he frequently conducted seminars in folklore. Katherine Luomala remarked on this too.[11] Lowie directed six master's theses in folklore. Included among these were Erminie Voegelin's "Kiowa-Crow Mythological Affiliations" (1930), and Katherine Luomala's "Turtle's War Party: A Study in Comparative Mythology" (1933). He directed eight doctoral dissertations in folklore, among which were the following: D. S. Demetracopoulou, "The Loon Woman Myth: A Study in Synthesis" (1931); E. W. Count, "The Earth-Diver: An Attempt at an Asiatic-American Trait-Correlation" (1935); E. K. Luomala, "Maui the Demi-God: Factors in the Development of a Polynesian Hero Cycle" (1936): F. J. Essene, Jr., "A Comparative Study of Eskimo Mythology" (1947) (Voegelin 1958, 150).

Frank Gouldsmith Speck (1881–1950) carried Boas's influence to the University of Pennsylvania. He did his undergraduate work at Columbia (B.A. 1904) where he studied with the linguist J. Dyneley Prince. Prince directed his student to Boas, and Speck completed his M.A. one year later. Under Boas's direction, he began his fieldwork in the Indian Territory of Oklahoma (Yuchi, Creek, Chickasaw, and Osage) (Hallowell 1951, 69). Speck went to the University of Pennsylvania on a newly established fellowship in anthropology (1907–1908) (Darnell 1970, 88). After he received his doctorate (1908), he was hired by George Gordon to be the Assistant Curator in Ethnology at the University Museum, University of Pennsylvania (1909–1911). In 1909, Speck began teaching courses as well.

Speck's writings on the Montagnais, Naskapi, Penobscot, Algonkian, and other American Indian groups provide detailed accounts of rituals, sensitive explanation of symbolism, native ethnoesthetics, and critical oral historical accounts. His classic, *The Naskapi* (1935), is a stunning account of the ritual and symbolism attached to the woodland life of hunting. His book, *The Penobscot,* which was written in 1915 but not published until 1940, provides crucial oral historical information on a group of native Americans whose way of life had almost passed when Speck began his interviews. Speck was a consummate fieldworker. He conducted annual summer fieldtrips among the Naskapi and among the Eskimo of southern Labrador (National Research Council 1938, 92).

His contributions to folklore studies were both extensive and creative. Weston LaBarre called Frank Speck "the major contributor in the field of folk sciences" (Hallowell 1951, 68). While Speck used the term ethnohistory in his later writings, Hallowell observed that he was always an ethnohistorian. He had a continuing interest in material culture (Hallowell 1951, 70); and in his works he linked material culture to the ceremonial and social life of the people. He also had an abiding interest in religion and ritual. This was reflected in the course called "Primitive Religion" that he taught for many years (Hallowell 1951, 74) and in his publications.[12]

Melville Jacobs (1902–1971) took his B.A. in history and philosophy at the City College of New York (1922) and his M.A. in American history at Columbia (1923). In 1924, he began course work in the Anthropology Department, where his fellow students were Ruth Benedict, Melville Herskovits, George Herzog, Alexander Lesser, Margaret Mead, and Gene Weltfish (Thompson, L. 1978, 640). With two summers devoted to his Sahaptin fieldwork, Jacobs completed the work for the doctorate in December 1927. The degree was not awarded until the Sahaptin grammar was published in 1931 (Thompson, L. 1978, 641). In 1928, Jacobs went to the University of Washington, where he would remain for the rest of his life.

Following the terms of his appointment, Jacobs was relieved of his teaching responsibilities for six months of every year so that he could conduct fieldwork. Much of this research was devoted to recording Indian languages soon to pass away with the deaths of the last surviving speakers.[13] The linguistic notes were taken with great care, and "following the

Boasian ideal," included "traditional texts—myths, tales, and ethnographic commentary." Jacobs used an Ediphone dictating machine to record songs on wax cylinders. In 1934, Jacobs had a portable electric phonograph recorder constructed which used the voltage from his car battery. "He put it to immediate use recording some of Annie Peterson's Coosan songs and narratives. Thus we have actual sound recordings of these largely extinct tongues" (Thompson, L. 1978, 641).

In his retiring presidential address to the American Folklore Society in 1964, Jacobs spoke on "A Look Ahead in Oral Literature Research." His remarks show both his theoretical concerns and an aspect of his personality to which his student, Laurence Thompson, referred—the "bitter side," the "caustic" criticism of others (Thompson, L. 1978, 643).

> In folklore, Boasian anthropologists seemed incapable of going beyond catch-word kinds of captions which historicogeographical folklorists were using for those rude assemblages or macro-units called "motifs." Even the terminology employed by the anthropological folklorists was inconsistent. Robert H. Lowie wrote about a father-in-law "test theme," but Thomas T. Waterman wrote about "explanatory elements," both in doctoral dissertations prepared under Boas.
>
> (Jacobs 1966b, 415)

Jacobs continued with a criticism of every anthropological folklorist from the 1890s to the moment he was speaking. Then he moved on to a criticism of the literary folklorists who had no concern "with building fundamental theoretical knowledge," or with studying non-Western oral literatures (Jacobs 1966b, 420–21).

Jacobs's theoretical orientation was expressed in the title of his work, *The Content and Style of an Oral Literature* (1959). As he explained, "I did not venture toward perfection in the linguistic aspect of my research, because of my overruling concern with folklore content and literary style" (Jacobs 1958, 3). Jacobs focused on a *specific* oral literature. As Thompson said, "He rejected the projection of West European values onto non-Western folktales" (Thompson, L. 1978, 643). Yet, ironically, Jacobs chose to use Western theatrical terms such as "play, acts, scenes, epilogues, and entr'actes" as captions for "each myth or tale recital" (Jacobs 1960, viii). He suggested that, although "oral literature recitals lack stage settings," still they resemble "in presentation and structuring of content those special performances of plays in which one speaker acts all the actors' roles" (Jacobs 1960, viii). His was an innovative and provocative approach, one that is now reflected in performance theory.

While Alfred Kroeber and Robert Lowie were establishing their sphere of influence on the West Coast at the University of California, Berkeley, and Frank Speck was building up the Anthropology Department at the University of Pennsylvania, Boas brought other individuals to the study of anthropology and folklore from his position at Columbia University. Some of these stayed with Boas in New York and added to his base of power there, and some moved on to establish other centers of anthropological study.

Melville J. Herskovits (1895–1963) came to Columbia University in 1921, after his undergraduate work in history at the University of Chicago. At the New School for Social Research in New York, Herskovits met Alexander A. Goldenweiser (Simpson 1973, 2), Elsie Clews Parsons, and Ruth Benedict (Simpson 1973, 2). At Columbia, he worked with Boas; he received his M.A. degree in 1921, and his Ph.D. in 1923. In 1927, he took a position at Northwestern where he remained until his death in 1963 (Merriam 1964, 83).

Margaret Mead, who was a senior at Barnard College when she first met Melville Herskovits, remembered his ebullient personality. "One of his famous remarks—when we had all gone to dinner in Chinatown—was 'I don't expect to be a Boas, but I do expect to be a Lowie or an Ogburn'" (Simpson 1973, 3).[14]

Along with his wife, Frances Shapiro Herskovits, Melville Herskovits conducted his first fieldwork in Suriname, Dutch Guiana in 1928, followed by a second expedition in 1929. Together they collected the Guiana narratives which appeared in *Suriname Folklore* (1936). Herskovits was fascinated by the relationship between the African cultures and the black cultures in the Western hemisphere. He continued his studies in Haiti (1934), and in Brazil (1941–1942).

As Melville and Frances Herskovits remarked, their work collecting and researching the Guiana narratives provided them with the expertise to launch their study of *Dahomean Narratives* (1958). This classic book was the result of their 1931 fieldwork in Aloney, Dahomey. The narratives were recited in Fon by the informants, rendered in English by the translator, and typed by the Herskovits, all in one sitting. Of this method, the Herskovits said,

> The use of the typewriter brought out interesting reactions. At first, both teller and translator, watching the play of the machine with fascination, spoke on and on; some of the fullest tales were recorded under the influence of the novelty of having what was said taken on the typewriter.
>
> (Herskovits and Herskovits 1966, 7)

As the informants grew more accustomed to the typewriter, they would at times "attempt to confound the *yovo*, the whites—that is, ourselves—by talking rapidly and including the elaborations of the actual story-telling session to test our typing skill" (Herskovits and Herskovits 1966, 7).

The opening lines of *Dahomean Narrative* mark the Herskovits as scholars in the Boasian tradition: "The narratives in this collection have taught us much about how the Dahomean sees his world and himself, and how his imagination plays on the realities of everyday life" (Herskovits and Herskovits 1966, v). Taking the narratives as a reflector of culture, they anchor their research in a nonbiased acceptance of the native view. As they say, fundamental to their approach "is the rejection of terms such as 'primitive' and 'savage'; as 'civilized' and 'barbarian' or 'backward'; as 'greater' or 'lesser' tradition" (Herskovits and Herskovits 1966, 4). As all good students must, Herskovits added to his mentor's work. Together with Frances Herskovits, Melville Herskovits formulated new questions that directed the work in narratives to the heart of concerns that are now central to much folkloristic research:

> What functioning role does the culture assign to its spoken arts? What is its attitude toward improvisation? Is it permissive, encouraging and rewarding it; or is it indifferent or even hostile toward its exercise? Does it have named criteria which distinguish the excellence of artistry from merely competent repetitions? What in the structure of the narrative form is dictated by the fact that it is spoken, and is thus more akin to drama than are written forms? How closely and in what situations does the teller's participant audience hold him to fixed versions?

> (Herskovits and Herskovits 1966, 4–5)

Herskovits trained an outstanding group of scholars. Among these was one—Herskovits's first Ph.D. student in anthropology—who was to make profound contributions to anthropology and folklore. William Russel Bascom (1912–1981) took his undergraduate degree in physics at the University of Wisconsin in 1933, and a master's in anthropology in 1936. He went to Northwestern University in 1936, to study anthropology "in a very small program under the dominant figure of Melville J. Herskovits, who 'first interested me in Africa, the Yoruba people, and the city of Ife'" (Ottenberg 1982b, 3). Greatly influenced by Herskovits, Bascom specialized in African religion, art, folklore, and Afro-American connections.

Bascom's first fieldwork was among the Kiowa of Oklahoma in 1936. This was followed by his work among the Yoruba in southwestern Nigeria (1937–1938). His interests in Afro-American and Afro-Cuban cultures led to his research among the Gullah Blacks of South Carolina and Georgia, and to his work in Cuba (Ottenberg 1982b, 4). After World War II, he carried out an economic study of the people of Ponape in the Caroline Islands.

Bascom's publications reflected his years of involvement with African cultures and Afro-Cuban and Afro-American cultures. Among these are the following: *African Art in Cultural Perspective* (1973), *African Dilemma Tales* (1975), and *Sixteen Cowries: Yoruba Divination from Africa to the New World* (1980). In 1969, Bascom was awarded the Giuseppe Pitre International Folklore Prize for *Ifa Divination: Communication Between Gods and Men in West Africa*.

Bascom began teaching with Herskovits at Northwestern in 1939 and continued until 1957. He served as Chairman of the Department of Anthropology and Acting Director of the Program of African Studies for the 1956–1957 academic year. In 1957, Bascom came to the University of California, Berkeley, as Professor of Anthropology and Director of the Robert H. Lowie Museum of Anthropology and remained in that position until

1979. As he said, his good friend and colleague, Archer Taylor, professor in the German Department, was instrumental in this change of university affiliation (Bascom 1981d, 285). Bascom taught the successor of Taylor's folklore course. During his years in the Berkeley department, he offered courses in prose narrative, African art, and African folktales.

During his initial fieldwork in Nigeria in 1937–1938, Bascom began his lifelong work with Yoruba proverbs. In World War II, he was stationed in West Africa. As he said, "My collection grew to around five thousand Yoruba proverbs. I had bitten off a very large morsel" (Bascom 1981d, 288). In 1950–1951, William Bascom and Berta Montero Bascom returned to Nigeria on a Fulbright Fellowship. While William Bascom conducted ethnographic work, Berta Bascom "worked with English-speaking Yoruba informants, translating the proverbs into English, exploring their social contexts, and probing for their deeper meanings" (Bascom 1981d, 288).

In a largely autobiographical account of his scholarly work, "Perhaps Too Much to Chew?" Bascom noted the lengthy nature of his undertakings:

> It does seem that I get involved in large projects with lengthy production times, but I did manage to complete *Ifa Divination* (1938–69) and *Sixteen Cowries* in twenty-nine years (1951–80). Meanwhile I have my teeth into another big project and, even in retirement, the proverbs have been neglected.
>
> (Bascom 1981d, 288–89)

Berta Bascom continues the work on the proverb, the project carried on with her husband for more than thirty years, and which Bascom himself had been engaged in for forty-four years.

Among those who were influenced by Boas and who stayed on to work with him in New York were Ruth Benedict, Elsie Clews Parsons, Ruth Bunzel, and Gladys Reichard. Elsie Clews Parsons (1875–1941) was a folklorist of independent means.[15] Generous with her support, she was also a patron of the American Folklore Society. Reichard said of her, "She was an anthropological institution because of her varied interests, her cooperation with many universities and museums, her incredible tolerance, her discrimination and her judgment, in short, because of her philosophy of life" (Reichard 1943a, 45).

Parsons came to folklore and anthropology after years of work in sociology. She took her B.A. at the newly established Barnard College in 1896. At Columbia University she studied sociology under Franklin H. Giddings, and received her M.A. in 1897, and her Ph.D. in 1899. Parsons served as a fellow at Barnard College from 1899 to 1902, and as a lecturer in sociology from 1903 to 1905.[16] In 1919, Parsons helped establish the New School for Social Research in New York, where she lectured on anthropology at one of the first sessions (Boyer 1971, 21; Chambers 1973, 182).

Parsons's career shifted from an earlier interest in American family life and feminist issues to an involvement in folklore and anthropology. This change of research focus manifested a long-term interest Parsons had in the Southwest. And it was also linked to a profound disillusionment with the ability to affect social and political change. As a committed pacifist, Parsons took the involvement of the United States in World War I as a sign that her movement had failed. She wearied of the struggle and took solace in her work in anthropology and folklore. This was a conscious change from a front-line political arena to an absorption in other cultures. Important for her work was her friendship with Pliny Earle Goddard of the American Museum of Natural History, who was also president of the American Folklore Society (1915) (Chambers 1973, 183; Hare 1985, 135–37). Even more crucial, as Leslie Spier said, she "fell in with" Franz Boas (Spier 1943, 246), and their relationship was one that grew in friendship and respect. The major focus of Parsons's work, however, remained essentially the same throughout her life: she was concerned with the control that custom and culture exerted over the individual.

In "Some Next Steps in the Study of Negro Folklore," Melville J. Herskovits remarked, "The contributions of Elsie Clews Parsons to the study of Negro folklore are so extensive as to comprise, in themselves, the bulk of the available materials in this field" (Herskovits 1943, 1). He added that "no significant work" could be done in this field without using Parsons's work as a foundation. Parsons had indicated her interest in working on black folklore in a letter to Boas: "I'd like to try it, particularly if it would require doing and directing field-work in the West Indies and getting correspondents there. From visits to Hayti and the Bahamas . . . I believe there is a rich, unexplored field" (Boas Papers, Parsons to Boas, 11/25/1915). Parson's involvement was formalized at the December 1915 meeting of the American Folklore Society. Boas reported, "The President was authorized to appoint Mrs. Elsie Clews Parsons upon the Editorial Board to assist in the publication of material on Negro folk-lore" (Peabody 1916, 297). By the next year and Boas's next editorial report, Parsons had collected "the material for the first Negro number" and publication was scheduled for the following year (Boas 1917a, 269–70; see also Hare 1985, 137). Not only did Parsons collect the material but she also paid the publication expenses (Dwyer-Shick 1979, 228). Further, she assumed the expenses for all subsequent *Journal of American Folklore* publications on Negro folklore.

Reichard called Parsons "a respecter of evidence," a trait that, when combined with collecting, yielded detailed works. Parsons once told Gladys Reichard that she thought of her own work "as a mosaic and that she hated to omit any detail" (Reichard 1943a, 47). "Dr. Parsons held the theory that many isolated details obtainable but perhaps not comprehended at the time of collection, should be preserved until a time when 'someone would know more and be able to interpret them'" (Reichard 1950, 309). She was also wary of generalizing. As she wrote to Boas, "I am so pleased you liked that chapter. I was afraid there might be too much guessing to suit you. There has to be some and the best one can do is to indicate plainly that a guess is a guess" (Boas Papers, Parsons to Boas, 9/8/1936).

Because of Parsons's emphasis in empiricism, fieldwork was crucial for her study of folklore. As Hare notes, "she came to recognize that psychological and philosophical generalizations were not enough and that rigorous empirical study . . . was necessary." It was Parson's belief that through her intensive fieldwork she "would ultimately illuminate her own society as well as the other cultures she so meticulously investigated" (Hare 1985, 20). She undertook extensive fieldtrips:

> to the Pueblo Indians, 1915–32, to Andros Islands, Balina, and many Negro communities in U.S., including Cape Verde Islanders, 1919, to Micmac of Cape Breton Island, 1923, to Pima Indians, 1926, to Kiowa Indiana, 1927, to Lesser Antilles, 1924, 1925, 1927, to Egypt and Soudan, 1926, to Zapotecan Indians, 1929–33.

> (National Research Council 1938, 77)

Parsons found in fieldwork the excitement and freedom that she felt was so dismally absent in the wealthy social circles of New York with which her family was associated. She also found in it the mental and physical challenge for hard work. And then at the end of a long day, she liked to enjoy a moment of relaxation. As Reichard remarked: "She used to say that her idea of complete comfort was to have *at the same time* a cigarette, a cup of coffee, and an open fire. And characteristically she added quietly, 'You know it is very hard to get all three together. It is easier among Indians than among ourselves" (Reichard 1943a, 48).

Parsons's wealth made it possible for her to maintain a large retinue of servants, to employ people to care for her four children, and to travel frequently and extensively (Rosenberg, 1982, 154; Chambers 1973, 193). She could also purchase items that would facilitate her work, such as the expensive sound recording equipment that she used to record the cantefables (Chambers 1973, 187) and a yacht for sailing to the Caribbean islands.

Parsons's work in folklore yielded many important works (Reichard 1943b; Hare 1985, 169; Voegelin 1943, 136). *Folk-Lore of the Sea Islands, South Carolina* (1923) and *Folk-Lore of the Cape Verde Islands* (1923) were published as memoirs of the American Folklore Society. *Hopi and Zuni Ceremonialism* (1933) and *Taos Tales* (1940) are among the many works from her fieldwork in the Southwest among the Pueblo Indians. Parsons's *Pueblo Indian Religion* (1939) was recognized as the most comprehensive piece of research on the subject (Kroeber 1943a, 254) in which the author "combed archaeological reports for clues to the interpretation of modern rituals and beliefs" (Reichard 1943a, 46). Parsons's extensive work in Mexico culminated with *Mitla, Town of the Souls* (1936) wherein she examined the connection between the Southwest Pueblo Indian culture and the Indian cultures of Mesoamerica. Parsons was also interested in the influence of the Spanish and of Catholicism on the Indians.

Parsons was exceedingly generous with her wealth. While contributions to the *Journal of American Folklore* from 1916 to 1941 were in excess of thirty thousand dollars, Chambers suggests that the actual sum of her contributions was substantially larger. As he remarks, "she quietly supported many individual scholars in large and small projects and resorted in some cases to the facade of anonymous donations" (Chambers 1973, 197). This is illustrated in a letter to Boas, where Parsons wrote, "Enclosed is a check for $60 to tide over Dr. Frachtenberg. I would prefer to have the matter remain private to you and me" (Boas Papers, Parsons to Boas, 1/3/1918). Parsons also funded Aurelio Espinosa's trip to Spain for an amount exceeding two thousand dollars (Boas Papers, Parsons to Boas, 11/4/1919).

Susan Dwyer-Shick stresses Parsons's key role as a benefactor of *The Memoirs of the American Folklore Society*. From 1917 to 1940, in addition to her support of the journal, Parsons contributed a recorded amount of $12,113.54. She also assumed the expenses for five volumes of this series for which the publication figures are not available (Dwyer-Shick 1979, 285). As Chambers notes, at the time of his writing in 1973, Parsons had paid for "nearly a third of the whole series from 1889 to 1973" (Chambers 1973, 197, n69).

Though as Leslie Spier remarked, Parsons "had no interest in formal recognition or personal aggrandizement for herself" (1943, 244), still she received much recognition during her lifetime. She was elected president of the American Folklore Society in 1918 to serve through 1920. As Boas commented, "In the Folk-Lore Society we have elected Mrs. Parsons president, in the hope particularly that she may be able to devise some means of increasing our membership. She is very energetic and resourceful" (Boas Papers, Boas to Tozzer, 12/30/1918). Parsons was associate editor of the *Journal of American Folklore* from 1918 until her death. In 1928, Reichard wrote to Parsons,

> My dear Dr. Parsons,
>   At the meeting of the American Folk-Lore Society on December 29, 1927, the Council requested the Secretary to send you a letter expressing the deepest thanks of the Society to you for the large amount of help and interest which you have rendered us particularly during the last year. It was decided that a letter to this effect be sent you and that a copy be laid upon the minutes.
>
> (UPFFA, Reichard to Parsons, 2/18/1928)

Ruth Benedict (1887–1948) was first a student of Elsie Clews Parsons and then a student of Franz Boas. In 1919, Benedict began taking courses from Alexander Goldenweiser and Elsie Clews Parsons at the New School for Social Research (Mintz 1981, 144). As Virginia Briscoe says in "Ruth Benedict, Anthropological Folklorist," "she approached the academic life very cautiously, taking one course a semester for two years at the New School for Social Research" before going on to Columbia to study with Boas (Briscoe 1979, 446). Benedict came to Boas on Elsie Clews Parsons's recommendation. "With Boas' blessing, she completed her doctorate at Columbia in three semesters" (Mintz 1981, 144). After taking her degree, Benedict became a teaching assistant at Barnard College (Mead 1974, 20). It was here that she had as a student the young Margaret Mead. Years later, Mead wrote an article entitled "Ruth Benedict, a Humanist in Anthropology." This title, in fact, encapsulates much of Benedict's contribution to anthropology and folklore. She brought to her work in the social sciences a background in the humanities. Her undergraduate degree from Vassar College (1909) had been in literature. She remained throughout her life a poet, publishing under the pen name of Ann Singleton. Ruth Benedict was conscious of her dual approach to anthropology and folklore. In December 1947, she delivered her retiring presidential address to the American Anthropological Association on "Anthropology and the Humanities." She maintained that, not only were the humanities compatible with the study of anthropology, but *necessary* for the vitality and sensitivity of the discipline (Benedict 1948).

Ruth Benedict had a formative impact on her students. Margaret Mead recalled, "The intensity of her interest, combined with the magnificent clarity of Boas' teaching, made anthropology . . . something of a revelation to me" (Mead 1974, 3). Another of Benedict's students, Sidney Mintz, remembered the first time he saw her in the fall of 1946:

> Benedict stood before us, tall, spare, seemingly rather distant, her voice startlingly low and slightly hoarse, plainly dressed, her silver hair short and severe, what I judged to be her shyness heightened by the contrast between the penetration of her ideas and the somewhat absent gaze with which she regarded us. I was astonished by her, and by her lecture. It simply had never occurred to me before that a total culture might be looked upon as if it were a work of art, something coolly contemplated, something utterly unique and distinctive, yet available to be studied, analyzed, understood.

> (Mintz 1981, 156)

Margaret Mead's and Sidney Mintz's recollections of their teacher convey the intellectual power and style of this remarkable anthropologist and folklorist. They present the reader with Ruth Benedict the humanist—the one who studied "a whole culture as a work of art"—as well as with Ruth Benedict the scientist.

Benedict's dissertation, "The Concept of the Guardian Spirit in North America," brought praise from an anthropologist who was to become a close colleague and life-long friend. Edward Sapir wrote to her from Ottawa,

I read your paper yesterday in one breath, interrupted by supper, most necessary distractions, only. Let me congratulate you on having produced a very fine piece of research. It makes a notable addition to the body of historical critiques that anthropology owes to Boas. I put it with such papers as Goldenweiser's "Totemism" (1910) and Waterman's "Explanatory Element in American Mythology" (1914) except that it impresses me as being decidedly more inspiring than either of these.

(Mead 1974, 22)

Ruth Benedict is remembered primarily for her book *Patterns of Culture*. Published in 1934, the book was an immediate success. Indeed, it has become a classic in anthropological literature. Benedict discussed individual cultures as wholes composed of patterned social and expressive behavior, of style and design that are replicated in every area of life. As Benedict said in a letter to Reo Fortune in 1932, "The theme of course is cultural configuration again" (Mead 1974, 41). According to Benedict's analysis, each culture had its own pattern; each culture was personality writ large. She examined Zuni culture as Apollonian; Kwakiutl culture as Dionysian; and Dobuan culture as schizophrenic. Her critics pointed to the labeling of non-Western cultures by terms laden with Western value-judgments, that is, schizophrenic, Dionysian, and Appolonian. But the power in the book lay in the elucidation of the symbolic patterning of social behavior and expression. From folktales, to dance, to child rearing practices, the same patterns or configurations emerged.

In the introduction to *Zuni Mythology*, Benedict stressed that "the intensive study of one body of folklore" had been neglected in both European and American scholarship. With a stress on "far-flung comparative studies," scholars had missed the opportunity to examine "a living folklore" (Benedict 1968, 103, 102, 106). There had been exceptions that illustrated "the great amount of cultural material in myth," and those that stressed "the value of folklore for an understanding of the culture" (Benedict 1968, 103). This approach was present in Boas's work on the Tsimshian (1916) and the Kwakiutl (1935).

For Benedict, a "profitable" study would result from an intensive examination of a single body of mythology and of folktales. These "should hold an important place in the tribal life" (Benedict 1968, 103). There should be a large body of tales recorded over a period of time; the culture should be adequately studied; and "folklore among that people should be a living and functioning culture trait" (Benedict 1968, 103–104). These conditions were met at Zuni.

Benedict examined the themes in the narratives and their relationship with the culture. She found that certain themes did not correlate with Zuni life and values. Though she did not phrase it in this way, Zuni mythology provided an imperfect reflection of Zuni culture. "It has always been obvious to students of every theoretical persuasion that folklore tallied with culture and yet did not tally with it" (Benedict 1968, 105). An oft-used explanation stressed the retention in folklore of past customs: "cultural survivals of earlier ages are perpetuated in folklore." Benedict eschewed this approach. A body of lore which reflected only "long-discarded customs" was "a dead lore rather than a living one" (Benedict 1968, 105).

What, then, was the explanation for the emphasis on polygamy in Zuni tales, when Zuni marriage was monogamous? Why the recurrent theme of the abandoned infant when this was not condoned in real life? In the first instance, Benedict suggested that the narratives provided both "mythological exaggeration" and "compensatory daydreams." Though in life, one had a single partner, in folktales, one could indulge. "Just as the hero of folktales kills a buck every day, or four in a single day, so he also is courted by eight maidens and marries them" (Benedict 1968, 107–08).

The explanation for the popularity of the theme dealing with the abandonment of children lay in "the fact that the hearer's identification is with the child, not with the mother." The hearer, in fantasy, becomes a child again and punishes the aberrant mother (Benedict 1968, 108–09).

Ruth Benedict taught courses in folklore and anthropology at Columbia from 1926 until her death in 1948 (Briscoe 1979, 446). In her teaching, she was known not only for her rigor and expertise, but also for the concern and support given her students. The personal guidance that Benedict extended to her students is conveyed in the following excerpt from a letter written to Margaret Mead in March 1926:

> Then this week Klineberg—do you remember the very fair, neat-minded boy in psychology—reported on psychoanalytic treatment of myth. I told him to do it as sympathetically as possible, and he thought at first that with the best will in the world that was impossible. But with the help of Malinowski's work and of suggestions we cooked up, he gave an exceedingly interesting report.

> (Mead 1974, 28)

Still another mark of the personal encouragement she gave her students was in material support. After the death of her husband, Stanley Benedict, she used her considerable inheritance to help finance her students' fieldwork.

In addition to her teaching, research, and writing, Ruth Benedict served in many other professional capacities. She contributed articles on "Animism," "Dress," "Folklore," "Magic," and "Myth and Ritual" to the first edition of the *Encyclopedia of Social Science* (Briscoe 1979, 445–46). In the late 1920s and the 1930s, Benedict worked with Gene Weltfish and Erna Gunther on a project funded by Elsie Clews Parsons which involved a compilation of a Southwest Indian mythology concordance (Briscoe 1979, 464). And in the 1940s, Benedict was one of the anthropologists working for the United States government as part of the war effort. In 1943, she took a position at the Office of War Information; she moved to Washington, D.C., and began her studies of "cultures viewed at a distance" (Mead 1974, 61).

Her book, *The Chrysanthemum and the Sword, Patterns of Japanese Culture* (1946), was the result of her wartime work.

From 1925 to 1939, Ruth Benedict served as editor—indeed, as the first woman editor—of the *Journal of American Folklore* and of the *Memoirs* of the American Folklore Society.[17] Benedict encouraged the publication of ethnic folklore collections. But, unlike Newell, her stress was not on British folk communities (Briscoe 1979, 463). In 1936, she wrote to Katherine Luomala saying, "What is needed is Finnish, Greek, Swedish and French folklore and the like" (Briscoe 1979, 463).[18]

Benedict received national and international recognition as an outstanding American anthropologist. In 1933, she was listed in the official register *American Men of Science.* As a further mark of her esteemed position, her name was starred as a leading scientist. She was among a group of seven out of one hundred scientists who were so designated as leading scholars. And she was the only living woman anthropologist to be listed—but then the register only listed three women (Briscoe 1979, 457–58). In addition to this, Benedict received many awards and held many offices. She was president of the American Ethnological Society (1927–1929); fellow at the Washington School of Psychiatry (1945); vice-president of the American Psychopathological Association (1946); president of the American Anthropological Association (1947); and fellow of the American Academy of Arts and Sciences (1947). In 1946, she received the American Design Award for War Services and the Achievement Award, from the American Association of University Women; in 1947, she was awarded an honorary D.Sc. from Russell Sage College (Mead 1949, 35); and in the summer of 1948, Benedict attended a UNESCO seminar in Czechoslovakia.

Yet it was only in July of 1948 that Columbia University bestowed the title of full professor on Ruth Benedict. This was, as Sidney Mintz said, "a shamefully tardy attempt" on the part of Columbia "to make up for its previous treatment of a great scholar" (Mintz 1981, 144). Ruth Benedict had taught at Columbia for twenty-six years, twelve of those as an associate professor. She was never, however, to teach under the title of full professor. She died two months after she was named full professor, in September 1948, at the age of sixty-one.[19]

Gladys Reichard (1898–1955) was another of Boas's students who took her degree at Columbia (1925) and stayed on to conduct courses at Barnard College (Columbia). Marian Smith said of Reichard, her teaching was "patterned" after Boas and "her interests had the same breadth" (Smith 1956, 914). In 1922–1923, she had a research fellowship at the University of California, Berkeley, which enabled her to write her dissertation, "Wiyot Grammar and Texts." Reichard completed the Ph.D. in 1925; and did a year of post-doctoral work (1926–1927) at the University of Hamburg, Germany (Reichard 1963, 805). Reichard began research among the Navajos in 1923, and continued working with them for more than twenty-five years. She spoke the language fluently and learned Navajo weaving as well during her four summers spent with a Navajo family (Reichard 1963, 805). She also worked among the Coeur d'Alene Indians (1927, 1929). Her fieldwork among the Navajo resulted in numerous publications, among which were *Navaho Religion, a Study of Symbolism* (1950), and *Spider Woman, a Story of Navaho Weavers and Chanters* (1934). Reichard's *An Analysis of Coeur d'Alene Indian Mythology* (1947) was awarded the Chicago Folklore Prize in 1948.

Reichard's work was grounded on the solid rock of Boasian anthropology, but had expanded into areas of symbolism and worldview. In the introduction to *Navaho Religion*, Reichard explained her intent—to go beyond the dance, song, and sandpaintings and to explicate the religious system that has sustained the Navajos in a rapidly changing world. Her aim was "to show how and why these people are preoccupied with ritual, and further, how the principles of their system differ so radically from our own" (Reichard 1963, xxxiii). Her work was divided into three parts. In the first, on dogma, she examined Navajo categories, worldview, the nature of man, the supernatural beings, the theory of disease and curing, and ethics. The second part focused on symbolism, and the third, on ritual. The concordances dealt with supernatural beings, ritualistic ideas, and rites, and were followed with a list of concordance topics.

Paul Radin and Martha Warren Beckwith followed a professional course that differed from that of the other anthropological folklorists. Both were trained by Boas; both conducted fieldwork and published works in folklore. But Radin (1883–1959), described as a man "of everywhere and nowhere" (Goldenweiser 1922, vii), refused to attach himself to an institution. He moved from job to job—University of California (Berkeley), Mills College, Fisk, University of Chicago, Kenyon College, and Brandeis. Julian Steward said, "his charm got him about every job in Anthropology in the country" (Diamond 1981, 72). Radin, who criticized the academic as "dependent upon his official academy" and "linked to the ruling establishment" (Diamond 1981, 75), once boasted that "he had turned down more job offers than any other anthropologist" (Sapir 1961, 67).

Radin did his undergraduate work at City College of New York (1902–1907); he wrote his thesis on the embryology of sharks. In 1907, Radin went to Munich to pursue his interests in icthyology. Here he studied with Ranke and developed an interest in physical anthropology. He took course work at the University of Berlin with Karl von den Steinen, Eduard Seler, and Paul Ehrenreich. On his return to Columbia, Radin minored in history under James Harvey Robinson, while majoring in anthropology under Boas. He completed his doctorate in 1911. Diamond, who discusses the intellectual life of his mentor, suggests that "the combined effect of Robinson's skeptical humanism and Boas' empirical insistence upon the indivisible potential of primitive and civilized mentalities . . . originally led Radin to question all notions of primitive inferiority" (Diamond 1981, 71).

Radin's first fieldwork was with the Winnebago Indians in 1908. This became his area of intense specialization. He wrote *The Culture of the Winnebago: As Described by Themselves* (1923). A classic among his works was

Crashing Thunder; The Autobiography of an American Indian (1926). Radin claimed only to be the editor of this work. However, as Sapir remarked, Radin provided in the notes "the essential background material which makes the struggle of this Indian in the face of white culture fully intelligible" (Sapir 1961, 65).

In addition to the Winnebago, Radin worked with the Ojibwa, the Fox, the Zapotec, the Wappo, the Wintu, and the Huave. He also studied the Italians of the San Francisco Bay Area. The thrust of Radin's work was to give voice to the people. As Stanley Diamond explained, Radin's continual concern was "that the values of social science itself were only reflections of the dominant social and economic currents peculiar to the civilization in which they existed." Radin felt "that studies of primitive life continually face the risk of reflecting ourselves and the established framework of Western thought more than primitive society" (Diamond 1981, 79).

Radin's work in folklore was extensive. His analytical perspective on folktale as literature is exemplified in *Literary Aspects of North American Mythology* (1915), and "Literary Aspects of Winnebago Mythology" (1926). Radin used the native terms for the narratives, and attempted to analyze the narratives for style, theme, and cultural content. In "The Literature of Primitive Peoples," Radin represented oral literature as drama. He spoke of the raconteur as the impersonator of the actors in the drama, with the audience as a participant. In his appraisal of Radin's work, Sapir says, "One looks for dramatic interaction between audience and actors, between audience and raconteur, and between raconteur and actors" (Sapir 1961, 66). Sapir concludes, "Oral literature looked at this way should, in the future, come up with interesting results." Radin's work followed the innovative thrust of his mind. He focused on the individual in culture, both in terms of the creative and intellectual capacity. Dell Hymes said, "Boas had no peer in American anthropological work except his students, Sapir and Radin" (Hymes 1965, 334).

With her academic training in anthropology and literature, and her unique appointment as a research professor in folklore, Martha Warren Beckwith (1871–1959) perhaps best exemplified a scholar who later would be classified as a folklorist. She did her undergraduate work in English literature at Mt. Holyoke College, which was followed by ten years as an English instructor at Elmira, Mt. Holyoke, Vassar, and Smith. Beckwith completed her master's work with Boas in 1906, and in 1918, she received her Ph.D. On her return to Vassar College in 1920, Beckwith was given a special appointment as research professor for the Folklore Foundation. She was also assistant professor of comparative literature. While this latter position terminated in 1929, she retained her position with the Folklore Foundation until 1939, when she retired as professor emeritus of folklore (Luomala 1962, 341–42; Boas Papers, Beckwith to Boas, 12/14/1919).

The research professorship was created through an endowment. Only after Beckwith's retirement did the contributors become known: Mr. and Mrs. Alexander of Hawaii had donated funds solely for the employment of

Martha Beckwith. Beckwith, who had grown up on the island of Maui, was a friend of this family. She dedicated her final work on Hawaiian folklore, *The Kumulipo, A Hawaiian Creation Chant* (1951), "To the memory of Annie M. Alexander, Lifelong Friend and Comrade from early days in Hawaii, whose generous sponsorship has made the author's research possible" (Luomala 1962, 3341–42).

Beckwith worked extensively on Hawaiian folklore; her *Hawaiian Mythology* (1940) was a detailed work of 575 pages. Yet in the preface, Beckwith said, "The study covers, as any old Hawaiian will discover, less than half the story (Beckwith 1970, xxxi). Beckwith returned frequently to Hawaii to pursue research. She had a position as research associate in Hawaiian folklore at the Bishop Museum, where she translated Hawaiian manuscripts. In addition to her work on Hawaiian folklore, Beckwith contributed to studies of folklore and ethnography among Jamaicans, native Americans (Mandan, Hidatsa, and Oglala), and the Portuguese of Goa (Luomala 1962, 342).

Beckwith wrote *Folklore in America, Its Scope and Method* (1931), a work that as Luomala noted "has had less notice than it deserves" (Luomala 1962, 345). Beckwith's survey of the study of folklore in the United States was scholarly and comprehensive. She began with a "Definition of the Field," followed with "The Method of Folklore," and ended with "Folklore in America." In the first two sections, Beckwith included the European and American approach to folklore. Clearly in control of the scholarship, she reviewed the major works and discussed pertinent works that were neglected in many contemporary histories of folkloristics. (See Beckwith 1931, 1–52).

The work of the anthropological folklorists expanded from an initial concentration on North American Indians to a consideration of Central and South America, the Caribbean, the Philippines, and Africa. (See also Lowie 1960, 462.) The change of geographical focus had to do with a conscious expansion of research boundaries. This was reflected by Boas's suggestion in 1908 that the *Journal of American Folklore* be renamed the *American Journal of Folklore* in order to justify the inclusion of non-American material (Willis 1973, 317; Boas Papers, Boas to Tozzer, 3/18/1908). One such anthropologist who illustrates this move beyond the continental United States was Laura Watson Benedict (1861–1932). Pursuing her fieldwork with little support, she went to the Philippines where she taught school to Bagobo children in Santa Cruz in order to obtain funds for her ethnographic work. She remained there for fourteen months, enduring great hardships from the stress of rigorous fieldwork and a demanding teaching schedule. Benedict collected ethnographic specimens with a care for detail, a sense of native aesthetics that set her work apart from the often haphazard collecting of the time. Her observations of ritual show her sensitive appreciation of the people. After her return from the Philippines, she undertook the study of anthropology with Franz Boas at Columbia (See Bernstein 1982).

Boas's plan for anthropology involved establishing control of university teaching and research, editorial control of the *Journal of American Folklore*, and supervision of museum collecting (Boas Papers, Boas to Nuttall, 5/14/1901; Parmenter 1966, 98–99). Boas did gain control of university instruction in anthropology. Just as Child and Kittredge had done at Harvard, so Boas did at Columbia. He trained the young anthropologists who fanned out across the country and carried on his form of anthropology. As Darnell commented, "Boas' students . . . came to constitute the major power bloc in American anthropology early in the century, headed academic departments which looked to Columbia and to Boas for access to publication outlets and money for fieldwork" (Darnell 1969, 235).

For Boas and for his students, folklore was not separate from anthropology (Boas 1904, 520). Again, this is an attitude similar to that of the literary folklorists discussed in the last chapter. For them, folklore was not separate from their literary studies, but a part of their research and of their instruction. For neither the literary folklorists nor the anthropological folklorists was there a separate and independent study of folklore. It was a sideline for Stith Thompson; and it was a subarea for Franz Boas.

Boas remained faithful to his initial plan for the science of anthropology. As he confided to Zelia Nuttall in 1901, the success of his vision depended on his power to mold and direct academic concerns, "I believe that it will be of advantage to American anthropology if I can retain a certain amount of control in the direction of the various activities . . . for a few years" (Boas Papers, Boas to Nuttall, 5/14/1901). He added that he was opposed to a single man "retaining longer than is absolutely necessary" the power and control that were necessary to effect his "multitude of plans." Part of Boas's strategy was to develop anthropology in all areas—physical, archaeological, linguistic, ethnological—to the extent that a specialist would be needed for each. Further, he did not deviate from the position that he shared with William Wells Newell when they struggled to keep folklore under the wing of anthropology. It was not Boas's intent to develop a curriculum in folklore studies. He taught folklore related subjects as part of other anthropological instruction. As Melville Jacobs remarked, "For years Boas gave university courses on the mathematical tools for description of populations, on the science of languages, and on American Indian languages, but to my knowledge he never offered a course on folklore, though by 1910 he had set a commanding example by his publications" (Jacobs 1959b, 121). Thus, in doing linguistic translations, an anthropological folklorist would collect and transcribe folktales. Or in studying diffusion through distribution, one would examine style and form in art, in narratives, in ritual. In the Boasian view, folklore illustrated other anthropological concerns. It did not stand alone.

Ben-Amos remarks on the two forms of institutionalization: "the learned societies and the university departments and centers."

> Boas and Newell controlled the Society, but their ambition, particularly that of Boas, was to establish authority over university research and teaching. Indeed,

in due time Boas achieved his goal in anthropology, but folklore lagged behind and only many years later gained a stronghold at the university.

(Ben-Amos 1973, 122).

In truth, Boas, by establishing authority over university research and instruction in anthropology, brought to fulfillment the initial plan for folklore. That folklore should be kept under the wing of anthropology was first stated by Newell in his capacity as editor of the *Journal of American Folklore*. Further, it should be emphasized that folklore *was* taught in the early years by anthropologists—not by Boas, but by his students. Kroeber taught "Studies in Comparative Mythology." Goddard, Speck, Radin, and Lowie taught seminars in folklore and courses in primitive religion, which included a consideration of mythology, magic, and ritual; Radin taught a course on primitive literature. Clearly, anthropological folklorists did make major contributions to the academic study of folklore.

SIX

Approaches to Folklore

The Literary and
the Anthropological

In *Philosophy in a New Key*, Susanne Langer stresses the importance of "the nature of our questions." These questions taken together comprise our *basic concepts*, our intellectual framework. As she says,

> A philosophy is characterized more by the *formulation* of its problems than by its solution of them. Its answers establish an edifice of facts; but its questions make the frame in which its picture of facts is plotted. They make more than the frame; they give the angle of perspective, the palette, the style in which the picture is drawn—everything except the subject. In our questions lie our *principles of analysis*, and our answers may express whatever those principles are able to yield.
>
> (Langer 1970, 4)

Using Langer's metaphor, it is possible to examine the angles of perspective, the frames of reference used by the literary folklorists and by the anthropological folklorists in viewing folklore material. What questions did they bring to the material? And how did the nature of the questions asked shape the material studied?

The literary folklorists classified folklore into genres which were further divided into major and minor genres. And certain literary folklorists specialized in one area: Child and Kittredge in the ballad, Thompson in the folktale, Taylor in the proverb and riddle. The anthropological folklorists studied folklore as part of culture—a way of learning more about the culture history, as with Boas, or a way of learning more about cultural patterns, as with Benedict. For the literary folklorists, the frame for the study of folklore was the written tradition. Folklore was studied as it existed *within* the literate civilizations, mainly those of the Indo-European world. For the anthropological folklorists, the questions were not directed to folklore *per se*, but rather to culture: what was the nature of culture? and how was this reflected in folklore?

It is a matter of import to single out culture as the basic concept for the anthropological folklorists. If this is not established as the point of origin for the questions about folklore, the boundaries between the literary folklorists and the anthropological folklorists might be blurred. Both spoke of the oral literary aspect of folklore. But this oral literary aspect had a different point of reference for the anthropological folklorist than it did for the literary folklorists. The anthropological folklorist chose as their frame cultures without writing. They could not, then, delineate the body of material by saying it was oral, since all that was studied in a nonliterate culture was oral. But they could and they did stress the oral literary aspect of folklore. Erminie Voegelin called it "orally transmitted prose"; Herskovits, "unwritten literature"; and Bascom, "verbal art" (Leach 1949, 400, 403, 398).

The material of the anthropological folklorist and the literary folklorist was, indeed, common ground. But it was plowed and plotted in different ways, to different purposes. The cycle of inquiry for the literary folklorist was ultimately for the elucidation of written literature; and the cycle of inquiry for the anthropological folklorist was to augment the understanding of a particular culture, and/or culture in the universal sense.

In addition to their varying approach to the lore, the literary folklorists and the anthropological folklorists also had a different frame of consideration for the folk. For the literary folklorist, the folk were, for the most part, members of the peasant community. Thompson was the exception to this, since he, although a literary folklorist, studied native American material. For the anthropological folklorist, the folk were members of non-Western, tribal cultures. Yet, the literary folklorist and the anthropological folklorists did agree on one folk group, the black American. As Dundes notes in "The American Concept of Folklore," black folklore was a combination of European and African elements (Dundes 1966a, 230). Still, the literary folklorist emphasized the European elements and the anthropological folklorist emphasized the African. So in essence, they maintained their divided orientation, even though working with the same folk group.

In both cases, for the literary and for the anthropological folklorist, the folk were set apart from the scholars themselves. The folk were to be found in bucolic enclaves for Child, untouched by time and education—in life, on the Shetland Islands; in print, in unpublished ballad manuscripts. And for the anthropological folklorists, the folk (and they were likely to be referred to as the primitive) were to be found on the Northwest Coast with the remains of a once lavish culture, or in the Southwest in the pueblos or in the hogans. The folk were for both the literary folklorists and the anthropological folklorists *the other.*

In their scholarly work, the literary folklorists adopted a European orientation to their subject matter, theory, and form of presentation. Frequently this link between the American scholar and the European approach was clearly stated. In his preface to *The English and Scottish Popular Ballads,* Francis James Child said, "In the editing of these ballads I have closely followed the plan of Grundtvig's Old Popular Ballads of Denmark" (Child

1962, ix; see also Dundes 1966a, 240). Child corresponded with Grundtvig and sought his counsel for the five volumes of his ballad work. He also maintained extensive correspondence with Andrew Lang in Britain, Reinhold Kohler in Germany, Kaarle Krohn in Finland, Giuseppe Pitré in Italy (McNeil 1980, 541), and was influenced by Cecil Sharp of England (Dundes 1966a, 240). Kittredge, too, identified with European standards of scholarship and maintained a correspondence with Europe's leading folklorists. For Thompson, European folklore scholarship was crucial. As he said, "It is only by an emulation of these European colleagues that our folklore scholars can proceed with certainty and skill" (Thompson 1949, 244). As noted, both Stith Thompson and Archer Taylor traveled to Finland to meet with Kaarle Krohn. In fact, as Thompson emphasized, Finland was regarded as the center of folklore studies (Upadhyaya 1968, 112). In his memoirs Thompson noted that the trip to Finland was like a scholarly pilgrimage for American folklorists to visit Krohn, the leader of folktale studies.

The European orientation to the study of folklore was clearly evidenced at the Midcentury International Folklore Conference held at Indiana University from July 21 to August 4, 1950 (Thompson 1953). Of the four symposia, three began with addresses by European folklorists. In the first symposium, Stith Thompson, the organizer of the conference, introduced Sean O'Sullivan who spoke on the work of the Irish Folklore Commission in collecting folklore. In the second, Maud Karpeles from the International Folk Music Council, London, England, introduced Ake Campbell of the Dialect and Folklore Archive in Uppsala, Sweden, who spoke on the European systems of archiving folklore. In another, George Herzog of Indiana University introduced Sigurd Erixon of the University of Stockholm who spoke on the European study of folklore. In only one symposium, entitled "Making Folklore Available," was the lead speaker an American. Alan Lomax, listed with the affiliation of New York City, spoke about his work with radio programs and the use of folklore.

In "The Future of Folklore Research in the United States," Stith Thompson laid out the sequence for the study of folklore: "1. it must have its field defined; 2. the materials for study must be assembled; 3. the materials must be arranged and preserved; and 4. the materials must be interpreted" (Thompson 1949, 244). Thompson devoted a good deal of attention to the second and third category, touched on the first, and ignored the last. And in truth, this was generally true of the literary approach to folklore. The stress was on collection, classification, and preservation of text. The collection was viewed as crucial— to save the material from oblivion, to pass it on to future scholars. The classification provided a means of organizing a growing body of texts. This was done with genre classification, tale-type identification, and motif analysis. These three categories of the literary approach—collection, classification, and preservation—ultimately contributed to the establishment of folklore archives.

The Midcentury International Folklore Conference provided just such a forum for the study of folklore. The symposia encompassed the following: the collecting of folklore, archiving folklore, studying folklore (definition and theory), and making folklore accessible to the public. Referring to Thompson's four categories listed above, one notes that three of the four were included at the Midcentury International Folklore Conference: the definition of field, the assembling of the material, and the preservation of the material. The fourth category, the interpretation of the material, was not included. In its place was another category, "making folklore available."

Child's ballad scholarship was predicated on a *complete* collection of all versions. His emphasis was always on gathering together manuscripts of ballads—collecting, annotating, and editing them. Thompson was explicit about the importance of collecting.

> For folklore as for other subjects this is a continuing process and will never end. Collectors have now been busy for a century and, especially in ballads and folksongs, have published a great mass of material. They have filled many volumes of folklore journals and many cabinets with phonograph records.

(Thompson 1949, 245)

Archer Taylor noted, "The collecting of tales is, obviously enough, the prerequisite to their study, and in this direction scholars have been very active indeed" (Taylor 1940, 1).

Dan Ben-Amos, in the introduction to *Folklore Genres*, remarks on the link between collection and classification. "The genre orientation in folklore research is a direct continuation of the first stage of research—the very act of collecting" (Ben-Amos 1976, xi). And Dundes, in "Folk Ideas as Units of Worldview," notes, "Once any corpus of folklore has been collected, it is to matters of genre classification that folklorists invariably turn. Obviously the exigencies of archiving have forced the folklorists to think in terms of classification and genres" (Dundes 1978a, 106). Further, the genre orientation carries over from collecting to publication, and it provides the framework for most collections, anthologies, and indexes (Ben-Amos 1976, xi). Since the classification by genre framed the work of the literary folklorists, let us examine Child's concept of ballad, Taylor's concept of proverb, and Thompson's concept of folktale.

Walter Morris Hart, in an essay on "Professor Child and the Ballad," observed, "it is obvious that Professor Child already had in mind the conception of 'a real *traditional* ballad,' a 'specimen of authentic minstrelsy'" in his early work (Hart 1906, 799–800). Hart contrasted Child's work on the ballad over the forty year period from his first publication in *English and Scottish Ballads* (1857–1859) to the final volumes of *The English and Scottish Popular Ballads* (1882–1898). Though the earlier conception of the ballad was not so complete and rigorous as the latter, "the significant fact is that for at least forty years Professor Child retained without essential change his conception of the traditional ballad as a distinct literary type." For Child, the ballad was a "very important species of poetry" which preceded "the poetry of art," a term Child used to refer to written poetry. The ballad told a story in lyric verse; it was a narrative song (Hart 1906, 800, 756, 781).[1]

For the literary folklorists, the genres of folklore designated certain literary types. Though these types were at times hard to define, the scholar developed a "feel" so that one genre could be distinguished from another. Archer Taylor, whose book, *The Proverb* (1931), is a classic, was recognized as the authority on proverb scholarship. Yet he never defined the genre: "The definition of a proverb is too difficult to repay the undertaking." He felt that no definition would "enable us to identify positively a sentence as proverbial" (Taylor 1931, 3). Stith Thompson, the international expert on the folktale, remarked that "no attempt has ever been made to define [the folktale] exactly." He saw this lack of definition as a "great convenience . . . since it avoids the necessity of making decisions and often of entering into long debates as to the exact narrative *genre* to which a particular story may belong" (Dundes 1978a, 24–25).

The literary folklorists adopted both an evolutionary and a devolutionary explanation for the origin of folklore. As Dundes explains in "The Devolutionary Premise in Folklore Theory," while people were said to evolve, folklore was said to devolve or to degenerate: it passed from the higher to the lower classes (Dundes 1969a). And this is precisely Francis James Child's view of the evolution of society and the devolution of the ballad: "Whenever a people in the course of its development reaches a certain intellectual and moral stage, it will feel an impulse to express itself, and the form of expression to which it is first impelled is, as is well known, not prose, but verse, and in fact narrative verse" (Hart 1906, 756).[2] At this stage, according to Child, the people are not divided into classes by political organization or book culture: "There is such community of ideas and feelings that the whole people form an individual." The popular ballad, Child maintained, was "an expression of the mind and heart of the people as an individual."

Child did not concur with Wilhelm Grimm who said that the ballads "write themselves." An individual, after all, composed them, "still the author counts for nothing" and the ballad comes to us as an anonymous creation. This position he stated succinctly, "The fundamental characteristic of popular ballads is therefore the absence of subjectivity and of self-consciousness." Further, the popular ballad had its origin "in that class whose acts and fortunes they depict—the upper class." It "is not originally the product or the property of the lower orders of the people." Society, then, reached the right stage of development, and the ballad was created— by the upper class. At this stage, there was "no sharp distinction of high and low . . . in respect to knowledge, desires, and tastes." However, with "an increased civilization" and the beginning of "book-culture," there arose a division between the high and low classes. The high class turned away from the popular ballad to written poetry (what Child called "the poetry of art"). "The popular poetry is no longer relished by a portion of the people, and is abandoned to an uncultivated or not over-cultivated class—a constantly diminishing number" (Hart 1906, 756–57).

Taylor, while less explicit than Child, also adopted an evolutionary frame for certain genres. He identified jests as part of the "primitive narrative tradition." And in reference to Arthur Beatty's efforts to establish the marchen as prior to the ballad, Archer Taylor remarked, "I hasten to say that I, too, believe the ballad to be much younger than the marchen as a genre" (Taylor 1940, 20–21). In his caution, he remarked, "The question of ways and means to prove or disprove the correctness of such a belief needs serious thought." Ralph Steele Boggs's explanation of the development of folklore was succinct and evolutionary: "As folklore comes down through history it is modified by the cultural level in which it is found" (Boggs 1929, 9).

The European orientation which was adopted by the literary folklorists focused on the story of the text (Dundes 1966a, 243). The text was catalogued by type and broken down into components or motifs. Dan Ben-Amos discusses this early orientation to the study of folklore: "The formative years of folklore have been devoted to the construction of research tools such as classification systems, indexes, bibliographies, and annotated collections" (Ben-Amos 1973, 115). Certainly Thompson was active in these endeavors. He worked on *The Types of the Folktale* and the *Motif Index of Folk-Literature*. His work was directed, he said, toward facilitating archival work, toward building classificatory systems. Child's work on the ballad came to be associated with a type classification—the Child Ballad Number.

Ben-Amos notes that these organizational systems were originally developed to enable the folklorist to carry out research in a professional manner. Thompson in his early work on American Indian narratives recognized the need for a general reference work on motifs. As he said in "Narrative Motif-Analysis as a Folklore Method," there had been a lack of "adequate tools" for the study of traditional narrative. "Exact terms of reference have been needed, and a great deal of labor has been wasted because people were talking about different things under the same name" (Thompson 1955, 4). Thompson's works on folktale classification and motif elements have become standard tools of reference for folklorists. *The Types of the Folktale* and the *Motif-Index of Folk-Literature* have enabled scholars to communicate about narrative folklore with greater facility.

The *Motif-Index of Folk-Literature* catalogues the basic elements of narratives from all over the world. For example, from volume 1, part A, "Mythological Motifs" comes the following:

    A1. Identity of creator.
  A1.1. Sun-god as creator.
  A1.2. Grandfather as creator.
              A1.4. Brahma as creator. (Thompson 1955, 66)

Motifs are cross-referenced. Thus "A220. Sun-god" is listed in small print with "A1.1. Sun-god as creator." Volume 1 covers "Mythological Motifs," "Animals," and "Tabu." It also includes a "General Synopsis of the Index," a bibliography and abbreviations. Volume 6 provides an index, which facilitates the search for specific motifs.

Given this elaborate six volume reference work, still the question remains, what are scholars referring to when they talk of motifs? In his article "Narrative Motif Analysis as a Folklore Method," Thompson asked this same question. And he answered, "To this there is no short and easy answer" (Thompson 1955, 7). In order to select the material to be included in the *Motif-Index of Folk-Literature*, he used the following guidelines: "Certain items . . . are the stuff out of which tales are made. It makes no difference exactly what they are like; if they are actually useful in the construction of tales, they are considered to be motifs" (Thompson 1955, 7). The motif, then, cannot be defined, but is the basic element out of which a narrative is composed.

Thompson's intent for the *Motif-Index of Folk-Literature* was to provide a sensible arrangement of motifs. "The *Index* is merely an application of well-known principles of division and subdivision and is made so that it can be enlarged at any point without limit. . . . The principal end of the *Index* is to find a place for everything" (Thompson 1955, 7). Even Thompson's method of work illustrated his desire to find a place for every motif. As Dorson recalled:

> [Thompson] would sit at his work table in Room 40 of the old Indiana University library, piles of motif slips laid out on the table before him, and spin a poker chip container around in lazy Susan fashion until he found the right slot for the slip under consideration. But if it seemed an isolated and questionable motif he discarded it.
>
> (Dorson 1977c, 5)

The *Motif-Index of Folk-Literature*, a reference work that can expand *without limit*, provides the ultimate in the literary orientation to collecting and preserving folklore. Every element of every narrative from anywhere in the world can find a place in this reference work.

The reviewers of the *Motif-Index of Folk-Literature* recognized its strengths and its limitations. Gerould, in his review of the first edition of the *Motif-Index of Folk-Literature*, praised Thompson for undertaking a task that required not only fortitude but "scholarly intelligence of a high order" (Gerould 1936, 275). Kurt Ranke gave the second edition of the *Motif-Index* a mixed review. From his European perspective, it was "the typical product of an American mind as well as of American possibilities." The work had been done "in grand manner in a piece of humanistic research." However, a larger number of type indexes and handbooks had not been consulted and "no new motifs of great importance have been found" (Ranke 1958, 81,

83). Ranke remarked on the potential and the problem, "Thompson's great achievement is the planning, organization, and execution of his *opus magnum*, without question an enormously respectable work which places him among the greats of our discipline. But posterity must solve the problems which he has raised thereby" (Ranke 1958, 83). And to do this, the regional indexes would have to be completely incorporated to produce "a great universal index."

Another major contribution of the literary folklorists was the establishment of the tale-type indexes. Stith Thompson's translation and revision of Antti Aarne's *Verzeichnis der Märchentypen* (1910) is the foremost type index. As Thompson said in the preface to the second revision of *The Types of the Folktale*, Aarne's original classification was directed toward "arranging the great Finnish collections of tales." He further states that it served well for the tales of northern Europe. The countries of "southern and southeast Europe and of Asia over to India" were not included. Though attempts were made to extend the coverage in the 1928 revision, still, as Thompson himself said, the index was not inclusive. The appearance of "regional and national indexes of folktales from Russia, Spain, Iceland, and Lithuania brought suggestions of many new types" (Thompson 1961, 5). Thus the research for the 1961 revision started almost as soon as the 1928 work was published.[3]

The basic form of *The Types of the Folktale* was established by Aarne's work in 1910. Thompson's contributon was the translation and expansion of the index. The index categories—or as Thompson referred to them, the index numbers—establish the framework for the classification. In the first revision of *The Types of the Folk-Tale*, Thompson retained Aarne's original "Outline of the Classification of Tales": I Animal Tales—Nos. 1–299; II Ordinary Folk-tales—Nos. 300–1199; III Jokes and Anecdotes—Nos. 1200–2499 (Thompson 1928, 20–21). In the second revision of *The Types of the Folktale*, the outline follows the same numbering and categories, except that the third is further divided: from 2000 to 2399 fall the formula tales of part IV; and from 2400 to 2499 is part V, the unclassified tales (Thompson 1961, 20).

Each tale-type was assigned an Aarne-Thompson or AT number. On occasion, there was a further division by letter. Thus AT 314A is the tale of "The Shepherd and the Three Giants," which is summarized as follows: "He overcomes three giants, gets three horses at their castles and with these wins a tournament three times, defeats three ogres or helps the king thrice in battle" (Thompson 1961, 110). The tale summary is followed by a listing of the motifs which are found in the tale-type. For AT 314A the following entries appear:

L113.1.4. Shepherd as hero.
  G500. Ogre defeated.
  Z71.1. Formulistic number: three.
  B184.1. Magic horse.

B401. Helpful horse.
R222. Unknown knight (Three days' tournament).

And finally, there is a listing of the major bibliographic sources for the tale, the countries in which the tale was located, and the number of versions found.

Thompson's revision of Aarne's 1910 *Verzeichnis der Märchentypen* was received as a welcome expansion. Spargo said of the 1928 work, "In spite of whatever faults can be found, *The Types of the Folk-Tale* is the most useful single work for the student of the popular tale" (Spargo 1930, 444). And Warren Roberts called the 1961 revision a "primary research tool," a model for future indexes (Roberts 1977, 6).

Literary folklorists adopted a method for the study of folklore that combined their emphasis on the collection, annotation, and dissemination of the text. The name of this approach also indicated their European orientation. It was called the Finnish historic-geographic method. In this study of narrative folklore, the attempt was made to arrive at the original, or *Ur* form, and to trace the route of diffusion. The method involved the formidable task of collecting all available versions of a tale in print and ordering them chronologically, thus encompassing the historical aspect. The oral versions were then plotted according to geographic order. The scholar examined the corpus of texts and broke them down into principal traits, which were often represented by code to facilitate comparison of numerous versions. When the archetype for each trait had been determined, they were put together to comprise the hypothetical *Ur* form of the narrative. Basic to the historic-geographic method was the assumption that an item diffuses from the center of creation in a wave-like movement. Also implicit is the assumption that age can be correlated with distribution. A tale on the edge or periphery of the geographic mapping would be derived from and younger than the tale at the center. Thus, a trait that is more widely distributed is also assumed to be older.

Archer Taylor's *The Black Ox: A Study in the History of a Folk-Tale* illustrates that approach. At the time of writing in 1927, Taylor's intent was to introduce this "systematic method" from Finland to the English readers (Taylor 1927, 3). The principles of the historic-geographic method had been presented in Kaarle Krohn's *Die Folkloristische Arbeitsmethode* (1926). Taylor wrote an article on the historical background of this approach in 1928, "Precursors of the Finnish Method of Folklore Study." As his corpus, Taylor used more than a hundred recorded Finnish versions of the tale. "This number," Taylor said, "is sufficiently large to enable us to determine with some degree of accuracy both the details of the normal form and the various centers of distribution." Since there was not a great deal of variation in the form of the recorded tale, "it is possible to construct any prototypic form with more than the usual confidence." In order to reconstruct the original form of the narrative and to arrive at "its primitive form," each incident or trait was to be examined. The next step, then, was to put together the original incidents: "After establishing each element in this manner, we may by simple addition of the elements arrive at the outlines of the primitive form of the whole." Taylor warned the scholar to choose versions from one country and only then gradually to extend the geographical consideration. Such a tale from one country would yield "a local 'normal form'" and would eliminate "certain recalcitrant and apparently anomalous variations" (Taylor 1927, 1, 4, 6, 5).

Taylor emphasized that there were certain criteria that established a trait "as belonging to the normal or the primitive form": "A trait which appears in *many* variants is likely to be old and to be intimately associated with the tale. A trait's *wide distribution* weighs heavily in its favor" (Taylor 1927, 6). The *nature of the text* also gave credibility to the determination of the age of a trait. If it occurred in a "well preserved" narrative, one that was not "fragmentary or otherwise known to be corrupt or contaminated" then there was added assurance of its antiquity. Taylor noted that a trait could be considered as *demonstrably old* if it occurred in early versions or "implied ancient custom or superstition." And if a trait were *useful in the management of the story* it was likely to be older. Another indication of age had to do with the *cumulative* effect of traits, those established earlier influenced those later added to the narrative. As Taylor said,

> The readiness with which the varying traits may be derived from the one selected as primitive or normal may give a further indication of an earlier state of affairs, particularly when such derivation points to development in one direction and cannot be readily construed in a reverse sense.
>
> (Taylor 1927, 6–7)

Taylor addressed the hostile critics of this method and noted that they were mainly opposed to the criteria used for determining the age of the traits. He admitted that no single factor alone was sufficient to determine age, and that "a numerical preponderance" would not establish age. But, he said, even the most hostile critic would have to concede

> that a trait which is widely distributed, which appears frequently in the variants, particularly in the fuller and better ones, which is attested at an early period in the tale's recorded history, which is *per se* old (involving some ancient religious or superstitious idea), which is useful in the tale's economy, which permits competing forms to be derived from it by some natural and readily explicable alteration or substitution, which yields evidence in agreement with that deducible from other traits, and which shows a development in accord with a known or a probable cultural trend, *must* belong to the earliest ascertainable form of the tale. I insist upon the word *must*. Granted that the trait meets these requirements, one is compelled to accept it as original; no option is conceivable.
>
> (Taylor 1927, 7)

After providing an explanation and a defense of the method, Archer Taylor presented the most common version of the tale of the Black Ox.

> When he is plowing, a farmer throws a knife into a whirlwind, for he had heard that this causes the whirlwind to disappear. A Lapp orders him to come after his knife or all will not be well. The farmer arrives Christmas eve. While eating, he sees the knife and recognizes it. He wants to return for the holiday dinner. The Lapp promises to take him for the ox that stands at the door-post. The Lapp says, "Will you go like thought, like a bullet, or like a black cock?" The farmer answers, "Like a black cock." He is put in a trough drawn by reindeer. The trough bumps into a steeple. The farmer's cap flies off, but it is not recovered. . . . At home the farmer orders the maid to substitute a smaller black ox. But the Lapp and the ox are in the trough and the bellowing of the ox is audible as they disappear.
>
> (Taylor 1927, 16)

Abstracts of variants were given in the appendix. Taylor broke the narrative into traits, analyzed them, and determined the point of origin. "Ultimately the story is of Scandinavian origin; a closer localization is impossible with such scanty evidence, although indications favor Norway. From Sweden it was borne to Finland, where it attained a characteristic, highly elaborated form, and in Finland it passed from west to east" (Taylor 1927, 63–64).

Stith Thompson was also enthusiastic about the use of the Finnish historic-geographic method for the study of folk narrative. In his article, "The Star Husband Tale," Thompson attempted to still the objections of two leading European folklorists. Albert Wesselski argued that literary versions had such a powerful influence on oral versions as to make the reconstruction of the original oral version impossible. And C. W. von Sydow stressed the importance of linguistic and national boundaries and opposed the notion of wave-like diffusion of the tale (Thompson 1965b, 418). Thompson examined the eighty-six reported versions of the Star Husband Tale, and in his conclusions postulated the place of origin, path of diffusion, and age of the tale. He said, "The Central Plains would seem the most reasonable place of origin for the simple tale or basic type." As to the age, Thompson remarked, "It is, of course, quite impossible to tell just when this tale began to be told." Then after reviewing the types of the tale and the accompanying dates of the recorded versions, he added, "It would seem from these facts that this tale in its basic form must go back at least to the eighteenth century. But that is as close as we can come to an estimate of its age" (Thompson 1965b, 455–57).[4]

The Finnish historic-geographic method was not accepted unanimously and without reservations. Both Archer Taylor and Stith Thompson in their articles on the application of the method were attempting to counter criticism and to gain approval of a wider audience. Certainly there was opposition. And at the Midcentury International Folklore Conference, some of this opposition was articulated. Thompson lead the session devoted to a discussion and a debate about the Finnish historic-geographic method (Thompson 1953, 267–86). Many of the participants expressed their reluctance to accept the validity of the reconstructed archetype, to dismiss the complicating factors of differing linguistic groups and the effect of the printed versions on oral renditions. Alan Lomax was perhaps the most candid:

> I should like to ask a question which I am sure many people here would like some information on. What so far . . . are the achievements of the so-called historic-geographic method? From what has gone so far I can't make out what the method has brought forth in terms of scientific conclusions.
>
> (Lomax in Thompson 1953, 276)

What, indeed, were the achievements of the Finnish historic-geographic method? From the review of Taylor and Thompson's work, it is apparent that rigor is required to collect and study *all* the available versions of the item under scrutiny. But after this was done, what were the results? Taylor was able to suggest that the story of the Black Ox was of Scandinavian origin, probably from Norway. And Thompson was able to tell us that the Star Husband tale probably originated in the Central Plains sometime around the eighteenth century. These results were in keeping with the stated goals of this form of study. As Thompson said,

> The student using this method is attempting to find what the tale probably looked like at the beginning, before it started on its long wanderings. He is trying to find out vaguely in what part of the world it started, and also to make some guesses, not too wild guesses it is hoped, as to about what period of the world's history it may have originated.
>
> (Thompson 1953, 269–70)

Perhaps it is not fair to fault Taylor and Thompson and other advocates of the Finnish historic-geographic method for failing to consider that which was not part of their stated concern—the meaning of the material. However, a determination of origin and of age *was* among the goals of this method, and this was not accomplished with any degree of certainty. The method, though rigorous, was sterile and did not accomplish its purpose.

The final, and perhaps more serious, problem with this approach was the separation of the folk from the lore. Scholars talked of tales that migrated from country to country, but they excluded from the discussion the tellers of the tales and the effect they had on the creation and dissemination of folktales. This was part of the orientation of the literary folklorist, toward a study of the text and an elimination of the folk. Thompson said,

> One assumption I am making is that the student of folklore is resolved to study the history of the particular item that he is interested in. Now this does not

preclude an interest in the people who own the item or the people who tell it. It means merely that for the particular study the scholar is making, his interest is focused at least for the moment on the particular item he is working on.

(Thompson 1953, 268)

Thompson viewed this separation of the folk from the lore as a definite advantage. He referred to it as a dispassionate reading of the material; the scholar did not have to be distracted by people.

There were those among the literary folklorists, however, who did not let this exclusion of the folk occur without objection. During the symposium devoted to a discussion of the Finnish historic-geographic method at the Midcentury International Folklore Conference, Albert Lord, a member of the Slavic Department at Harvard University, raised an objection. "I wonder whether it is possible to arrive at any archetype of a tale or a song or an epic, if we consider that in every performance of an art form in oral tradition, whether it be a tale or an epic, the individual singer introduces variations" (Lord in Thompson 1953, 275).

For the anthropological folklorists, the concept of culture provided the crucial framing for their enterprise. As Kroeber said, "If there is a subject matter specific to our science, it is culture" (Kroeber 1940, 4). And Wirth, in his review of social science contributions to American scholarship, remarked, "Perhaps the most significant contribution which anthropology has made to social science and to popular intelligence centers around the concept of culture and the independence of culture from biology" (Wirth 1953, 64–65).

In 1871, Edward Burnett Tylor wrote what is now regarded as the classic definition of culture: "Culture or Civilization, taken in its wide ethnographic sense, is that complex whole which includes knowledge, belief, art, morals, laws, custom, and any other capabilities and habits acquired by man as a member of society" (Tylor 1871, vol. 1:1). George Stocking, in his detailed and penetrating examination of the culture concept, points to the evolutionary framework of Tylor's definition. Culture existed in the singular and was marked off in stages. Stocking directs us to Boas for the development of the culture concept, the idea of "cultures" in the plural, representing a way of life and not a stage of development. (See Stocking 1968, 69–90, 195–233.) Boas arrived at this view of the plurality of cultures through his early work on Northwest Coast Indian folklore. Here, as he noted in 1887, he observed tribes that were distinct linguistically, but shared "so great a similarity in myths and beliefs"; and tribes with the same language that had a different body of folklore (Stocking 1968, 206). This was the beginning of Boas's concern with the necessity for separating race, language, and culture—a concern that would become a central motivation in his work and in his teaching. As Boas explained it, his method was "to inquire into the peculiarities of the single tribes, which are obtained by a thorough comparison of language, customs, and folklore" (Stocking 1968,

206). In his introduction to the *Publications of the Jesup North Pacific Expedition*, Boas said, "before we seek for what is common in all culture, we must analyze each culture by careful and exact methods" (Lowie 1911, 604).

In a letter to Hodge, Boas stressed the holistic nature of culture: "the culture of each person forms a unit, all features of which are interdependent" (Darnell 1969, 179).[5] Thus, an aspect of culture could not be meaningfully studied outside the cultural context. Boas strongly opposed Otis T. Mason's arrangement of museum exhibits according to item, without regard for cultural integrity. As Boas said in 1887, "By regarding a single implement outside of its surroundings, outside of other phenomena affecting that people and its productions, we cannot understand its meaning" (Lowie 1948, 69; see also Jacknis 1985).

Though there were different domains for the literary folklorists and the anthropological folklorists—one deriving from literature, the other from culture—still there were shared concerns and similar approaches. For the anthropological folklorists, as for the literary folklorists, the collection of material was of primary importance. From the multitude of texts, the literary folklorists attempted to reconstruct the original text. And from the detailed linguistic texts, the anthropological folklorists tried to reconstruct the traditional culture—or as Lowie called it "reproduce [the] ancient culture" (Lowie Papers, Lowie to Risa Lowie, 6/23/1914). For both, the study of the material was largely devoted to a discussion of diffusion and an analysis of traits or motifs.

Gladys Reichard noted the importance of texts for Boas: "The strongest rocks in Boas' self-built monument are his texts, his belief that what people record of themselves in their own words will in the last analysis reveal their motivations and ideas most accurately" (Reichard 1943c, 55). Boas recorded the tales phonetically in the native language, and translated them interlineally. He was emphatic about the importance not only of collecting the texts in the native language, but also of publishing them. As he remarked, he came to his first disagreement with Newell over just this issue:

> I consider the publication of the Indian texts essential. Just as little as you would be satisfied with having only translations of European material, can we be satisfied with having Indian material in translation only. Even if the present use of Indian texts is limited to a few people, they are indispensable.

> (Boas Papers, Boas to Newell, 3/28/1906)

Boas's primary emphasis was on collection, or what he would term the complete description of a culture, which had to precede the formulation of general theories. In "The Growth of Indian Mythologies" (1896), Boas said, "If we want to make progress on the desired line, we must insist upon critical methods, based not on generalities but on each individual case" (Boas [1896] 1948, 435). The study of Indian mythology, and indeed by extension, the study of anthropology was based on the accumulation of individual cases, or information on single cultures.

However, Boas's stress on the particulars did not mean that he was inordinately opposed to theory. As he wrote to Kroeber, "all through my life I have discussed theoretical questions in connection with definite problems" (Kroeber Papers, Boas to Kroeber, 7/24/1917). Boas advised Kroeber to present the theory separate from the "detailed investigation," because "evidently no one reads this kind of material, but expects to get his theoretical point of view from general theoretical works." On this theme, Walens remarked, "it is a perennial mistake of anthropologists to believe that Boas's eclectic idea of culture prevented him from making any summary statements about Kwakiutl culture" (Walens 1981, 18).

Boas's early work in folklore shaped his later work in anthropology, especially in linguistics. (See Hymes 1963; Rowe 1962; Stocking 1974c; Darnell 1969, 338.) This is apparent in two articles in which Boas sets forth his method for the study of distribution: his 1891 article, "Dissemination of Tales among the Natives of North America"; and his 1896 article, "The Growth of Indian Mythologies." Ruth Benedict in "Franz Boas as an Ethnologist," said that his 1896 writing "was basic to all his work in this field. Dissemination of traits was one of the processes that always had to be taken into account before it was possible to understand the working of the human mind in its cultural creations." As Benedict said, the study of diffusion "was not an end in itself nor did it by itself furnish the key to the understanding of culture." But for Boas, it was a necessary precedent in order to understand how "each human group built up its own version of life and code of behavior" (Benedict 1943, 29).

In "Dissemination of Tales among the Natives of North America," Boas discussed narratives that were similar but widely dispersed among the native peoples of North America and that were shared among the Eskimos and Indians. After the presentation of the material, he remarked, "From these facts we conclude that diffusion of tales between the Eskimo and Indian tribes of the western half of our continent has been quite extensive." And if tales have spread, then, Boas suggested, other cultural elements as well "have spread from one center over the Arctic and the North Pacific coasts" (Boas [1891] 1948, 441, 443).

"The Growth of Indian Mythologies, a Study Based upon the Growth of the Mythologies of the North Pacific Coast," was delivered first as an address to the seventh annual meeting of the American Folklore Society, in Philadelphia, on December 27, 1895. In this, Boas had two concerns. First, he was arguing against the theories that explained similar elements in widely dispersed folklore, that is, solar mythology, radical diffusion, parallel development, and psychic unity. And second, Boas was presenting his own position, that "similarity of traditions in a continuous area is always due to dissemination." While willing to concede to the solar mythologists that "the grandeur of nature upon the mind of primitive man" might influence thematic elements of myths, he emphasized that it could not explain the form that myths would take (Boas [1896] 1948, 432, 433). Boas was also willing to admit the possibility of independent origin or parallel development in certain circumstances. For instance, when a tale, composed of a single incident, was found in numerous cultures from around the world, then this tale might have been invented independently in each culture. As he noted in his earlier article on the dissemination of tales, "The tale of the man swallowed by the fish, or by some other animal, which has been treated by Dr. E. B. Tylor is so simple that we may doubt whether it is due to dissemination" (Boas [1891] 1948:437, 438). However, when a tale was composed of several elements that were combined in a similar manner, then the explanation could not be parallel development or independent invention, but must be diffusion of the tale from one culture to another. Boas's emphasis was on diffusion—or dissemination as he called it—within a *contiguous* or limited area. He was not interested in discussing diffusion on a global scale, such as Schmidt and Rivers attempted with the *Kulturkreislehre*.

The diffusion of tales and other aspects of culture would, according to Boas, ultimately illustrate the connection between tribes, including their migration and their place of origin. In his later work in folklore, Boas developed the idea of the culture reflector method, that folk narratives mirrored aspects of the culture. As he said in the section on "Mythology and Folklore" in his textbook *General Anthropology,* "If it is true that myths are built on the experiences of everyday life, we may expect that the dominant cultural interests are reflected in them. The incidents mirror the life of the people and their occupations, and social life may in part be reconstructed from these tales" (Boas 1938, 622). Thus, through studying folklore, one could *see* a portion of the culture. This was especially valuable for cultures that were so changed by extensive white contact as no longer to be traditional. In his *Tsimshian Mythology* and *Kwakiutl Culture as Reflected in Mythology,* Boas used narrative folklore to reconstruct the past.

Unlike the scholars who codified the Finnish historic-geographic method, Boas did not formulate an explicit method for the study of diffusion in narratives. He did, on occasion, provide an indication of his assumptions about diffusion, as is evident in the following statement: "Whenever we find a tale spread over a continuous area, we must assume that it spread over this territory from a single center" (Boas [1891] 1948, 439). This assumption was basic to the age-area hypothesis in anthropology. In this approach, as in the Finnish historic-geographic method, the movement or diffusion of traits was conceptualized as concentric circles or waves, like ripples on water made when a rock is thrown. And just as with ripples, a trait diffused from a central point, unless an obstacle lay in the path.[6]

In order to study the diffusion of narratives, the anthropological folklorists used another approach similar to that used by the literary folklorists. It was necessary for Boas to break a narrative down into elements. As he explained, "A single element may consist of a number of incidents which are very closely connected and still form one idea" (Boas [1891] 1948, 438). Boas listed the elements of the dog-husband story of the Dog-Rib Indians from the Great Slave Lake as follows: "1. A woman mated with a dog. 2. Bears pups. 3. Deserted by her tribe. 4. Sees tracks of children. 5. Surprises them. 6. Takes their skins. 7. They become a number of boys and one girl. 8. They become the ancestors of a tribe of Indians" (Boas [1891] 1948, 438). These eight elements from the narrative of the Dog-Rib Indians have been combined in a similar way by the Indians on Vancouver Island. Boas remarked that "The elements may have arisen independently in various places, but the sameness of their combination proves most conclusively that the whole combination, that is, the story, has been carried from Arctic America to Vancouver Island, or *vice versa*" (Boas [1891] 1948, 438).

Boas was determined that others would work on this project. On August 31, 1907, he wrote to Kroeber, "Have you been able to do anything about the catch-words concerning which I wrote last spring? I am very anxious that our committee should present a report at the Christmas meeting and should be very much indebted for contributions" (Kroeber Papers, Boas to Kroeber, 8/31/1907). Boas mentioned Ehrenreich's *Mythology of South America*, Stucken's *Astral Myths,* and Frobenius's *Das zeitaltendes Sonnengottes* as works that Kroeber might consult. Boas again corresponded with Kroeber on the subject, "It is my idea to try to devise a number of catch-words for discussion by the Committee when we meet this winter, or, probably better, later on by correspondence. . . . I will send you a short list which will indicate perhaps more clearly what I mean" (Kroeber Papers, Boas to Kroeber, 9/17/1907).

The concept of narrative elements was developed further by Robert Lowie in an article entitled "Catch-Words for Mythological Motives": "The advantages of uniform terminology—of brief, unequivocal designations for wide-spread elements which are constantly referred to in mythological discussions—are obvious" (Lowie 1908a, 24). Lowie had compiled the list "at the suggestion of Professor Boas." His intention was to use catch-words which were already sanctioned by usage. In one category, "Catch-Words in General Use, or already Suggested," Lowie gave twenty-nine categories. Included among these were the following: Orpheus, visit (journey) to the sky, bear and deer, theft of fire, rolling skull (head), rolling rock, evil father-in-law, tar-baby, world-fire, turtle's war party. He also gave thirty-two "proposed catch-words" (Lowie 1908a, 24–27).

Lowie had hoped to stimulate "revision and collaboration" (Lowie 1908a, 24). Kroeber responded in "Catch-Words in American Mythology," a paper delivered to the California Branch of the American Folklore Society. He referred to Lowie's article and then credited Boas with the stimulus for pursuing this attempt at classification: "The idea has for some years been agitated by Dr. Boas, to whom credit is due for the realization of the value of this method of approaching the problem of handling so large a body of material" (Kroeber 1908a, 222). Kroeber offered a few modifications to Lowie's catch-words, and then provided a "designation of concepts occurring in myths and tales of the California Indians." Kroeber's catch-words include a description:

1. *Theft of sun (luminaries, light).*
   Analogous to theft of fire. The Yurok tell also of the theft of night, of water, of food.
2. *Creation in a vessel (under cover).*
   Creation of men, or animals, in a basket, from a bundle, under a blanket.
3. *Skunk-shaman.*
   The skunk, pretending to be a shaman, kills his patient by shooting.
4. *Abandonment on tree.*
   Son or younger brother abandoned on tree which grows upward or the branches of which are blown away.

(Kroeber 1908a, 223)

His list continued with a total of fifty-three concepts that he had found useful in his study of California mythology.

The work of Kroeber, Lowie, and Swanton on catch-words of American Indian narratives was part of a larger plan, that of compiling a myth concordance. Lowie referred to "Professor Boas' " suggestions as spurring him on in his work. Kroeber noted Boas's "agitation" on this subject. Actually the plans for a reference work on American Indian mythology had been present from the early days of the Bureau of American Ethnology. As Darnell notes, "One of the Bureau's first projects was an abortive attempt to classify the mythology of North America. The First Annual Report included a summary of American mythology written by Powell. . . . The concordance was pursued by Jeremiah Curtin between 1883 and 1892" (Darnell 1969, 59). Curtin's plan for his work on mythology was to "reveal the mental systems of various groups of American Indians" (Darnell 1969, 59). He would use his work in mythology to aid in his classification of "these nations at successive periods."

Frank Boas suggested a collaboration between the American Folklore Society and the Bureau of American Ethnology on a general work in American mythology (BAE, Boas to Henshaw, 12/6/1890; Darnell 1969, 290). Boas envisioned this on a grand scale with the following people responsible for specific groups: John Murdoch (Eskimo), Garrick Mallery (Atlantic Algonkian), Daniel Brinton (southern and central Algonkian), Reverend McLean (Blackfeet), Horatio Hale (Iroquois), James Mooney (Cherokee), A. S. Gatschet (southeastern tribes), J. O. Dorsey (Sioux), John W. Powell (Shoshone), Jesse Walter Fewkes (Zuni), Washington Matthews (Navajo), John Bourke (Apache), Jeremiah Curtin (California), Alice Fletcher (Sahaptin), Boas (Northwest Coast). As Darnell noted, "The plan was abortive for a combination of reasons, including lack of publication funds and difficulty of eliciting appropriate material from the would-be contributors" (Darnell 1969, 290).

Though this work did not materialize, still Boas did not give up the idea. He headed a committee of the American Anthropological Association which included Dorsey, Kroeber, and Swanton. Working also through the American Folklore Society, Boas appointed Swanton as head of the committee composed of Boas, Swanton, and Dixon. Though serving on both committees, Swanton did not know how to proceed. He wrote Boas, "As yet I haven't a clear idea of the method of identifying myths by catch words, and should like an example" (Boas Papers, Swanton to Boas 8/3/1907). Boas expanded on the concept in a letter to Swanton:

> The principal thing is to find a very simple catch-word which represents either an incident in a myth or a whole type of myths; for instance, the numerous tests of son-in-law or nephew or suitor might be called "test myths," or the tales of the ascent to the sky by a chain of arrows might be called "arrow-chain."

> (Boas Papers, Boas to Swanton, 8/10/1907)

Dixon caught on and compiled "a practically complete list" with ease: "Cannibal-head; Canoes of enemy bored with holes; Time miraculously shortened; House miraculously enlarged; Pitch on belly to imitate fat. . . ." However, there was still the question of judgment: "how minute do you wish the analysis to be?" (Boas Papers, Dixon to Boas, 9/30/1907). Dixon asked whether the catch-words should be large elements or small.

The project was overwhelming. The quantity of material made the organization difficult. And, even more central to the problem, there was disagreement as to the method of classification. Swanton despaired of finding a "connection between more than a thousandth part of our myths"; but even such minimal resemblance would be "sufficient for some sort of classification that is vastly better than our present chaos" (Kroeber Papers, Swanton to Kroeber, 9/23/1910).

In his 1907 article, "A Concordance of American Myths," Swanton addressed both the benefits and the difficulties of such an undertaking. He foresaw "great additions . . . to the fund of human knowledge" should a suitable method be devised for organizing all North American myths into appropriate categories. "The accomplishment of such a work would involve the compilation of a concordance in which all the genuine unaffected American myths should find a place." He anticipated three obstacles: "(1) the difficulty of classifying accurately and uniformly throughout, (2) the difficulty of knowing where to draw the line in admitting myths and mythic elements, and (3) the danger of making the work so cumbersome as to be practically useless" (Swanton 1907, 220).

In 1909, Swanton delivered his presidential address to the American Folklore Society on "Some Practical Aspects of the Study of Myths." He referred again to the importance of compiling a concordance of American myths: "Here it is proposed to classify all myths under types, each type to have some suitable catch-word; i.e., its technical term in the science, such as 'magic flight,' 'Potiphar,' 'rolling-stone,' " (Swanton 1910, 5).

Along with the classification of "myths and larger elements," Swanton stressed the need to study "mythic formulae" (Swanton 1907, 221). These were "conventional modes of expression and conventional mythic ideas" that were unique to a tribe.

> Thus, among the Haida a mythic town is described by saying that it was "a five-row town," while the neighboring Tlingit call it "a long town." Among the Haida, again, an incarnate deity indicates his supernatural origin by clamoring for a copper bow and arrows, but his Tlingit counterpart is content to "hunt all the time."
>
> (Swanton 1907, 222)

Swanton called the compilation of a myth concordance "a crying need in the further study of folk-lore and anthropology." He was enthusiastic about the prospects, but recognized the difficulties in bringing together such a work. He concluded his article, "A Concordance of American Myths," with the following questions: "(1) is such an undertaking practicable; (2) how comprehensive can a concordance be made without destroying its usefulness, or in other words how much shall be included in it; and (3) granted its desirability, what steps can be taken by anthropologists and students of folk-lore to make it an actuality" (Swanton 1907, 222).

Waterman, who had written his dissertation at Columbia on the explanatory element in American mythology, hoped to pursue a myth concordance. Waterman was under the impression that the Bureau of American Ethnology had been working on a classification of myths, and he wrote to Hodge to inquire. He suggested "a concordance of occurrence and diffusion of every tale" (Darnell 1969, 293).[7] Kroeber learned of Waterman's interest and wrote to him: "Your plans for a handbook on mythology interest me greatly but I fear you will find it a bigger undertaking than you imagine. I have played around the fringe of the problem enough to be impressed by it" (Darnell 1969, 293).[8]

In 1913, Stith Thompson wrote to Boas to inquire about the myth concordance. He told Boas of his dissertation topic on "European Borrowings in American Indian Tales," and asked if there was "any reason why the investigation of this topic would not be advisable" (Boas Papers, Thompson to Boas, 5/29/1913). Boas responded to Thompson, "I am interested to hear that you are taking up the question of borrowing of European folklore in America" (Boas Papers, Boas to Thompson, 5/29/1913) and advised him concerning current research.

The anthropological folklorists continued their interest in a catch-word concordance. On November 5, 1926, Boas wrote to Parsons, "Since you left we have been considering the question of the Concordances" (Boas Papers, Boas to Parsons, 11/5/1926). Parsons took this up as a project and directed it specifically toward a concordance of Southwest mythology (Boas Papers, Boas to Reichard, 11/4/1926). However, in spite of the enduring enthusiasm, the plans for a concordance of Indian mythology were never realized, perhaps because of the nearly insurmountable difficulties (Kroeber Papers, Kroeber to Swanton, 9/3/1910).

Thompson carried on in a tenacious fashion. And in a sense, Thompson's work was a continuation of the anthropological work on catchwords. Thompson on several occasions acknowledged his debt to anthropologists. In his letter to Kroeber, he had characterized his dissertation as "about equally in the fields of comparative literature and anthropology" (Kroeber Papers, Thompson to Kroeber, 7/5/1914). He also noted that in his attempt to make a distribution map for North American Indian tales he was aided by Clark Wissler's map of culture areas which arranged "tribes by culture rather than linguistic families" (Thompson 1953, 271).

While the literary folklorists compiled collections and anthologies according to genres, the anthropological folklorists were likely to compile their material either by focusing on a single culture or on several cultures. Boas's *Kwakuitl Culture* is an example of the encyclopedic approach to the study of one culture, with folklore as an integral part of the study. Gladys Reichard in writing on "Franz Boas and Folklore" stressed this nature of his work:

> The title *Franz Boas as Folklorist* might seem proper but would actually be inappropriate. Professor Boas did not study folklore because he was a "folklorist" nor by studying it did he become one. He used it as an important part of the whole which he envisioned; a description of the tribes in which he was interested and an interpretation of their culture.
>
> (Reichard 1943c, 52)

The anthropological folklorist might also study a single aspect of folklore as it was manifested in several cultures. Elsie Clews Parsons's *Pueblo Religion* and Ruth Benedict's "The Concept of the Guardian Spirit in North America" exemplified this comparative approach.

On occasion, the anthropological folklorist focused on a genre of folklore. For example, Paul Radin wrote *The Trickster, a Study in American Indian Mythology* (1956) and Ruth Benedict produced two volumes on *Zuni Mythology*. However Radin's and Benedict's work were not intended as investigations of folklore genres—a concept that was not used by the anthropological folklorists—but as explorations in cultural patterning. In the prefatory note to *The Trickster*, Radin said, "Manifestly we are here in the presence of a figure and a theme or themes which have had a special and permanent appeal and an unusual attraction for mankind from the very beginning of civilization" (Radin 1972, xxiii). Benedict's intent in *Zuni Mythology* was to explore the pattern or theme in Zuni culture through a study of their mythology. And mythology was conceptualized more as a system of belief, that is, customs and practices and sacred narratives, than as a collection of narratives.

The emphasis on cultural patterns was critical for the shift that took place in American anthropology, a shift from an earlier focus on detailed description to a focus on theme and meaning. Thus folklore manifested certain themes that resonated in other areas of culture as well. In Benedict's terms, it was part of the personality of the culture.

Ruth Benedict, Paul Radin, and Melville Jacobs were the innovators in this new approach to folklore. And their contributions had an impact that is still reverberating in folklore theory. The three were characterized by Lowie—rather coolly, it should be noted—as scholars of folklore who were "not averse to psychoanalytic interpretation" (Lowie 1960, 467). Together they sparked the psychological interpretation of folklore.

This innovation in folklore studies combined three approaches: the psychological, the cultural, and the folkloristic. Radin's remarks in the opening to *The Trickster* clearly show this:

> Our problem is thus basically a psychological one. In fact, only if we view it as primarily such, as an attempt by man to solve his problems inward and outward, does the figure of Trickster become intelligible and meaningful. But we cannot properly and fully understand the nature of these problems or the manner in which they have been formulated in the various Trickster myths unless we study these myths in their specific cultural environments and in their historical settings.
>
> (Radin 1972, xxiv)

Fieldwork has long been regarded as a distinctive part of the anthropological endeavor. And the stress on the importance of fieldwork has been present in American anthropology from the early years: "The Bureau took the fieldwork of its staff extremely seriously. When Frank Cushing needed a scalp for his initiation at Zuni, it was provided from the museum collection" (Darnell 1969, 68).

Franz Boas, in his own research and in the training of his students, also encouraged fieldwork. He worked among the Eskimo of Baffinland from 1883 to 1884, and among the Indians of the Northwest Coast for nearly two and a half years (Rohner 1966, 159). Alexander Lesser notes another of Boas's contributions to fieldwork. Referring to the Torres Straits Expedition of the British under W. H. R. Rivers and A. C. Haddon, Lesser says, "somewhat overlooked in this historical view are the monumental field researches of the Jesup North Pacific Expedition, which was mounted under Boas' inspiration, direction, and editorship while he was at the American Museum of Natural History and at Columbia" (Lesser 1981, 11). The Jesup Expedition, which was contemporary with the Torres Straits Expedition, resulted in seventeen volumes on Siberia and the Northwest Coast. Triloki Pandey noted the importance of the American anthropologists to the development of fieldwork. "One should not belittle the importance of earlier field workers such as Boas and Cushing among others, in making anthropology an observational science" (Pandey 1972, 322, n8).

If culture was, as Kluckhohn said, like water for fish, then fieldwork was cultural immersion. The assumption was made that through the process of immersion, the anthropologist would learn the culture through the voices, eyes, and lives of the people. For the anthropological folklorists, this meant studying the folklore in context. As Voegelin said, the anthropological folklorist was "interested in the function of folk tales, in the various other interpretations of folk tales in their setting, and in their meaning to the teller" (Voegelin in Thompson 1953, 283).

While fieldwork has been long associated with the anthropological approach to the study of folklore, still it would be a skewing of intellectual history to use this as the major point of division between the literary and the anthropological approaches. There has been just such a tendency to equate the literary approach with library research and the anthropological approach with field research. While this might frequently be the case, still it does not take into account those literary folklorists who recognized the importance of fieldwork for capturing the life of the material. Phillip Barry was such a person. He emphasized the need to go to the folksingers themselves. And because Barry did this, he knew that, contrary to what the academicians were saying, ballads were still present as songs, and were not just recited as poems. He was also cognizant of more pressing problems for ballad study than the tired consideration of the communal theory (Alvey 1973, 71).

Another scholar who belied the equation between the literary approach and library research was Milman Parry. As Bynum noted in his work on oral literary studies at Harvard, "Though a Classicist by profession, he preferred to think of himself as a professional hybrid—a 'literary anthropologist.' It was an apt expression" (Bynum 1974, 28).

From the appraisal of the literary and the anthropological approach, one can see the shared ground. The anthropological folklorists were early concerned with the dissemination of narratives. In order to study this dissemination, they attempted to compile an index of catch-words and a concordance of myths. Thompson, along with other literary folklorists, began a study of the diffusion of folktales and an analysis of motif elements. In his work, Thompson was influenced *both* by the work of the American anthropologists and the European folklorists. His work on American Indian narratives was a continuation of the work done by Boas and his students. Contemporary with the work done by the anthropological folklorists in the United States, was the work in Finland on tale type. While Boas and his students attempted to compile a myth concordance, Antti Aarne was compiling his tale-type index. In 1913, Thompson wrote to Boas about the possibility of pursuing work on a myth concordance. And Thompson did just that. In 1924, he was invited by Kaarle Krohn to continue the work of Antti Aarne. In his work on the *Motif-Index of Folk-Literature*, he pursued in expansive detail the beginning attempts by Boas, Lowie, Swanton, Waterman, Dixon, and Kroeber to index elements or catch-words for American Indian narratives. Thompson chose the folk literature of the entire world for his corpus. Thus, in a real sense, he carried on work in the early tradition of the American anthropologists and the Finnish folklorists.

Both the literary folklorists and the anthropological folklorists were concerned with the *collection* of a large quantity of material. For the literary folklorist, the emphasis had been on the collection of folklore and the classification according to genre or tale type or motif. For the anthropological folklorists, the emphasis was on the collection of the material—in the earlier years, on the reconstruction of culture history; and in the later years, on pattern and meaning. The starting point for the two was different. For the literary folklorists, it was literature; for the anthropological folklorists, it was culture. But the cognitive approach to the material was strikingly similar: it was the collection and classification of folklore.

The literary folklorists in their study of the diffusion of a narrative focused on the narrative itself. It was the text that interested them. And it was the *origin* of the text that concerned them. They asked: What is the *Ur* form and from whence did it come? For the anthropological folklorists, the text was a conduit. And their questions were phrased: What does the narrative tell about the people and from whence did they come? The focus was different: for the literary folklorists, the text; for the anthropological folklorists, the people. But the underlying framework sustained the same assumptions. Through the study of diffusion, age and origin could be ascertained. The original narrative could be reconstructed; and the traditional culture could be described.

The anthropological folklorist and the literary folklorist have shared more common ground in their study of folklore than has been recognized, either by intellectual historians or by the folklorists of the two persuasions themselves. It cannot be denied that there are very significant differences between the two. However, under close scrutiny, one realizes that there are also shared concerns and shared orientations. The two roots of American folkloristics feed from a common source, the material of folklore. And both the literary and the anthropological approaches shared in the intellectual orientation of the time, which were the concerns with the point of origin, with the past, and with the original.

To close the consideration of the orientations to folklore, Archer Taylor's critique of the work in folktales and Melville Jacobs's suggestion for a combined scientific and literary approach should be examined. Archer Taylor in "Some Trends and Problems in Studies of the Folk-Tales," concluded, "The quality of the essays devoted to describing the collecting of tales and to interpreting the significance of tales in folk-life is depressingly low and rarely rises above the level of conversation at an afternoon tea" (Taylor 1940, 23). He suggested that a freshness might be gained if "the study of the forms of tales is allied to the classification of tales." And he added, "enlargement of our knowledge of the forms of tales would improve our systems of classification" (Taylor 1940, 12–13). Taylor wanted to take the work in narrative beyond Thompson's *Gerüst* or framework (Upadhyaya 1968, 113), beyond a mere classification of motifs and types. He was suggesting a combination of type and form, a combination that Vladimir Propp had accomplished in his work *Morphology of the Folktale*. Though written in 1928, this was unknown to the English-reading public until the 1958 translation. Taylor, attuned to structure through his work on formula tales, was also anticipating the approach taken by Lee Haring in *Malagasy Tale Index*, a classification of tales according to form or structure. Using von Sydow's work in oikotype as an inspiration, Taylor suggested that comparisons could be made between countries for differences in meaning (Taylor 1940, 14). Taylor's critique indicated his dissatisfaction with the work of the literary folklorists and his desire to move beyond mere classification to form and meaning.

Melville Jacobs posed another challenge for the anthropological folklorists. He asked, "Can both scientific and literary function be combined in publication of folktales and still adhere to rigorous standards?" And he answered, "I believe that they can, if interpretive comments supplement the stark translations and if the additions are written so as to include, readably and pleasurably, associations and sentiments which the native audience experienced" (Jacobs 1959b, 124). Jacobs in this statement was proposing a blending of humanities and science, a combined approach suggested by Ruth Benedict a decade earlier. He was also anticipating the development of performance theory in folklore. The text could be combined with the context, and both could add meaning to the other. His query and response provide a tantalizing suggestion of what is to be gained through a combination of the literary and the anthropological approach to the study of folklore.

SEVEN

Remnants of the Past in the Present

Conflict in Contemporary Folklore Theory

In 1965, Alan Dundes commented on the assumed division between the literary and the anthropological in folklore studies:

> Many of those outside the discipline of folklore and even some of those within tend to divide folklorists into literary or anthropological categories. With this binary division comes a related notion that each group of folklorists has its own methodology appropriate for its special interests; hence there is thought to be a method for studying folklore in literature and another method for studying folklore in culture.

(Dundes 1965b, 136)

Dundes stresses that the study of folklore in literature and in culture is "almost exactly the same." And this shared approach comes from "the discipline of folklore" which "has its own methodology applying equally well to literary and cultural problems." The dichotomy, Dundes says, is false, persistent, and divisive.

As noted in the preceding chapter, there had been a remarkable similarity between the literary and anthropological approach to folklore. While this similarity was veiled, and not necessarily recognized, it did exist. And certainly with the emergence of folklore as an independent discipline, the two branches of folklore study would grow together. Still, the roots of conflict ran deep; the tension between the literary and the anthropological persisted. Francis Lee Utley spoke of this in "Conflict and Promise in Folklore," his presidential address delivered at the sixty-third annual meeting of the American Folklore Society on December 27, 1951: "Nothing has disturbed your president more in this year . . . than the disintegrative quarrels which make our society function at only a small fraction of its potential." Utley listed four major conflicts that threatened "to deluge our society." The first was "the literary folklorists versus the anthropologists—

speaking bluntly the . . . Modern Language Association versus the . . . American Anthropological Association." He continued, "Broadly speaking, the source of the battle is a preoccupation with differing subject matters— the folklore of the native White and the Southern White (with a brief glance at the immigrant White) as opposed to the folklore of the aboriginal Indian." Utley further noted that "the best of the anthropologists seem to me to be more aware of the absurdity than we are—at least they seem more anxious to resolve the conflict so that folklore studies can proceed with direction and accomplishment" (Utley 1952, 111).

Very often this resentment ran like static through scholarly debates. A controversy that has been stilled in recent years was once energetically pursued as the myth-ritual debate. In 1966, Joseph Fontenrose wrote, "Myth has a great vogue today, and nowhere so much as in literary criticism. Some critics are finding myth everywhere, especially those who follow the banner of the 'myth-ritual school'" (Fontenrose 1971, i). He points out that there is diversity of opinion within the myth-ritual school. For the most part, he adds, all agree that "myths are derived from rituals and that they were in origin the spoken part of a ritual performance." The myth-ritual theory was given impetus in 1912 by the publication of Jane Harrison's *Themis*. She presented myth as the *legomena* or the spoken part of *dromena*, the rites. The true myth for Harrison was the sequence of words which accompanied the rites.[1]

In 1934, Fitzroy Richard Somerset, the Fourth Baron of Raglan, delivered an address to the English Folklore Society entitled "The Hero of Tradition" (Raglan 1965). This formed the basis of *The Hero: A Study in Tradition, Myth, and Drama* (1936). Lord Raglan studied the lives of Robin Hood, the heroes of the Norse Sagas, King Arthur, Cuchulainn, and the Greek heroes. He found that the accounts of the heroes' lives conformed to a pattern composed of twenty-two features, among which were the following:

1. His mother is a royal virgin.
2. His father is a king, and
3. Often a near relative of his mother, but
4. The circumstances of his conception are unusual, and
5. He is also reputed to be the son of a god.

The hero's life ends with the following features:

18. He meets a mysterious death.
19. Often at the top of a hill.
20. His children, if any, do not succeed him.
21. His body is not buried, but nevertheless
22. He has one or more holy sepulchers.   (Raglan 1965, 145)

Raglan suggested that this pattern emerged from the rituals associated with the rites of passage, specifically those concerned with birth, accession to the throne, and death.

Raglan's discussion of the pattern in the hero cycle is important. In the headnotes to Raglan's "The Hero of Tradition," and in "The Hero Pattern and the Life of Jesus," Dundes situates Lord Raglan with others who have worked on pattern in folklore, and on pattern in the life of the hero (Dundes 1965b, 142–44; 1978b). Johann Georg von Hahn published *Arische Aussetzungs-und-Ruckkehr-Formel* (Aryan Expulsion and Return Formula) in 1876. Von Hahn used the biographies of fourteen heroes and arrived at sixteen incidents. In 1909, Otto Rank, after a study of fifteen biographies, published *The Myth of the Birth of the Hero*. Raglan was unaware of the work of von Hahn and Rank (Dundes 1978a, 231). Vladimir Propp's *Morphology of the Folktale*, which appeared in 1928 in Russian, was also part of the pattern approach to the study of narrative.

Joseph Campbell, author of *The Hero with a Thousand Faces* (1949) was certainly the most popular of those who studied pattern. Campbell divides the hero's adventures into the formula of separation, initiation, and return. He truncates the heroes' biographies, never examining the life of one person in its entirety. His major conclusion, in keeping with the tenor of the myth-ritual school, denies historicity to the heroes of tradition. As Dundes notes, Campbell was, like Raglan, unaware of the body of scholarship. While he included one footnote on Otto Rank, he did not make any reference to von Hahn, Propp, or Raglan (Dundes 1965b, 143).

Raglan makes this same point in support of the ritualistic interpretation in "Myth and Ritual," an article that was included in the 1955 issue of the *Journal of American Folklore*, entitled *Myth: A Symposium*. "Myths as a rule are untrue historically, because most rituals have been developed gradually, and not as a result of some historical incident." Raglan focuses on ritual because he believes that action must be prior to thought. As he says, "Nobody can possibly imagine anything which has not been suggested to him by something which he has seen, heard, or read" (Raglan 1955, 454, 455). This stance allows for no creativity among the folk. Nothing can come as an expression of the mind and the soul except that which has gone before. And this precedent in event must be ritual: "My general theory . . . is that there arose, probably in southeast Asia, and at least 6000 years ago, a religion centering about the cult of a divine king who was periodically killed" (Raglan 1957, 360). The religion spread, though the king was no longer killed. Yet the initial killing was retained symbolically in rituals and myths. This could also be found in folktales and legends which, for Raglan, were merely myths severed from ritual. An example of the vestigal remains can be found in the folktale "Llewellyn and His Dog" (AT 178A). In this tale, the faithful dog has saved a child from a serpent. The master returns home, sees the bloody mouth of the dog, and shoots it, thinking that it has killed the baby. According to Lord Raglan, this tale records the substitution of animal for human sacrifice.

William Bascom in "The Myth-Ritual Theory" (1957) and Joseph Fontenrose in *The Ritual Theory of Myth* (1971) provide a careful critique of Lord

Raglan, Stanley Edgar Hyman, and others of the ritualist school. Bascom remarked on Raglan's two major points in favor of ritual interpretation of myths—that myths lack historicity, and that the folk lack creativity. In short, myths could not be connected with historical events because, in Raglan's words, "tradition never preserves historical facts" (Bascom 1957, 36). Raglan had "after much consideration . . . fixed on the term of one hundred and fifty years as the maximum" for folk memory (Bascom 1957, 36; see also Raglan 1949, 12). Bascom counters this argument with a reference to the Gwambe of Mozambique, and their legends about early European contacts:

> [One legend tells of] a disagreement among the chiefs of the Delagoa Bay area as to whether Europeans should be refused permission to pass through their territories, since they were so dirty, disease ridden, and destructive. Another legend . . . tells of the killing and prompt burial of white cannibals in the region south of Delagoa Bay.

(Bascom 1957, 105–06)

The details in both of these legends have been confirmed in Portuguese records "referring to historical events 400 years ago."

Addressing Raglan's argument denying the creativity of the folk, Bascom refers to the statement Raglan made in *The Hero*: "No popular story-teller has ever been known to invent anything" (Bascom 1957, 106; See also Raglan 1949, 134). Following Bascom's critique, Raglan's second point was that the incidents in folktales were the same the world over. And finally, folktales treat subjects of which the folk have no knowledge, such as castles and kings. Thus, for Raglan, the folk could not create the stories because they were not capable. And the proof that they were not the creators lies in the content of the tales, which involved things not of their life. Raglan argues for diffusion from the center of origin where the ritual killing of the king was first enacted. From the ritual arose the myth; and from the myth, the tales.

Bascom, in his critique, counters Raglan, point by point. First he notes there are societies where the tellers of the tales embellish and elaborate: "it cannot be maintained that creativity is lacking in all societies" (Bascom 1957, 106). Further, Bascom notes, the fanciful elements in folktales are just that—the fantasy of the folk. Thus, the castles, kings, and queens allow the folk to escape from their everyday life. The presence of the fanciful and the absence of the mundane does not, as Raglan maintains, prove that the folk could not have been the creators of the tales. Addressing Raglan's diffusion argument, Bascom makes two observations. To say a trait or tale has diffused does not mean that (1) it could not have been the creation of one person, or (2) that it could not have been of secular origin. And finally, Bascom finds the best evidence of the creativity of the folk in their own creations: "If the aborigines of the Americas could invent the igloo, snowshoe, toboggan, smoking, *cire perdue* casting, the zero concept, and so forth, could they not also have composed a folktale?" (Bascom 1957, 107, 108).

Bascom's critique of Raglan in "The Myth-Ritual Theory," though pointed, was balanced and reasoned. It brought forth a bitter reply from Stanley Edgar Hyman, an ardent supporter of the ritualist interpretation of myth. Hyman pondered why Bascom had chosen to review Raglan's *The Hero* "more than two decades after publication"; and why the selection of a general work, *The Hero*, rather than a book that focused on a specific area in greater detail, "such as Jane Harrison's *Themis*, which Bascom quotes at one point?" (Hyman 1958, 152). Having asked the question, Hyman responded,

> The question answers itself. Bascom cannot debate Greek drama with Harrison, or New Testament myth with John M. Robertson, or medieval romance with Jessie Weston, or Homeric epic with Rhys Carpenter, or Scandinavian Edda with Bertha Phillpotts; he is not informed on such matters; *he is an anthropologist, not a folklorist.*
>
> (Hyman 1958, 152; emphasis added)

Hyman's initial and concluding remarks stress that an anthropologist—in this case, Bascom—is unqualified to judge the work of a folklorist. Indeed, Hyman goes so far as to say that the anthropologist is not equipped to *understand* the folklorists' subject matter. As he says, "Many factors keep anthropologists from being adequate folklorists, and some day I hope to write about them in more detail." Hyman continues:

> The American Folklore Society decided, with dubious wisdom in the infancy of both fields, that this problem was no problem; the membership and activity of anthropologists in our society has been encouraged; and it has been the informal custom to choose alternate presidents from that field.
>
> (Hyman 1958, 154)

Hyman inveighs against the attention paid to Bascom due to his position in the American Folklore Society. "Thus Bascom can speak and publish encyclicals on the subject in the JOURNAL." Hyman adds that most of Bascom's contributions "like this paper on the Myth-Ritual Theory, display the tendency of his own field, as Franz Boas and others have shaped it in America in our century, toward atomism and nominalism, wary of any theory or generalization." And finally, Hyman says, "anthropologists tend to see folklore as a minor subdivision of anthropology, a body of materials for cultural profiling" (Hyman 1958, 154).

Hyman's "A Reply to Bascom" was followed immediately by Bascom's "Rejoinder to Hyman." Bascom regrets, "that Hyman has brought what had been a respectable discussion of theory down to the level of vulgarities of mind, ignorance of literature, and arguments about who is and who is not a folklorist." Bascom vigorously protests Hyman's portrayal "that I regard folklore as a minor tool of social science, as a minor subdivision of anthropology." And referring to Hyman's critique of Boas, Bascom says, "In renewing his attack on Boas, Hyman adds little that is new except to do me the honor of including me with him." "But by attacking the potential contributions of anthropologists to the study of folklore . . ., Hyman does a disservice both to our Society and to the ritual theory of myth." Bascom points to the crucial contribution which can and must be made to folklore through anthropology. The proponents of the myth-ritual theory speak in universal terms. But in order to prove its universality, scholars need to consider material beyond the influence of western civilizations "where the research of anthropologists will be important if not indispensable" (Bascom 1958, 155, 156).

Joseph Fontenrose in *The Ritual Theory of Myth* says, "The ritual interpretation of myths is by no means confined to literary criticism. It has a wide influence in many fields, although few anthropologists, folklorists, or classicists accept it, despite ritualists assertions to the contrary" (Fontenrose 1971, i). Yet, as Fontenrose traces the origin of the ritual theory, he finds the major influence in James George Frazer, the classicist and anthropologist, author of *The Golden Bough.* Jane Harrison, one of the leading figures of the ritualists, "was a classical scholar much influenced by the findings of anthropology." Thus, both Frazer and Harrison, drawing inspiration from classics and anthropology, were the sources for those propounding a ritual origin for myths. While willing to accept Frazer's anthropology, the scholars of the ritualist school were unwilling to incorporate twentieth-century ethnographic material in their consideration. For example, Hyman referred to Bascom's example of the creativity of the American Indians as "muddying the waters of theory with irrelevant defenses of primitive potentiality" (Hyman 1958, 154). It is likely that Frazer was considered a safe source. From his library at Trinity College, Cambridge, Sir James George Frazer penned the thirteen volumes of the *The Golden Bough,* protected by his wife, Lily Grove Frazer, from the distraction of the world outside his door (Kardiner and Preble 1961, 76). And he was certainly removed from the world beyond Cambridge, as a legend about him illustrates. When asked if he had ever met any savages, Frazer remarked curtly, "God forbid!" (Beattie 1964, 7). Frazer's anthropology was penned in the style of the nineteenth century. It was refined and to the liking of the scholars of the myth-ritual theory. But still, it was anthropology. So it is doubly ironic that Hyman protested so against Bascom as an anthropologist daring to appraise the work of folklorists. Indeed, Bascom was both a folklorist and an anthropologist.

In this debate the sabers crossed as they had been crossed before. But this time, the opposition as drawn by Hyman was between the anthropologists and the folklorists. Hyman was speaking as a literary critic and a folklorist and he claimed the field. No anthropologist would be admitted. And why? Because they did not have the proper credentials—they were not folklorists. The past inclusion of anthropologists in the

American Folklore Society was, in Hyman's judgment, a mistake. The hostility toward Boas and his successors was explicit. But Bascom was speaking as an anthropologist and a folklorist. He was proud of this dual affiliation and of his position as an anthropologist whose intellectual tradition linked him to Boas.

The myth-ritual debate focused on the origin and diffusion of narratives, concerns that had been present in both the literary and the anthropological approach to the study of narrative. The concern of origin and diffusion of narratives, and the underlying tension between two differing approaches was present in another major theoretical conflict, the debate about the origin of Afro-American folktales. As Dundes says in his headnote to "African Tales among the North American Indians,"

> The positions regarding the origin of American Negro folktales fall along the all too familiar traditional lines. Africanists generally claim that the tales are African survivals while specialists in European folklore argue that the majority of American Negro folktales are borrowed from the European repertoire.

> (Dundes 1973, 114)

Dundes discusses the orientation of the American folklorists, who looked to Europe for their scholarly inspiration. Thus, Thompson wrote about *European Tales among the North American Indians* (1919). Other folklorists of the literary persuasion, following Thompson's lead and the accepted European orientation, identified Afro-American folktales as largely European in origin. This "European-centered orientation" was intensified by another factor, "their tendency to neglect African folklore" (Dundes 1973, 115).

The divided orientation between Europe and Africa is illustrated by an account given by Dorson in *American Negro Folktales* concerning his collections from the loquacious raconteur, James Douglas Suggs: "On one occasion I played a tape recording of Suggs to Melville Herskovits, who exclaimed, 'Those are some remarkable African tales!' Shortly after, I played the same tape to Stith Thompson, who exclaimed, 'Those are some remarkable European tales!' " Dorson says "these comments reflect the strong biases of the two masters, whom I equally admired." In the next sentence, he gives his own opinion, "But the question of origin is susceptible of proof, and the proof of European origins lies in my notes" (Dorson 1967, 16).

Dorson's position is clear: the majority of Afro-American narratives are of European origin. There is, he stresses, very little evidence to support the theory of African origin. Concerning the 244 narratives presented in *American Negro Folktales*, Dorson remarks,

> The first declaration to make is that this body of tales does not come from Africa. It does not indeed come from any one place but from a number of dispersal points. . . . Many of the fictions, notably the animal tales, are of demonstrably European origin. Others have entered the Negro repertoire

from England, from the West Indies, from American white tradition, and from the social conditions and historical experiences of colored people in the South.

(Dorson 1967, 15–16)

He adds, "Only a few plots and incidents can be distinguished as West African."

In the chapter on "The Negro" in *American Folklore*, Dorson refers to "the sharp break between African and American tradition," which was localized in the West Indies. There Anansi, the spider, figures in hundreds of narratives. "But no Anansi stories are found in the United States" (Dorson 1959a, 185). Dorson suggests that the Negro narrative tradition falls into two groups. The area of the Atlantic and Caribbean islands as well as northeastern South America draw their tradition from Africa, while the southern part of the United States draws its tradition from Europe and Anglo-America (Dorson 1967, 17).

In the "Origins of American Negro Tales," Dorson reviewed the position of the nineteenth-century writers, Joel Chandler Harris and William Owens. Harris, author of *Uncle Remus: His Songs and Sayings*, had said, "One thing is certain—the Negroes did not get them from the whites: probably they are of remote African origin." Owens had written "Folk-Lore of the Southern Negroes" in *Lippincott's Magazine,* and stated that the fables of talking animals were of African origin (Dorson 1967, 13). There was the precedent set in the nineteenth century for the position taken by scholars of the twentieth century. Those who most ardently supported the claim of African origin, as Dorson said, were the anthropologists: "When American anthropologists such as Melville J. Herskovits and his students turned their attention to Africa, they reinforced the thesis of African origins with the best scholarly credentials (1967, 13). Dorson noted that Herskovits had traced the rich and elaborated traditions of Dahomey, that he had attacked the white supremacists who denied this cultural inheritance to blacks.

While Dorson clearly admired Herskovits, he was opposed to the anthropological stress on Africa as a possible source for Afro-American traditions. In *American Folklore*, Dorson criticized what he thought was a negative aspect of this anthropological explanation: "The argument for African origins is fully as racist as that for white origins, for it assumes that an original American Negro tradition can only emanate from black-skinned Africans" (Dorson 1959a, 185).

In the introductory remarks to the panel on Afro-American studies at the International Congress of the Americanists held in Paris in 1976, William Bascom stated his view of the search for African origins: "For moral and political, as well as for scientific reasons, it is important that African retentions be identified and documented beyond reasonable doubt" (Bascom 1979, 593). This was crucial, Bascom said, "because their existence has so often been denied." Sometimes this denial was supported by explicitly racist explanations (there could be no African retentions because there had never been an African culture; the inferior African culture gave way to the superior European cultures) and sometimes by an explanation that the uprooting of the blacks was so brutal as to wipe out all cultural heritage. Bascom was suspicious of those who were so adamantly opposed to the search for African origin. "I question the motives of some of those who attack the search for Africanisms as academic antiquarianism." He offered a possible explanation, "I suspect that some of them wish to discourage the search, for fear of what may be found. There are some who are unable or unwilling to recognize Africanisms in their own data, or even in their own personal lives" (1979, 593).

In "African Folktales in America: I. The Talking Skull Refuses to Talk," Bascom addresses both the issue of origin and the charge of racism: "In this article, I will try to establish as a fact, beyond dispute, that the folktale which I call "The Talking Skull Refuses to Talk" was brought to the United States from Africa" (Bascom 1981a, 184). As Bascom notes, this is the tale that Dorson designated as coming "straight from West Africa" (Dorson 1967, 188–89). Bascom begins with the Talking Skull "not simply because Dorson admits that it comes from Africa, but to demonstrate that it is a tale type, and not just a motif, and also to show the kind of documentation that can be provided, in some instances, for African origins" (Bascom 1981a, 188). Further documentation of the origin of this tale is not redundant, nor is it, Bascom adds, an "antiquarian search for African 'survivals' in the New World; nor is it racist. It is, I submit, important not only for Afro-Americans, but for folklorists, for Africans, and for all Americans to recognize the African contributions to America's folklore" (Bascom 1981a, 184). In the series on "African Folktales in America," Bascom presents forty-three tales: twenty-four from Africa, one from Haiti, and eighteen from the United States. Of these, Bascom says, none appear in the Aarne-Thompson *Types of the Folktale*. And only "United States Negro versions" are cited in the *Motif-Index of Folk-Literature*. He concludes, "Thus they could not have come from Europe or from India" (Bascom 1981a, 193).

In his Archer Taylor Memorial Lecture, "Perhaps Too Much to Chew?," Bascom told how he had become interested in the search for Africanisms.

> As a student of Herskovits I had thought that this century-old debate had been settled long ago. But Dorson says that in his own collection of over one thousand Negro narratives, primarily from Michigan and Arkansas, there is only one motif that surely came from Africa. Not even one tale type or even one folktale!
>
> (Bascom 1981d, 289)

Of the series of articles on "African Folktales in America" Bascom added, "I began this project with very little knowledge of Afro-American folktales." He continued, in this first article ["The Talking Skull Refuses to Talk"] I said, "I believe that I can show that more than twenty folktales must have come to the United States from Africa rather than from Europe." I now think that the number will exceed fifty. In fact, I am currently examining ninety tale types.

(Bascom 1981d, 289–90)

Bascom noted that a number of these tales he had found in Dorson's own collection.

In his work on Afro-American tales, Bascom included all of the Americas. He pointed out that the existence of the same tale type in other areas where African slaves were transported would add credibility to "the argument for the African sources of tale types in the United States" (Bascom 1981d, 290). Of his approach to the study, Bascom said, "My method is simple." He searched the literature for folktales that had been recorded both in the United States and in Africa. Then he referred to Thompson's *Types of the Folktale* and to his *Motif-Index of Folk-Literature*. "If I do not find such a tale type in either of these two indexes, which provide good coverage of Indo-European folktales, I conclude that it could not have come from Europe and must have come from Africa." Bascom did not claim to be providing the origin for all Afro-American narratives. He notes, "Fifty, or even a hundred tale types from Africa do not represent a majority of the folktales in the repertoire of the Negroes of the United States" (Bascom 1981d, 291). Included in this repertoire are also tales from Europe and tales that originated in the United States.

In the Archer Taylor Memorial Lecture, "Perhaps Too Much to Chew?," Bascom read twelve tales which were grouped into six tale types. For each tale type, he gave versions from Africa and from the United States. He preceded this presentation with the comment, "I assume that many of you will be familiar with the American folktales from Harris, Fortier, and Dorson, but that fewer will know their African counterparts" (Bascom 1981d, 292). In the first, "Inside Elephant's Belly," Bascom read a version from Upper Volta which involved the characters Hare, Elephant, and Hyena. Hare makes Elephant laugh, enters his body through his anus, and stuffs himself with Elephant's fat. The next time, Hyena joins Hare, and they both enter Elephant's stomach to steal fat. Elephant falls dead because Hyena does not follow Hare's instructions—he pierces Elephant's heart. It is only through his quick wits that Hare escapes and Hyena is beaten to death. Immediately following the reading of this African tale, Bascom read a tale from Arkansas that was taken from Richard Dorson's *Negro Tales from Pine Bluff, Arkansas, and Calvin, Michigan*. In this tale, Rabbit took a bucket of lard from Elephant. Bear joined Rabbit and they both jumped in Elephant's mouth to gather fat. Elephant died. Rabbit through his quick wits escaped and caused Bear to be beaten to death. The similarity between the tale told in the Upper Volta and the tale told in Arkansas cannot be denied.

Bascom noted that Dorson had linked this tale to "Tom Thumb" and "Jonah and the Whale." Tom Thumb was the tiny hero swallowed by a cow; and, of course, Jonah ended up in the whale's stomach. Bascom continued: "Dorson says of his Arkansas tale, 'The substitution of the elephant for the cow . . . is curious.' There is nothing curious when it is recognized that his tale came from Africa, where the animal involved is usually an elephant or a cow" (Bascom 1981d, 294).

After Bascom had delivered the Archer Taylor Memorial Lecture, one prominent folklorist remarked, "I don't know how Dick [Dorson] is going to counter that. I think he's beat!" Yet Bascom in his address disclaimed this competitive aspect of the dispute:

> Some students and colleagues have seen it as a personal attack on Richard M. Dorson, but it is not. I see it as a possible way of helping to end the century-old debate about the African sources of American folktales. The evidence has been sitting on library shelves, waiting to be analyzed. It is a challenge that I have not been able to resist.
>
> (Bascom 1981d, 291)

Florence E. Baer in *Sources and Analogues of the Uncle Remus Tales* says,

> A century has passed since publication of the first serious collection of American Negro folktales—Joel Chandler Harris' *Uncle Remus: His Songs and Sayings, 1880*. The book contains thirty-four tales in the dialect in which they were told. Folklorists at once began the search for parallels from other countries and cultures.
>
> (Baer 1980, 7)

Baer notes that in the last two decades of the nineteenth century, the tales were accepted as genuine folklore, though the sources were disputed. It was in 1919, that Elsie Clews Parsons decided Harris had rewritten the tales in *Uncle Remus Returns*. "She quickly disposed of the matter of origins; one was not a true folktale, three were of European provenience, and one had analogues in Africa and the West Indies" (Baer 1980, 9). The majority of the scholars in the twentieth century followed Parsons's judgment, and viewed Harris's writings as his own creation.

Baer's is the first systematic study of Uncle Remus tales. Other scholars, though convinced of their position, have offered us only speculations. After a consideration of "Joel Chandler Harris (1848–1908), an 'Accidental' Folklorist," Baer presents the tales along with Thompson's tale type and motif numbers for each and notes discussing analogues and possible origins. In the explanation to Table I, "Uncle Remus tales with tale types, motifs, distribution of analogues, source," Baer says,

> Of the 184 separate tales there is evidence that the immediate source of 122 (66.3%) is Africa. Twenty-eight (15.2%) probably came from Europe (this

includes the British Isles); seventeen (9.2%) seem to have arisen in the New World . . . three are too synthesized to determine a predominant influence; four could have come from either Europe or Africa; and for nine I have found no analogues, and in some cases must question whether they are true folktales.

(Baer 1980, 168)

She also notes that "there is one myth, three folktales and two tales that contain American Indian elements." Baer suspects that the influence of the American Indians might well have been much greater than indicated by her survey, but this she cannot substantiate.

The debate over the origin of Afro-American folktales did span the century. Perhaps now with Baer's definitive work on the *Sources and Analogues of the Uncle Remus Tales* and Bascom's convincing compilation of Afro-American tales with African analogues, scholars will recognize the undeniable, that African oral narratives have a significant place in Afro-American folklore.

One aspect of the debate was soon to be over, the dialogue between Richard Dorson and William Bascom. On September 11, 1981, these two great folklorists died. And yet the debate was not quite through. In November 1981, Bascom's twelfth article in the series "African Folktales in America" appeared, this one on "The Dogs Rescue Master in Tree Refuge." And his last contributions in this series were published in the 1982 issue of *Researches in African Literatures*.

In the myth-ritual debate and in the conflict over the origin of Afro-American narratives, a new dichotomy was emphasized, that of the folklorist and the anthropologist. This latter is not just a subtle change of phrasing from what had been referred to as the split between the literary and the anthropological folklorists. In essence, Hyman and Dorson were denying the validity of the anthropological perspective to the study of folklore. Hyman was explicit about this. Anthropologists were lacking; they could not adequately study folklore. Dorson explained it another way: "the anthropologists have enough of their own work to do; the point is that they are not equipped to do the work of folklorists" (Dorson 1963b, 2).

Dorson's attitude toward Boas was ambivalent. He held him in high esteem. He talked of "the massive figure of Boas" and referred to "the heroic age of Boas" (Dorson 1963b, 101; 1963d, 2). Yet, he resented his position of power. Consistent in Dorson's accounts is the separation of the anthropologists from the folklorists. On one occasion, he refers, with all politeness, to "our anthropological friends." And he remarks, "The tradition of American anthropological friendliness to folklore goes back to Boas, who edited our journal from 1908 to 1923" (Dorson 1971a, 18). Dorson portrays Boas as an outsider, one who was not seriously interested in folklore.

In the foreword to *American Folklore*, Dorson presented the anthropologists' contributions to the society and to folklore studies not as an act of friendship, but as an usurping of the folklorists' concerns: "After an initial thrust of interest propelled from England, which led to the founding of an American Folklore Society in 1888, the subject languished, going by default to the anthropologists, who concentrated on North American Indian tales" (Dorson 1959a, 2). Dorson dismissed the study of folklore when anthropologists were involved. Folklore "languished" with the anthropologists—that would be Boas, Kroeber, Lowie, Swanton, Dixon, Parsons, and others who were working with such diligence and dedication toward the development of a myth concordance, a catch-word index, and the thorough study of American Indian narrative tradition. In truth, Dorson provides a very selective view of what is and what is not part of American folkloristics. Without concern of omission, he could skip the period between 1888 and 1910, and continue his account, "In the first two decades of the present century interest picked up, with the publication of cowboy songs in 1910 by John A. Lomax and of old English ballads from the southern Appalachians by Cecil Sharp in 1917."

Dorson gave a more impartial representation of the contributions of anthropologists to the study of folklore in "Current Folklore Theories," perhaps because the essay was written for an anthropological audience, the readership of *Current Anthropology*. Here he refers to Boas's position as editor of the *Journal of American Folklore*, his influential studies in the folklore of nonliterate cultures, and the continuation of his scholarly tradition among his students: "Through his students Benedict, Parsons, and Herskovits, and in turn through the students of Herskovits, the Boas line of American anthropology has valued the tales and other oral traditions of Indians and Africans" (Dorson 1963b, 101). He remarked that after Boas, the number of cultural anthropologists who were "sensitive and sympathetic to folklore has steadily decreased" (Dorson 1963d, 2). Many "drew apart from folklorists" and turned "to such questions as social organization and personality and culture" (Dorson 1963b, 102). Further, Dorson says, the anthropologist is often "blind to the very existence of folklore" (Dorson 1963d, 2).

In "Current Folklore Theories," Dorson refers to "the widening gap" between folklorists and anthropologists. In an earlier article, "A Theory for American Folklore," he spoke of this division and of Bascom's attempts to draw the two sides together. "Recently Bascom has attempted to close the widening gulf between anthropological and humanistic folklorists in a series of meaty papers. No humanist has accepted his invitation to respond in kind, and his articles underscore the difficulty of cross-disciplinary communication" (Dorson 1971a, 18). Bascom's articles to which Dorson referred were "Folklore and Anthropology" (1953), "Four Functions of Folklore" (1954), and "Verbal Art" (1955). In the first article, Bascom spoke of "the intellectual isolationism" that existed between the literary folklorists and the anthropological folklorists. He hoped "to bridge the gap by presenting the anthropological approach to folklore" and he invited a reciprocal response from folklorists in the humanities (Bascom [1953] 1965a, 25–26). "Four Functions of Folklore," Bascom's presidential address to the American Folklore Society, followed by one year his invitation to the literary folklorists to present their approach to the study of folklore. His opening remark echoed this plea: "In a paper at the El Paso meetings last year I expressed the ópinion that the most effective way to bridge the gap between the anthropological and the humanist points of view towards folklore is through a common concern with common problems . . ." (Bascom [1954] 1965b, 279). This, Bascom thought, would be more effective in unifying the two approaches to folklore than the traditional reliance on a shared body of material. He was convinced that an open discussion, if conducted "moderately and rationally," would ultimately be beneficial for the American Folklore Society.

In "Verbal Art," Bascom once again attempted to clarify the position he held of an anthropologist who studied folklore. The term "verbal art," suggested by Bascom and Waterman (1949, 398, 403) as an appropriate frame for an anthropological approach, had stirred up resentment against the anthropological folklorist. Bascom attempted to assuage the offended:

> I agree . . . that it is unfortunate that anthropologists have tried to pre-empt the word folklore to designate a portion of the total body of culture. I am willing to go even further and say that anthropologists were somewhat presumptuous in twisting the meaning of folklore to fit in with their own needs in classifying the aspects of culture.

> (Bascom [1955] 1981e, 66)

Bascom stressed that the term "verbal art" was "meant to encompass only a segment of folklore and a segment of culture, and not the whole of either." He reiterated his point made in "Folklore and Anthropology," that Thoms had defined folklore twenty years before Tylor had defined culture. "We are even more presumptuous if we refer to verbal art as 'folklore proper,' or if we suggest that folklorists as a whole should accept the anthropological definition of folklore, when the responsibility for these terminological difficulties seems to lie clearly with anthropology" (Bascom [1955] 1981e, 66).

Instead of attempting to lessen the gap, as Bascom had done, Dorson emphasized it. Referring to the students of Boas, Dorson says, "In their addresses we see the Boasian emphasis on folklore as a mirror of culture—a mirror that distorts as well as reflects—and on folktales as an art form" (Dorson [1959] 1971a, 18). This reference most likely was to Bascom's presidential address to the society, "Four Functions of Folklore," and "Verbal Art," the latter first presented at the sixty-sixth annual meeting of the American Folklore Society in December 1953. For Dorson, the anthropologists were not part of the folklore circle. They were apart, on the other side of the divide that separated them from what Dorson calls "the

American folklorist." As he says, "Some of [Herskovits's and Bascom's] counsel lights up the distance between anthropological and American folklorists."

The mark of Boas was on the anthropological folklorists. And the new breed of scholars who claimed the identity of folklorists resented the past control of the American Folklore Society and the *Journal of American Folklore* by Boas and his students. This would not be forgotten. Indeed this resentment is still felt. In his 1980 dissertation, "The History of American Folklore Scholarship to 1908," William K. McNeil, a student of Richard Dorson, refers to the stranglehold of the anthropologists on the *Journal of American Folklore*. Michael Bell said that with the demise of the Chicago Folklore Society folklore became "the handmaiden to anthropology." And at the 1981 business meeting of the American Folklore Society, a leading folklorist made a passing, but telling comment. With reference to the plans for future sites for annual meetings, he shrugged and said, "Now that we have sold our souls to the American Anthropological Association. . . ." The American Folklore Society had contracted the American Anthropological Association to arrange future meeting sites. This was perhaps a bit too reminiscent of the past control of the American Folklore Society by anthropologists.

In light of this continued resentment directed toward those in anthropology, it is interesting that a recent theory in folklore should derive inspiration from anthropology. In performance theory, those who stress the importance of context for the creation of the event are amplifying on an anthropological concern. In the concluding remarks to *Frontiers of Folklore*, Richard Bauman says, "To make explicit what is probably clear from my remarks thus far, the frontiers of folklore as I conceive them are bound up largely with anthropology and linguistics" (Bauman 1977b, 128).

In the introduction to *New Perspectives in Folklore*, Bauman discusses the "highly self-conscious reorientation" in the study of folklore. This involved a movement from the stress on text, to a stress on the context; "from the traditional focus upon folklore as 'item'—the things of folklore—to a conceptualization of folklore as 'event'—the doing of folklore" (Bauman 1972, xi). As Ben-Amos says in "The Context of Folklore,"

> The aim of the "new perspectives" is the discovery of the possible and acceptable varieties of folklore performances by the members of a society, and the explanation of existing differences and similarities in folklore in terms of self-regulatory rules, with reference to social structure, cultural cosmology and symbols, and general verbal behavior.

> (Ben-Amos 1977a, 37)

Clearly the "new perspectives" draw from anthropology, as from linguistics with the study of the social aspects of verbal behavior. And, of course, the "new perspectives" are situated within the discipline of folklore.

Dan Ben-Amos notes that former definitions have all grouped folklore either as a body of knowledge, a mode of thought, or a kind of art (Ben-Amos 1972, 5). An alternative that stresses the mode of transmission—the oral nature of folklore—does not, according to Ben-Amos, solve the problem. Past definitions and theories have all perpetuated the "dichotomy between processes and things." This dichotomy is eliminated in performance theory where the item, or text, and the process, or context, are united in the whole.

Those who formulated performance theory constantly reiterate the importance of context. Bauman says, "The kind of focus on the doing of folklore, that is, on folklore performance, is the key to the real integration between people and lore on the empirical level" (Bauman 1972, 33). Ben-Amos says, "In sum, folkore is artistic communication in small groups" (Ben-Amos 1972, 13). Elli Köngäs Maranda takes an extreme position. She emphasizes that culture is a living thing and that folklore forms cannot be fixed: "folkloric utterances are created whenever they are made" (Maranda 1972, 60). Abrahams stresses the need for a close observation of individual performances in their social context. But he also cautions that limiting the study of folklore to performance alone would diminish the understanding "of the relationship between traditions and the uses of traditional expressions" (Abrahams 1972, 29).

Dorson referred to the creators of performance theory as "the young Turks" (Dorson 1972b, 45). They have stirred up the community of folklore scholars. In part this is due to the stress on context—certainly an anthropological concept—and the de-emphasis on text. If there can be no text outside of context, if folklore does not exist as an item or a text, then there can be no tale type, no genre. If the emphasis is on the present, the moment of creation, then there is no importance attached to the past, to culture history in the Boasian sense or to reconstruction of the original text. Performance theory lays to rest the past concerns of both the literary and the anthropological folklorists. The genre and tale type of Thompson are no longer a crucial consideration. The collection of texts, as stressed by the literary and anthropological folklorists, is no longer a focus of fieldwork. And a reading of the past through the folkloric present, the Boasian culture reflector, is no longer central to the study.

Ben-Amos says this quite succinctly: "The 'new perspectives' represent a transition from historical and comparative to descriptive folklore" (Ben-Amos 1977a, 36). The thrust of performance theory is on meaning in a specific context and a specific culture. Thus, both the historical study "across time periods" and the comparative study "across cultural boundaries" are replaced by descriptions of folklore performances in their setting.

The articulation of the performance theory has led to the text-context controversy. This involves the conflict between those who insist that folklore is text, and those who insist that folklore is context. In his 1972 presidential address to the American Folklore Society, D. K. Wilgus stressed the importance of text in "The Text is the Thing" (Wilgus 1973).

Steven Jones, in "Slouching Towards Ethnography: The Text/Context Controversy Reconsidered" (1979), accused those who focused on the importance of context of ignoring the traditional basis of folklore studies—the text. Dan Ben-Amos countered with "The Ceremony of Innocence" (1979), where he emphasized the importance of the study of process.[2]

In "Toward a Resolution of the Text/Context Controversy," Robert Georges says "In my view, the distinction between text- and context-oriented researchers is distortive and does more harm than good. It suggests the existence of warring factions, each vying for dominance over, if not the complete annihilation of, the other" (Georges 1980, 35). Yet, Georges agrees with Jones that there are those who are "slouching towards ethnography"—indeed, there are some who "have already arrived." "These individuals are *not* interested in the kinds of phenomena or questions that folklorists have considered historically. Instead, they are intent on determining the nature of culture." They study folklore "as a means of better understanding the cultures of individual societies or social groups." They are not interested in "the essence of narrative or narrating, song or singing, games or playing," but rather in the concerns of the anthropologist, "the rules or dynamics of culturally-determined behaviors of groups or particular peoples." "For all intents and purposes, they should be identified *as* ethnographers or cultural anthropologists, not as folklorists, for they are cultural relativists in the most extreme sense of that term. . . . Just why they call themselves folklorists . . . I do not know" (Georges 1980, 36). Georges says that "the text/context controversy in contemporary American folkloristics" is "deeply rooted, complex, and varied" (p. 39).

There were those in literature who laid claim to folklore. Francis Lee Utley called the English Department the "mother of folklorists" (Utley 1970, 112). Wayland Hand, in his presidential address delivered to the American Folklore Society in December 1958, said, "As we all know, folklore's earliest and strongest ties are with literature" (Hand 1960, 4). Hand stressed the precedent established by literary folklorists: "Long before there were folklore curricula anywhere, or even concentrations of work in the subject, students in these departments were busy writing masters' theses and doctoral dissertations in various aspects of popular literature and folklore, foreign as well as domestic" (Hand 1960, 4).

Still, while the literary folklorists were studying the ballad, the anthropological folklorists were studying myths. While Child and Kittredge taught their courses on the ballad, Boas trained his students in collecting folklore texts, Kroeber taught his course on world mythology, Lowie, his seminar on folklore, and Radin, his course on primitive literature. In the case of the study of diffusion of American Indian narrative elements and myth types, the anthropological folklorists preceded the literary folklorists and, in a sense, passed the study on to them. And certainly in terms of master's theses and doctoral dissertations, the anthropological folklorists made substantial contributions as well.

This representation of the literary and the anthropological folklorists as parallel and powerful contributors to American folkloristics is offered as a new reading of intellectual history. It is also hoped that it has been a fair reading of intellectual history. A detrimental result of the split between the literary and the anthropological folklorists has been a tendency to divide and claim the intellectual territory of folklore. When folklorists and historians of folkloristics highlight the contributions of one group and neglect the contributions of the other, a skewed picture of the past develops.

Just such a distorted picture has developed from Dorson's and Baker's review of folklore courses. In "The Growth of Folklore Courses," Dorson considered only courses taught in departments *other* than anthropology: "I have omitted courses offered by Departments of Anthropology, which concentrate chiefly on the traditions of nonliterate peoples. The dynamic interest in folklore in recent years has come outside of anthropology, from students of European and American culture and society" (Dorson 1950, 351). The list of folklore courses that Dorson compiled was heavily weighted toward the English departments, with a few courses offered in history, folklore, and foreign language departments. Ronald Baker, in his "Folklore Courses and Programs in American Colleges and Universities," offers a review of folklore courses in English departments. His survey "was concerned with only 'straight' folklore courses and not with classical mythology or with literature or anthropology courses with some folklore content" (Baker 1971, 221). Baker notes,

> The results of this survey would be much more impressive if such courses were included; however, since usually neither the material nor the approach in these units is strictly folkloristic, often the nature of folklore is distorted and the development of real folklore courses impeded, just as the development of anthropology courses and programs is hindered when anthropology is taught within sociology.
>
> (Baker 1971, 221)

No equivalent survey of folklore courses taught in anthropology departments has been done. Rather there has been the assumption that anthropologists did not teach folklore—or, at least, that what they taught was not *real* folklore—an assumption that is not borne out by the record.

The inclusion of one group or one approach, and the exclusion of another, results in a weakening of the entire fabric of folkloristics. This has been evidenced in the discussion of the anthropological folklorists and their carefully executed control of the American Folklore Society and the *Journal of American Folklore*. While Boas and his students exercised editorial power, the anthropological folklorists had the voice. But the denial of access to power bred resentment among the literary folklorists. This resentment was reversed. The first generation of folklorists, who in large part were trained by literary folklorists, by Stith Thompson and Archer Taylor (Dundes 1966a), minimized the important contributions made to the development of American folkloristics by the anthropological folklorists.

American folkloristics is a unique hybrid, drawing from differing intellectual currents. From the literary comes the concern with recorded text, with folklore as part of the literate tradition. From the anthropological comes the focus on function and meaning in cultural context, with folklore as part of culture. Each approach, the literary and the anthropological, opened a rich store of scholarship for American folkloristics. Further, the history of American folkloristics is not merely a matter of two divergent intellectual traditions. In fact, there are many approaches to the study of folklore—literary, anthropological, historical, sociological, psychological, political—and these approaches draw from and feed into one another.

The variety of approaches, the interdisciplinary nature of folklore studies, has been both a source of creative strength and a source of organizational weakness. Certainly it has posed a problem for the identity of the folklorists. For those outside the discipline, there has been a feeling that somehow the discipline of folklore is suspect because it draws from such a wide spectrum. It crosses boundaries. And, within the discipline, there is a concern about the proprietorship of theories. Folklore "shares" theories rather than "owning" them. Ben-Amos included this critique of folklore in "A History of Folklore Studies—Why Do We Need It?" He referred to Dorson's "Current Folklore Theories." In this article, Dorson differentiated the folklorists from "the anthropologist, the historian, the literary critic, the sociologist, the psychologist, the historian, the political scientist" and he did this on the basis of the folklorists' skills. "This is particularly revealing since Dorson sets out to discuss not so much the techniques as the theories of the discipline. . . . However, it soon becomes apparent that while the theories of folklore are all borrowed from other disciplines, the techniques are all its own (Ben-Amos 1973, 115). This "consuming interest with techniques" of folklore study resulted in the neglect of theories and philosophical issues. "Consequently, folklore has become a craft, not a science." Ben-Amos related the eclectic approach of folklorists, the use of theories from other disciplines, to "an enormous academic inferiority complex" (Ben-Amos 1973, 117); folklorists quote works and borrow theories from other disciplines in an attempt to assume a higher status.

While Ben-Amos links the eclectic approach of folklorists to feelings of inferiority, a search for academic status through association, it is also possible to view the eclectic nature of folklore as a source of strength. The blending of approaches in folkloristics could be said to bring a creativity to the enterprise. Merle Curti in *American Scholarship in the Twentieth Century* remarks, "In the last two decades many scholars have, in thinking of knowledge as a whole, reacted against its narrow compartmentalization" (Curti 1953, 4). It has been suggested that the greatest contributions to a field of knowledge occur when a scholar crosses "conventional boundaries" and draws from other disciplines.

Dundes, like Ben-Amos, is critical of American folklore theory. In "The American Concept of Folklore," he says, "Very few important original theoretical works in folklore have been penned by American folklore scholars." He gives a list of the important contributions by European folklorists, and adds: "One gets the impression that not only is much American folklore—the materials—essentially transplanted European folklore, but many of the theories and methods of studying folklore employed traditionally by American folklorists are likewise European borrowings" (Dundes 1966a, 239).

While Ben-Amos bemoans the lack of theory, and Dundes identifies what theory there is as European, Dorson finds "no books of theory, no continuity, no consensus" in the history of American folklore (Dorson 1973a, 125). In the midst of this critique by folklorists, Wayland Hand asks, "Why should we be so defensive about our discipline, and why should we be so self-effacing?" (Hand 1960, 9). In part, this self-effacement, to use Hand's term, seems to be tied to the European orientation which has been so prevalent in American folklore scholarship. Though American folklorists have adopted European methods and techniques, still they are not European folklorists. They have not done things the same way. They have followed the model, but they do not fit the mold. For Dorson, the history of American folklore lacks the continuity he was able to trace in the *British Folklorists*. And for Dundes, American folklorists have not made significant contributions in kind to match the European model. The pattern of American folkloristics and the contributions of American folklorists are matters for serious consideration, certainly a suitable topic for an extended work. Here it is appropriate to note the components of the comparison: American folkloristics and American folklorists have been compared to the European model and have been found lacking.

Another aspect of this harsh self-critique has to do with the proprietorship of theory. Yet theories are not "owned" by a discipline. The social sciences share theory. The functionalist theory is not solely an anthropological theory that has been pirated by folklorists. Sociologists have used it too. Psychological theory was blended with anthropological in the culture and personality school. Students of social welfare and education use it too. Structuralism, developed by the anthropologist Claude Levi-Strauss, has had a marked impact on comparative literature, literary criticism, art, film, history, and folklore.

Three of the leading American folklorists point to serious lacks in American folkloristics, a lack of identity, a lack of theory, and a lack of continuity. Returning to Hand's question, why is there this defensive posture and self-effacement among American folklorists? The answer might lie in the time. Dundes wrote "The American Concept of Folklore" in 1966. Dorson and Ben-Amos both were contributors to the special issue of the *Journal of the Folklore Institute* in 1973. Since the time of these publications, a new generation of folklorists has been trained who have for models folklorists such as Ben-Amos, Dundes, Dorson, and others, such as Abrahams, Bauman, and Georges. This senior generation of folklorists has formulated theory and applied it in dynamic ways. Current students of folklore are enough removed from the period of emphasis on techniques—the indexing and annotation—to view it with distance. They have an established identity as folklorists. And this established identity, this sense of security in a discipline, is due to the solid scholarship, both in theory and research, of their mentors. The feelings of inferiority, if they did exist, have passed away and are replaced by feelings of independence.

Susan Dwyer-Shick notes, "there has been a shift away from the identification with either an anthropological or a literary approach . . . within folklore study in the United States" (Dwyer-Shick 1979, 4). And here Ben-Amos's statement is apt when applied to our trio of critics, Ben-Amos, Dundes, and Dorson. The folklorists who have shaped American folklore "hardly recognize the new phase to which they themselves have brought the field of folklore" (Ben-Amos 1973, 116).

In a sense, the conflict between the literary and the anthropological folklorists was laid to symbolic rest one-half century after it first surfaced: George Lyman Kittredge died in 1941, and Franz Boas, in 1942. The dissension between the two groups continued in the 1940s; the discussion in the correspondence of the American Folklore Society remained bifurcated between those aligning themselves with the literary, and those with the anthropological.[3] This was the aftermath, the residue of the battle. Stresses and strains still remain. These surface from time to time as echoes of the past when the clash between the two groups concerned a real struggle for dominance and control.

The roots of conflict have twined together and have become, as Erminie Voegelin said, "part of our strength" (UPFFA, Voegelin to Leach, 1/30/46). The creative tension—which verged, at times, on destructive force—between the literary and the anthropological folklorists has helped to forge the hybrid of American folklore scholarship.

Notes

PREFACE

1. The chronic fallacy is David Fischer's term; see *Historians' Fallacies: Toward a Logic of Historical Thought* (1970, 152). For Ben-Amos's discussion of "the chronic fallacy," see Ben-Amos (1973, 114).

1. DISCIPLINE AND IDENTITY

1. Daniels quotes a letter from John L. LeConte to Charles Wilkes, March 7, 1847, and one from John Torrey to John L. LeConte, April 9, 1849 (LeConte Papers, American Philosophical Society).

2. Daniels quotes a letter from Charles Sanders Peirce to J. M. Peirce, dated December 18, 1859, located in the collection of the Houghton Library, Harvard.

3. Webster's *New World Dictionary* defines scientism as "1. the techniques, beliefs, or attitudes characteristic of scientists. 2. the principle that scientific methods can be applied in all fields of investigation; often a disparaging usage." The term scientism is employed here with the second definition, without the disparaging connotation.

4. This dispute over intellectual territory was not limited to the United States. It was occurring in Europe as well. For England, see Dorson (1968a). For France, see Clark (1973); Zumwalt (1978, 1982); Siegel (1965). For Germany, see Ben-David (1968–1969).

5. Recent dissertations on the history of American folklore scholarship are the following: William K. McNeil, "A History of American Folklore Scholarship before 1908" (Indiana University, Folklore Institute, 1980); Susan Dwyer-Schick, "The American Folklore Society and Folklore Research in America, 1888–1940" (University of Pennsylvania, Department of Folklore and Folklife, 1979); Peter T. Bartis, "A History of the Archive of Folk Song of the Library of Congress: The First Fifty Years" (University of Pennsylvania, Department of Folklore and Folklife, 1982); and Wendy Leeds-Hurwitz, "Jaime de Angulo, an Intellectual Biography" (University of Pennsylvania, Department of Folklore and Folklife, 1983). See also the special issue of *Journal of the Folklore Institute, American Folklore Historiography*, volume 10 (1973); as well as Reuss (1971); de Caro (1972); Chambers (1973); Thoresen (1973); Gillespie (1975, 1980); Briscoe (1979); and Baer (1980).

2. AMERICAN FOLKLORE STUDIES

1. For an appraisal of Newell's crucial contribution to the founding of the American Folklore Society and the shaping of the *Journal of American Folklore*, see Vance (1893, 595); "First Annual Meeting" (1890, 6); Dwyer-Shick (1979, 15). For a discussion of science as a gentleman's avocation in the nineteenth century, see Daniels (1967, 1700).

2. See Dwyer-Shick (1979, 17), and Dundes (1966a, 239, 248), for the identification of Newell with this anonymous contribution. For a review of the beginnings of

folklore in the United States, England, and Europe, see Herskovits's presidential address to the American Folklore Society, "Folklore after a Hundred Years: A Problem in Redefinition" (1946).

3. This emphasis on the oral aspect of folklore has been present throughout the twentieth century. See Utley (1961), and Leach (1949).

3. THE SCHISM IN FOLKLORE

1. See de Vries (1985), and Dorson (1955a) for a discussion of this theoretical approach.

2. For additional correspondence concerning the publication of obscene material, see Boas Papers, Newell to Boas, 3/1/1898.

3. In 1892, Chamberlain received the first Ph.D. in Anthropology granted in the United States. This was after Boas had already resigned from his position in the department of graduate education at Clark University (Dwyer-Shick 1979, 199; Dwyer-Shick and Bailey 1977, 2).

4. For additional correspondence concerning the change in editorship, see Boas Papers, Boas to Chamberlain, 1/10/1908; and Chamberlain to Boas, 1/15/1908.

5. See Dwyer-Shick for a review of the records of the American Folklore Society: Appendix A, "Presidents of the American Folklore Society and the American Anthropological Association, from the Founding of Each to the Present" (Dwyer-Shick 1979, 341–46); and "Policy of Rotation of Society Presidency," pages 49, 59–62.

6. Personal communication, Wayland Hand, 1981.

7. This pattern of joint annual meetings is strikingly displayed in Appendix C, "Annual Meetings of the American Folklore Society, 1889–1978," in Dwyer-Shick's work (1979, 353–62).

4. THE LITERARY FOLKLORISTS

1. M. A. De Wolfe Howe has compiled *A Scholar's Letters to a Young Lady*, a delightful selection of Child's correspondence to a young lady friend. This covers the period from 1883 through August 14, 1896, less than a month before he died. The letters bring out in a touching way the sensitivity of this great scholar, his dedication to his roses, which he called by name, his love of his friends, and his continuing concern with his ballad publications.

2. See Appendix A of Sigurd Bernhard Hustvedt's *Ballad Books and Ballad Men* (1930) for a collection of the correspondence between Child and Grundtvig.

3. Child to Grundtvig, March 26, 1872.

4. For a more detailed discussion of Child's use of manuscript sources see Kittredge, "Francis James Child," (1898, xxvii–xxviii); and also the list of manuscript sources (397ff.) of the fifth volume of *The English and Scottish Popular Ballads*. See also Hustvedt, *Ballad Books and Ballad Men* (1930, 213ff.). And in Appendix A of this book, the Child-Grundtvig correspondence testifies to a continuing concern with the acquisition of ballad manuscripts.

5. See Hustvedt (1930, 256), for Child's preference of unprinted manuscripts.

6. Child to Grundtvig, March 26, 1872.

7. Marian Michael is quoting a circular of Child, dated January 29, 1881, filed in the Harvard Library.

8. Ibid.

9. For a further discussion of Kittredge's early publications and his years of instruction at Phillips Exeter Academy (1883–1887), see Clyde Kenneth Hyder, *George Lyman Kittredge Teacher and Scholar,* chap. 3, "Phillips Exeter" (Hyder 1962, 33–40).

10. In *American Scholarship in the Twentieth Century,* Merle Curti mentioned the

recognition in Europe of American scholars. Among those named were Willard Gibbs, William James, Franz Boas, J. H. Breasted, and George Lyman Kittredge (Curti 1953, 5).

11. For information on the courses taught by Kittredge, see Hyder (1962, 42–44), and Thompson (1956, 57–60).

12. Hyder is quoting a letter from George Lyman Kittredge to Dr. Cabot, dated May 14, 1926.

13. This theory, of course, was influenced by nineteenth century romanticism, by Herder and the Grimms, and the idea of the spirit of the folk. See Wilgus (1959, chaps. 1, 2), and McNeil (1980, 522–602), for a discussion of the communal theory of ballad origin and the controversy surrounding it.

14. Thompson mimeographed two installments of his memoirs, "Folklorist's Progress" (1956), and "Second Wind" (1966). See also the interview, "Reminiscences of an Octogenarian Folklorist," (Upadhyaya 1968); Thompson's "Notes on an Itinerant Folklorist" (1957); and Peggy Martin, "Stith Thompson: His Life and His Role in Folklore Scholarship" (n.d.).

15. Lecture notes from Thompson's "The Folktale and Allied Forms" have been published as "Informal Notes on Transactions and Lectures of Second Folklore Institute of America" (Bloomington: Indiana University, Privately Multigraphed, 1946). For a discussion of these notes, see Martin (n.d., 40, n30).

16. John Lomax perpetuated the study of folklore in his family. He was the father of Alan Lomax and Bess Lomax Hawes. Alan Lomax graduated from Harvard in 1931. Bess Lomax Hawes took her M.A. in folklore at the University of California, Berkeley, in 1970.

17. These few pages that Milman Parry had written before his death are included in Lord's article, "Homer, Parry, and Huso" (1948).

18. In his tribute to his teacher, Henry Glassie quoted remarks made by MacEdward Leach at the close of a program given by the Philadelphia Folksong Society, held in honor of his retirement.

19. MacEdward Leach's crucial contributions to the American Folklore Society were remarked on by many of his colleagues. See the MacEdward Leach Memorial Issue of the *Journal of American Folklore* (1968); Fenton (p. 104), Garbaty (p. 106), James (p. 112), Laws (p. 115), Luomala (pp. 115–16), and Richmond (p. 117).

20. For additional correspondence in the Boas Papers concerning Espinosa's fieldwork, see Espinosa to Boas, 5/31/1913, 7/15/1913, 12/1/1913, 3/21/1915, 9/5/1920, 10/21/1920.

21. Anne C. Burson reported on Krappe and his contributions to folklore scholarship at the 1981 Meeting of the American Folklore Society.

5. THE ANTHROPOLOGICAL FOLKLORISTS

1. Personal communication, George Foster, 1976.

2. The conflict between Franz Boas and W. J. McGee over the establishment of the American Anthropological Association was played out between the two in private correspondence and in published accounts. It gave voice to concerns over the place of amateurs in anthropology, the power of professionals, and the direction and control of anthropology. (See Stocking 1960.) For Boas's plans concerning the development of American anthropology, see Parmenter (1966, 100).

3. Rohner is quoting from Boas's diary entry of 9/30/1886.

4. Darnell is quoting correspondence from Pilling to Boas (5/16/1887), and Hodge to Boas (3/31/1917), on file at the Bureau of American Ethnology.

5. For "A Bibliography of Franz Boas in Folklore," see Lowie (1944b, 65–69). See also the selective bibliography of Boas's major works in Herskovits, *Franz Boas, The Science of Man in the Making* (1953).

6. For Boas's discussion of the development of anthropology courses at Columbia from 1893 to 1896, see "Instruction in Anthropology," Boas Papers, attachment from Boas to Butler, 11/15/1902. For a discussion of the way in which Boas saw anthropological instruction linked to museum work, see Jacknis (1985, 88).

7. Buzaljko is quoting a letter from Kroeber to Hearst, dated March 29, 1902, on file in the Phoebe Apperson Hearst Papers at the Bancroft Library.

8. For Barrett's work in folklore, see *Pomo Myths* (1933), *Material Aspects of Pomo Culture* (1952), and *The Dream Dance of the Chippewas and Menominee of Northern Wisconsin* (1911).

9. The information on courses offered in the Department of Anthropology at the University of California, Berkeley, was taken from a catalogue compiled by Kroeber. It consisted of a photostat copy of the University of California Catalogue beginning in 1901, and continuing past Kroeber's retirement, when John Rowe followed Kroeber's pattern of recording anthropology courses, adding notes in the margin with pertinent information about course or professor. John Howland Rowe graciously made this catalogue available to me.

10. Darnell is quoting a letter from Putnam to Newell, dated May 6, 1905, filed among the Frederick Ward Putnam papers.

11. Personal communication from Katherine Loumala in 1981.

12. See Witthoft (1951) for Speck's bibliography.

13. See Thompson (1978, 641) for a list of these languages and the dates of the fieldwork.

14. Simpson is quoting a letter from Mead dated April 12, 1973.

15. Peter Hare notes that there is confusion about the actual date of Parsons's birth. While 1875 is given in all reference works as the correct date, 1874 is recorded as the year of her birth in the family Bible. The latter date was regarded by Parsons as correct (Hare 1985, 27).

16. For additional information on Parsons, see Chambers (1973); Hare (1985); National Research Council (1938, 78); and Reichard (1943a).

17. See Dwyer-Shick (1979, 240–50) for a detailed account of Benedict's tenure as editor.

18. Briscoe is quoting a letter from Ruth Benedict to Katherine Luomala, dated July 3, 1936, on file in the Benedict Papers at the Vassar College Library.

19. For a touching account of his memories of his teacher, see Sidney Mintz, "Ruth Benedict," in Sydel Silverman, *Totems and Teachers* (Mintz 1981, 141–68). For more information about Columbia University's reluctance to grant full professorship to a woman, see Mead (1974); and Lynd (1949, 22–24). Robert Lynd in his memorial to Ruth Benedict recalled, "When there was the problem of the moving of the Department of Anthropology into the Faculty of Political Science, the Faculty at Columbia under which the other social sciences are grouped, the shift was desirable and long overdue from the point of view of all of the other social disciplines. But there was an obstacle, around which gray-haired professors tip-toed, whispering anxiously: it would involve bringing a woman into the Faculty. And as a distinguished colleague, now dead, had remarked, 'The Faculty of Political Science is a very exclusive gentlemen's club' " (Lynd 1949, 23). Mead remarked, "The Faculty of Political Science, to which Anthropology had been transferred from the Faculty of Philosophy, Anthropology, and Psychology, felt that the addition of a woman to their ranks as a full professor would lower their academic standing" (Mead 1974, 55).

In addition to Columbia's reprehensible treatment of one of the outstanding scholar's of the twentieth century, there was also the matter of Ralph Linton's overt hostility toward Ruth Benedict. Two people had been considered to replace Boas on his retirement from Columbia: W. Lloyd Warner and Ralph Linton. Ruth Benedict favored the appointment of W. Lloyd Warner. She thought that she and Linton were so similar in their approach that Warner would provide a new perspective for the students. Linton learned that she had not supported him; and when he was appointed head of the department, he never missed an opportunity to show his hostility (Mead 1974, 55–56). Sidney Mintz recalled, "I never heard Ruth comment on Linton, but his hostility toward her was intense . . . when he referred to Benedict, it was always with a good deal of animus. He would occasionally boast publicly that he had killed her, and he produced for me, in a small leather pouch, the Tanala material he said he had used to kill Ruth Benedict" (Mintz 1981, 161).

6. APPROACHES TO FOLKLORE

1. Hart was quoting Child's passage on the ballad published in the *Universal Cyclopoedia*.

2. Ibid.

3. For a history of the type index, see Fritz Harkort, "Zur Geschichte der Typenindex," in *Fabula* (1962). Thompson also gives a brief background in *The Types of the Folktale* (1961).

4. See Dundes's note 10 to Thompson's "The Star Husband Tale" for a discussion of an attempt to find an earlier version of this narrative (1965, 457–58). For works on a related narrative, the star wife tale of Central and South America, see Howe and Hirschfeld (1981); Schorer (1962); Metraux (1946); Wagley (1940); Krause (1911). For a survey of the criticisms of the Finnish historic-geographic method, see Utley's "The Folktale: Life History vs. Structuralism" (1978).

5. Darnell is quoting a letter from Boas to Hodge, dated March 2, 1900, on file at the Bureau of American Ethnology.

6. Boas changed his position on diffusion theory later in life. In 1935, he wrote to Kroeber, "It is by no means certain that a center in which widely distributed phenomena reach their greatest intensity, must be their home. . . . Unless other reasons can be given, the distribution alone does not indicate place of origin" (Rukyser, Boas to Kroeber, 8/5/1935).

7. Darnell is quoting a letter from Waterman to Hodge, dated May 29, 1912, which is part of the records of the University of California Archives, Department of Anthropology.

8. Darnell is quoting a letter from Kroeber to Waterman, June 17, 1913, which is part of the records of the University of California Archives, Department of Anthropology.

7. REMNANTS OF THE PAST IN THE PRESENT

1. See Fontenrose (1971, 26–35) for a discussion of Harrison and Hyman.

2. See also Yigal Zan, "The Text/Context Controversy: An Explanatory Perspective" (1982).

3. Much of the correspondence of the American Folklore Society is on file at the University of Pennsylvania Folklore and Folklife Archives.

Archival Sources

American Philosophical Society Library (Philadelphia, Pennsylvania)
  Franz Boas Papers
  A. Irving Hallowell Papers
  Elsie Clews Parsons Papers
  Gladys Reichard and Elsie Clews Parsons Correspondence
  Muriel Rukyser Materials
  William Willis Collection
Bancroft Library (University of California, Berkeley)
  Alfred Louis Kroeber Papers
  Robert H. Lowie Papers
  Anna Gayton Spier
  University of California Archives, Department of Anthropology
National Anthropology Archive (Washington, D.C.)
  Bureau of American Ethnology
University of Georgia Libraries (Athens, Georgia)
  Archer Taylor Collection, Hargrett
  Rare Book and Manuscript Library
University of Pennsylvania (Philadelphia, Pennsylvania)
  Folklore and Folklife Department Archives

Abbreviations

AA	*American Anthropologist*
AAA	American Anthropological Association
AAAS	American Association for the Advancement of Science
AFS	American Folklore Society
ARBAE	Annual Report of the Bureau of American Ethnology
AT	Aarne-Thompson.
BAE	Bureau of American Ethnology
FFC	Folklore Fellows Communications, Helsinki, Finland
JAF	*Journal of American Folklore*
JFI	*Journal of the Folklore Institute*
KAS	*Kroeber Anthropological Society Papers*
NYFQ	*New York Folklore Quarterly*
PMLA	*Publications of the Modern Language Association*
SFQ	*Southern Folklore Quarterly*
UPFFA	University of Pennsylvania Department of Folklore and Folklife Archives
WF	*Western Folklore*

Bibliography

Aarne, Antti
1910   *Verzeichnis der Märchentypen*. FFC, no. 3. Helsinki: Suomalainen Tiedeakatemia.

Abrahams, Roger D.
1972   Personal power and social restraint in the definition of folklore. In *Toward new perspectives in folklore*, edited by Bauman and Paredes, 16–30. Austin: The University of Texas Press.
1977   Toward an enactment-contextual theory of folklore. In *Frontiers in folklore*, edited by William Bascom, 79–120. Boulder, CO: Westview Press.

Abrahams, Roger D., and John F. Szwed
1977   After the myth: Studying Afro-American cultural patterns in the plantation literature. In *African folklore in the New World*, edited by Daniel Crowley, 65–86. Austin: The University of Texas Press.

Alvey, R. Gerald
1973   Phillips Barry and Anglo-American folksong scholarship. *JFI* 10:67–95.

Amsler, Mark E.
1975   A bibliography of the writings of Francis Lee Utley. *Names* 23:130–46.

Arewa, Erastus Ojo
1961   A classification of the folktales of the northern East Africa cattle area by types. Unpublished Ph.D. dissertation in anthropology. University of California, Berkeley.

Baer, Florence E.
1980   *Sources and analogues of the Uncle Remus tales*. FFC, no. 228. Helsinki: Suomalainen Tiedeakatemia.

Baker, Robert L.
1971   Folklore courses and programs in American colleges and universities. *JAF* 84:221–29.

Barbeau, Marius
1943   The folklore movement in Canada. *JAF* 56:166–68.

Barrett, Samuel Alfred
1911   *The Dream Dance of the Chippewas and Menominee of northern Wisconsin.* Bulletin of the Public Museum of the City of Milwaukee, 1:251–406.
1933   *Pomo myths.* Bulletin of the Public Museum of the City of Milwaukee, 15:1–608.
1952   *Material aspects of Pomo culture.* Bulletin of the Public Museum of the City of Milwaukee, 20 (1):1–260, (2):261–508.

Bascom, William R.
1953   Folklore and anthropology. *JAF* 66:283–90. Reprinted in Alan Dundes, ed., *The study of folklore*, 25–33. Englewood Cliffs, NJ: Prentice-Hall, 1965.

| 1954 | Four functions of folklore. *JAF* 67:33–49. Reprinted in Alan Dundes, ed., *The study of folklore*, 279–98. Englewood Cliffs, NJ: Prentice-Hall, 1965. |

1954   Four functions of folklore. *JAF* 67:33–49. Reprinted in Alan Dundes, ed., *The study of folklore*, 279–98. Englewood Cliffs, NJ: Prentice-Hall, 1965.

1955   Verbal art. *JAF* 68:245–52.

1957   The myth-ritual theory. *JAF* 70:103–14.

1958   Rejoinder to Hyman. *JAF* 71:155–56.

1964   Folklore research in Africa. *JAF* 77:12–31.

1965a   Folklore and anthropology. In *The study of folklore*, edited by Alan Dundes, 25–33. Englewood Cliffs, NJ: Prentice-Hall.

1965b   Four functions of folklore. In *The study of folklore*, edited by Alan Dundes, 279–98. Englewood Cliffs, NJ: Prentice-Hall.

1965c   Folklore and literature. In *The African world: A survey of social research*, edited by Robert Lystad, 469–560. New York: Frederick A. Praeger Publishers.

1965   The Forms of folklore: Prose narratives. *JAF* 77:3–20.

1969   *Ifa divination: Communication between gods and men in West Africa*. Bloomington: Indiana University Press.

1973   *African art in cultural perspective*. New York: W. W. Norton.

1975   *African dilemma tales*. The Hague: Mouton.

1977a   *Frontiers of folklore*. AAAS Selected Symposia 5. Boulder, CO: Westview Press.

1977b   Frontiers of folklore: An introduction. In *Frontiers of Folklore*, edited by William Bascom, 1–16. AAAS Selected Symposium 5. Boulder, CO: Westview Press.

1977c   Oba's ear: A Yoruba myth in Cuba and Brazil. In *African folklore in the New World*, edited by Daniel Crowley, 3–19. Austin: The University of Texas Press.

1979   Afro-American studies. *Proceedings of the International Congress of Americanists* 6:591–95.

1980   *Sixteen cowries: Yoruba divination from Africa to the New World*. Bloomington: Indiana University Press.

1981a   African folktales in America: I. The talking skull refuses to talk. In *Contributions to Folkloristics*, 185–211. Meerut, India: Folklore Institute. Reprinted from *Research in African Literatures* 8 (1977): 266–291.

1981b   African folktales in America: XII. Dog rescues master in tree refuge. *Research in African Literatures* 12:460–519.

1981c   *Contributions to folkloristics*. Meerut, India: Folklore Institute.

1981d   Perhaps too much to chew? *WF* 40:285–98.

1981e   Verbal art. In *Contributions to Folkloristics*, 65–75. Meerut, India: Folklore Institute. Reprinted from *JAF* 65:245–52.

Bascom, William, and Richard Waterman

1949   African and New World Negro folklore. In *Funk and Wagnalls standard dictionary of folklore, mythology and legend*, edited by Maria Leach, 18–24. New York: Funk and Wagnalls.

Bassett, Fletcher S.

1892a   Department of literature, preliminary address of the committees on a folk-lore congress. *JAF* 5:249–50.

1892b   *Sea phantoms: Or legends and superstitions of the sea and of sailors*. Chicago: Morrill, Higgins and Company.

1898   Preliminary address of the committee on a folk-lore congress. *The international folk-lore congress of the World's Columbian Exposition*, 17–23. Chicago: Charles H. Sergel Co.

1973a [1892]   *The folk-lore manual*. Reprint. Darby, PA: Norwood Editions.

1973b [1892]   Introductory. *The folk-lorist*, vol. 1, 5–12. Reprint. Norwood, PA: Norwood Editions.

Bassett, Fletcher S., ed.
1892–1893   *The folk-lorist*, Journal of the Chicago Folk-Lore Society, 1, nos. 1–4.
1973   *The folk-lorist*, Journal of the Chicago Folklore Society. Norwood, PA:
             Norwood Editions. Reprint of original 1892–1893.
Bassett, Helen Wheeler, and Frederick Starr
1898   *The international folk-lore congress of the World's Columbian Exposition*,
             vol. 1. Archives of the International Folk-Lore Association. Chicago:
             Charles H. Sergel Co.
Bauman, Richard
1972a   Introduction. In *Toward new perspectives in folklore*, edited by Richard
             Bauman and Americo Paredes, xi–xv. Austin: The University of Texas
             Press.
1972b   Differential identity and the social base of folklore. In *Toward new
             perspectives in folklore*, edited by Richard Bauman and Americo Par-
             edes, 31–41. Austin: The University of Texas Press.
1977a   Settlement patterns on the frontiers of folklore. In *Frontiers in folklore*,
             edited by William Bascom, 121–31. AAAS Selected Symposia 5.
             Boulder, CO: Westview Press.
1977b   *Verbal art as performance*. Rowley, MA: Newbury House.
Bauman, Richard, and Americo Paredes, eds.
1972   *Toward new perspectives in folklore*. Austin: The University of Texas
             Press. Originally published in *JAF* 84 (1971).
Bayard, Samuel P.
1953   The materials of folklore. *JAF* 66:1–17.
Beattie, John
1964   *Other cultures*. New York: The Free Press.
Beck, Horace
1951   Frank G. Speck 1881–1950. *JAF* 64:415–18.
1978   Duncan Emrich (1908–1977). *JAF* 91:701–03.
Becker, Ernest
1971   *The lost science of man*. New York: George Braziller.
Beckwith, Martha Warren
1930   Mythology of the Oglala Dakota. *JAF* 43:339–442.
1931   *Folklore in America, its scope and method*. Poughkeepsie, NY: Vassar
             College, The Folklore Foundation.
1951   *The Kumulipo, a Hawaiian creation chant*. Chicago: The University of
             Chicago Press.
1970   *Hawaiian mythology*. Honolulu: The University of Hawaii Press. Orig-
             inally published in 1940 by the Yale University Press for the Folklore
             Foundation of Vassar College.
Bell, Michael J.
1973   William Wells Newell and the foundation of folklore scholarship. *JFI*
             10:7–21.
1979   The relation of mentality to race: William Wells Newell and the Celtic
             hypothesis. *JAF* 92:25–43.
Ben-Amos, Dan
1971   Toward a definition of folklore in context. *JAF* 84:3–15.
1972   Toward a definition of folklore in context. In *Toward new perspectives
             in folklore*, edited by Richard Bauman and Americo Paredes, 3–15.
             Austin: The University of Texas Press.
1973   A history of folklore studies: Why do we need it? *JFI* 10:113–24.
1976   *Folklore genres*. Austin: The University of Texas Press.
1977a   The context of folklore: Implications and prospects. In *Frontiers of
             folklore*, edited by William Bascom, 36–53. AAAS Selected Symposia

5. Boulder, CO: Westview Press.

1977b   The history of folklore and the history of science. *Midwestern Journal of Language and Folklore* 3:42–44.

1979   The ceremony of innocence. *WF* 38:47–52.

1983   Foreword. *Twenty-four years of the Department of Folklore and Folklife at the University of Pennsylvania, a dissertation profile*. Sue Samuelson, ed., Occasional Publications in Folklore and Folklife, no. 1:5. Philadelphia: Department of Folklore and Folklife, University of Pennsylvania.

Ben-Amos, Dan, and Kenneth S. Goldstein, eds.

1975   *Folklore: Performance and communication*. The Hague: Mouton.

Ben-David, Joseph

1968–69   The universities and the growth of science in Germany and the United States. *Minerva* 7:1–35.

Benedict, Ruth

1931   *Tales of the Cochiti Indians*. ARBAE, no. 98. Washington, D.C.: U.S. Government Printing Office.

1934a   Editor's report. *JAF* 47:261.

1934b   *Patterns of culture*. Boston: Houghton Mifflin Co. Reprinted in 1959 with a preface by Margaret Mead.

1939   Edward Sapir. *AA* 41:465–68.

1943   Franz Boas as an ethnologist. In *Franz Boas 1858–1942*, edited by Alfred Kroeber. Memoirs of the AAA, no. 61:27–34. Washington, D.C.: AAA.

1948   Anthropology and the humanities. *AA* 50:585–93.

1968   Introduction to Zuni mythology. In *Studies in mythology*, edited by Robert Georges, 102–36. Homewood, IL: The Dorsey Press. Reprinted from *Zuni mythology*, Columbia University, Contributions to Anthropology. Vol. 21 (2 vols.). New York: Columbia University, 1935.

1981   *Tales of the Cochiti Indians*. Introduction by Alfonso Ortiz. Albuquerque: The University of New Mexico Press. Originally published in 1931 as ARBAE, no. 98.

Bernstein, Jay

1982   The perils of Laura Watson Benedict: A forgotten pioneer in anthropology. Manuscript. Department of Anthropology, University of California, Berkeley.

Birdsall, Esther K.

1973   Some notes on the role of George Lyman Kittredge in American folksong studies. *JFI* 10:57–66.

Boas, Franz

1884   Sedna und die religiösen Herbstfeste. *Berliner Tageblatt*. (November 16)

1885   Die Sagen der Baffin-Land-Eskimos. *Verhandlungen der Berliner Gesellschaft für Anthropologie, Ethnologie und Urgeschichte* 17:161–66.

1887a   Die religiösen Vorstellungen und einige Gebräuche der zentralen Eskimos. *Petermanns Mitteilungen* 33:302–16.

1887b   Poetry and music of some North American tribes. *Science* 9:383–85.

1888   *The central Eskimo*. ARBAE, no. 6. Washington, D.C.: U.S. Government Printing Office.

1891   Dissemination of tales among the natives of North America. *JAF* 4:13–20. Reprinted in Franz Boas, *Race, language, and culture*. New York: The Macmillan Company, 1948.

1894   *Chinook texts*. ARBAE, no. 20. Washington, D.C.: U.S. Government Printing Office.

1896 The growth of Indian mythologies. *JAF* 9:1–11. Reprinted in Robert Georges, ed., *Studies in mythology*, 15–26. Homewood, IL: The Dorsey Press, 1968. Also reprinted in Franz Boas, *Race, language, and culture*. New York: The Macmillan Company, 1948.

1902a The foundation of a national anthropological society. *Science* 15:804–09.

1902b The Smithsonian Institution and its affiliated bureaus. *Science* 16:801–03.

1904 The history of anthropology. *Science* 20:513–24.

1906 The mythologies of the Indians. *The International Quarterly* 12:157–73.

1907a Some principles of museum administration. *Science*, 25:921–33.

1907b Tribute to W. W. Newell. *JAF* 20:63–66.

1914 Mythology and folktales of the North American Indians. *JAF* 27:374–410.

1916 *Tsimshian mythology.* ARBAE, no. 31. Washington, D.C.: U.S. Government Printing Office.

1917a Editor's report. [Twenty-eighth annual meeting of the AFS.] *JAF* 30:269–70.

1917b *Kutenai tales.* ARBAE, no. 59. Washington, D.C.: U.S. Government Printing Office.

1930 Review of *Tales of the North American Indians*, Stith Thompson, Cambridge, MA: Harvard University Press, 1929. *JAF* 43:223–24.

1935 *Kwakiutl culture as reflected in mythology.* New York: H. E. Stechert. Memoirs of the AFS, vol. 28.

1936 History and science in anthropology: A reply. *AA* 38:137–41.

1938 Mythology and folklore. In *General anthropology*, edited by Franz Boas, 609–26. Boston: D. C. Heath and Co.

1942 Elsie Clews Parsons. *Scientific Monthly* 54: 480–82.

1948 [1940] *Race, language, and culture.* Reprint. New York: The Macmillan Company.

Bock, Kenneth

1956 *Acceptance of histories: Toward a perspective for social science.* Berkeley: University of California Press.

Boggs, Ralph Steele

1929 Folklore, An outline for individual and group study. University of North Carolina Extension Bulletin, vol. 9, no. 6. Chapel Hill: University of North Carolina.

1940 Folklore in university curricula in the United States. *SFQ* 4:93–109.

1949 Folklore classification. *SFQ* 13:161–226.

1981 Reminiscences on the prenatal care and birth of the curriculum. *Curriculum in Folklore Newsletter*, 1–3. Chapel Hill: University of North Carolina.

Botkin, Benjamin

1939 WPA and folklore research. *SFQ* 3:7–15.

1959 Louise Pound (1872–1958). *WF* 18:201–02.

Boyer, Paul S.

1971 Elsie Clews Parsons. In *Notable American women, a biographical dictionary 1607–1950*, edited by Edward T. James, vol. 3, 20–22. Cambridge, MA: Belknap Press of Harvard.

Boyer, Ruth M.

1978 Anna Hadwick Gayton (1899–1977). *JAF* 91:834–41.

Brinton, Daniel

1895 The aims of anthropology. *Proceedings of the AAAS* 44:1–17.

Briscoe, Virginia Wolf

1979 Ruth Benedict: Anthropological folklorist. *JAF* 92:445–76.

Bronson, Bertrand
1959–1972   *The traditional tunes of the Child ballads.* 4 vols. Princeton, NJ: Princeton University Press.
Brown, Rollo W.
1948   "Kitty" of Harvard. *Atlantic Monthly* 182 (4):65–69.
Browne, Ray B., and Donald M. Winkelman
1964   Folklore study in universities. *Sing Out* 14:47–49.
Brunvand, Jan Harold
1978   Maria Leach (1892–1977). *JAF* 91:703.
Burstein, Sona Rosa
1958   Eighty years of folklore: Evaluations and revaluations. *Folklore* 69:73–92.
Buzaljko, Grace
1982   "I took California": Anthropology at Berkeley, 1901–1921. Unpublished manuscript. Department of Anthropology, University of California, Berkeley.
Bynum, David E.
1974   "Child's legacy enlarged: Oral literary studies at Harvard since 1856. Preprint from *The Harvard Library Bulletin* 22 (3).
Cabral, María Clementina Pires de Lima
1970   Os oitento anos do professor Archer Taylor. *Revista de Etnografia* (Museo de Etnografia e Historia, Porto, Portugal) 12 (2):498–99.
Campbell, Joseph
1949   *The hero with a thousand faces.* New York: Pantheon.
Cashion, Gerald, ed.
1974   Conceptual problems in contemporary folklore study. *Folklore Forum* no. 12.
Chambers, Keith S.
1973   "The indefatigable Elsie Clews Parsons—folklorist. *WF* 32:180–98.
Chandler, Mary E.
1949   Ruth Fulton Benedict, 1887–1948; Bibliography 1922–1948. *AA* 51:463–68.
Child, Francis James
1857–1859   *English and Scottish ballads.* 8 vols. Boston: Little Brown and Company.
1882–1898   *The English and Scottish popular ballads.* 5 vols. in 10 parts. Boston and New York: Houghton, Mifflin and Co.
1920   *A scholar's letters to a young lady.* Boston: The Atlantic Monthly Press.
1962   *The English and Scottish popular ballads.* 5 vols. New York: Cooper Square Publisher. Originally published 1882–1898.
Clark, Joseph D.
1964   Fifty years of meetings and programs of the North Carolina Folklore Society. *North Carolina Folklore* 12:27–32.
Clark, Terry Nichols
1973   *Prophets and patrons: The French university and the emergence of the social sciences.* Cambridge: Harvard University Press.
Claudel, Calvin
1944   History of the Louisiana Folklore Association. *SFQ* 8:11–21.
Cocchiara, Giuseppe
1954   *Storia del Folklore in Europa.* Torino: Einaudi.
1981   *The history of folklore in Europe.* Translated from Italian by John N. McDonald. Philadelphia: Institute for the Study of Human Issues.
Cole, Douglas
1983   "The value of a person lies in his Herzensbildung," Franz Boas'

Baffin Island letter-diary, 1883–1884. In *Observers and observed, Essays on ethnographic fieldwork,* edited by George W. Stocking, 13–52. Madison: University of Wisconsin Press.

Conclusion to Department of Literature's Preliminary Address of the Committees on a Folk-Lore Congress.

1892   *JAF* 5:252.

Congress of Anthropology in the Columbian Exposition

1893   *JAF* 6:67–68.

Congresses at the Columbian Exposition

1892   *JAF* 5:247–49.

1893   *JAF* 6:158–59.

Corso, Raffaele

1951   La Coordination des differents points de vue du folklore. *Laos* 1:20–27.

Cothran, Kay L.

1977   Meta-folkloristics and the history of the discipline. *Midwestern Journal of Language and Folklore* 3:44–47.

Crane, Thomas F.

1888   The diffusion of popular tales. JAF 1:8–15.

Crowley, Daniel J.

1966   *I could talk old-story good: Creativity in Bahamian foklore.* Folklore Studies, no. 17. Berkeley: University of California Press.

Crowley, Daniel J., ed.

1977   *African folklore in the New World.* Austin: The University of Texas Press.

Cullin, Stewart

1893   Exhibit of games in the Columbian Exposition. *JAF* 6:205–27.

Curti, Merle

1951 [1943]   *The growth of American thought.* Reprint. New York: Harper and Brothers.

Curti, Merle, ed.

1953   *American scholarship in the twentieth century.* Cambrdge: Harvard University Press.

Daniels, George H.

1967   The pure-science ideal and democratic culture. *Science* 156:1699–1705.

1971   *Science in American society, a social history.* New York: Knopf.

Darnell, Regina Diebold

1967   Daniel Garrison Brinton: An intellectual biography. Master of Arts thesis in anthropology. University of Pennsylvania.

1969   The development of American anthropology 1879–1920: From Bureau of American Ethnology to Franz Boas. Ph.D. dissertation in anthropology. University of Pennsylvania.

1970   The emergence of academic anthropology at the University of Pennsylvania. *Journal of the History of the Behavioral Sciences* 6:80–92.

1971   The professionalization of American anthropology. *Social Science Information* 10:83–103.

1973   American anthropology and the development of folklore scholarship. 1890–1920. *JFI* 10:23–39.

1974   *Readings in the history of anthropology.* New York: Harper and Row.

de Caro, Francis Anthony

1972   Folklore as an "historical science": The Anglo-American viewpoint. Ph.D. dissertation in folklore. Indiana University.

1977   Introduction to the history of folkloristics: An exchange of views. *Midwestern Journal of Language and Folklore* 3:41–42.

Dégh, Linda, ed.
1976   *Folklore today, a festschrift for Richard M. Dorson.* Bloomington: Indiana
            University Press.
De Laguna, Frederica, ed.
1960   *Selected papers from the American Anthropologist 1888–1920.* Evanston,
            IL and Elmsford, NY: Row, Peterson and Co.
De Vries, Jan
1984   Theories concerning "nature myths." In *Sacred narrative, Readings in
            the theory of myth,* edited by Alan Dundes, 30–40. Berkeley: Univer-
            sity of California Press.
Dexter, Ralph
1966   Putnam's problems popularizing anthropology. *American Scientist*
            54:315–32.
Diamond, Stanley
1981   Paul Radin. In *Totems and teachers,* edited by Sydel Silverman, 66–99.
            New York: Columbia University Press.
Dixon, Roland
1930   Anthropology 1866–1929. In *The development of Harvard University
            since the inauguration of President Eliot, 1869–1929,* edited by Samuel
            Eliot Morrison, 205–215. Boston: Harvard University Press.
Dorsey, George A.
1900   The Department of Anthropology of the Field Columbian Mu-
            seum—A review of six years. *AA* 2:247–65.
Dorson, Richard M.
1950   The growth of folklore courses. *JAF* 63:345–59.
1951   The great team of English folklorists. *JAF* 64:1–10.
1955a   The eclipse of solar mythology. *JAF* 68:393–416.
1955b   The first group of British folklorists. *JAF* 68:1–8, 333–40.
1957   Standards for collecting and publishing American folktales. *JAF*
            70:53–57.
1958   *Negro tales from Pine Bluff, Arkansas, and Calvin, Michigan.* Indiana
            University Publication. Folklore Series, no. 12. Bloomington: Indiana
            University Press.
1959a   *American folklore.* Chicago: University of Chicago Press.
1959b   Theories of myth and the folklorist. *Daedalus* 88:280–90.
1959c   A theory for American folklore. *JAF* 72:197–242. Reprinted in
            Richard Dorson, *American folklore and the historian.* Chicago: Univer-
            sity of Chicago Press, 1971.
1961   Folklore studies in England. *JAF* 74:302–12.
1962   Folklore in higher education. *NYFQ* 18:44–54.
1963a   The American folklore scene, 1963. *Folklore* 74:433–49.
1963b   Current folklore theories. *Current Anthropology* 4:93–112.
1963c   Melville J. Herskovits, 1895–1963. *JAF* 76:249–50.
1963d   Should there be a Ph.D. in folklore? *American Council of Learned
            Societies Newsletter* 14 (4):1–8.
1965   Folklore and folklife studies in Great Britain and Ireland: Introduc-
            tion. *JFI* 3:239–43
1967 [1956] *American negro folktales.* Reprint. Greenwich, CT: Fawcett Publication.
1968a   *The British folklorists: A history.* Chicago: The University of Chicago
            Press.
1968b   *Peasant customs and savage myths.* 2 vols. Chicago: The University of
            Chicago Press.
1969a   Fakelore. *Zeitschrift für Volkskunde* 65. Reprinted in Richard Dorson,
            American folklore and the historian, 3–14. Chicago: The University of
            Chicago Press, 1971.

1969b   A theory for American folklore reviewed. *JAF* 82:226–44. Reprinted in Richard Dorson, *American folklore and the historian*, 49–77. Chicago: The University of Chicago Press, 1971.

1970   American folklorists in Britain. *JFI* 7:187–219.

1971a   *American folklore and the historian*. Chicago: The University of Chicago Press.

1971b   Elsie Clews Parsons: Feminist and folklorist. *AFFword* 1:1–4.

1972a   The academic future of folklore. *JAF Supplement*, Annual Report of the AFS (May 1972):105–10.

1972b   *Folklore and folklife: An introduction*. Chicago: The University of Chicago Press.

1972c   *Folklore, Selected essays*. Bloomington: Indiana University Press.

1973a   Afterword. *JFI* 10:125–28.

1973b   Archer Taylor. *Folklore Forum* 6 (4):ii.

1973c   Is folklore a discipline? *Folklore* 84:177–205.

1976   *Folklore and fakelore, Essays toward a discipline of folk studies*. Cambridge: Harvard University Press.

1977a   The African connection: Comments on *African folklore in the New World*. In *African folklore in the New World*, edited by Daniel Crowley, 87–91. Austin: The University of Texas Press.

1977b   Comments on the history of folkloristics. *Midwestern Journal of Language and Folklore* 3:50–53.

1977c   Stith Thompson (1885–1976). *JAF* 90:3–7.

1978   *Folklore in the modern world*. The Hague: Mouton.

Du Bois, Cora, ed.

1960   *Lowie's selected papers in anthropology*. Berkeley: The University of California Press.

Dundes, Alan

1964a   Robert Lee J. Vance: American folklore surveyor of the 1890's. *WF* 23:27–34.

1964b   Texture, text, and context. *SFQ* 28:251–65.

1965a   *The study of folklore*. Englewood Cliffs, NJ: Prentice-Hall.

1965b   The study of folklore in literature and culture: Identification and interpretation. *JAF* 78:136–42. Reprinted in Alan Dundes, *Analytic essays in folklore*, 28–34. The Hague: Mouton, 1975.

1966a   The American concept of folklore. *JFI* 3:226–49. Reprinted in Alan Dundes, *Analytic essays in folklore*, 3–16. The Hague: Mouton, 1975.

1966b   Introduction, *The complete bibliography of Robert H. Lowie*, 2–5. Berkeley: The Robert H. Lowie Museum of Anthropology.

1967   North American Indian folklore studies. *Journal de la Société des Américanistes* 56:53–79.

1969a   The devolutionary premise in folklore theory. *JFI* 6:5–19. Reprinted in Alan Dundes, *Analytic essays in folklore*, 17–27. The Hague: Mouton, 1975.

1969b   Thinking ahead: A folkloristic reflection of the future orientation in American worldview. *Anthropological Quarterly* 42:53–72. Reprinted in Alan Dundes, *Analytic essays in folklore*, 226–38. The Hague: Mouton, 1975.

1971   Folk ideas as units of worldview. *JAF* 84:93–103.

1973   African tales among the North American Indians. In *Mother wit from the laughing barrel*, edited by Alan Dundes, 114–125. Englewood Cliffs, NJ: Prentice-Hall. Originally published in *SFQ* 29 (1965):207–19.

1974   Comments to Francis Lee Utley's, The migration of folktales: Four
                channels to the Americas. *Current Anthropology* 15:16–17.
1975   *Analytic essays in folklore.* The Hague: Mouton.
1976a   Folkloristic commentary. In Alfred Kroeber, *Yurok myths*, xxxi–xxx-
                viii. Berkeley: The University of California Press.
1976b   Structuralism and folklore. *Studia Fennica* 20:75–93.
1977   African and Afro-American tales. In *African folklore in the New World*,
                edited by Daniel Crowley, 35–53. Austin: The University of Texas
                Press.
1978a   *Essays in folkloristics.* Delhi: Folklore Institute.
1978b   The hero pattern and the life of Jesus. In Alan Dundes, *Essays in
                folkloristics*, 223–62. Delhi: Folklore Institute.
Dwyer-Shick, Susan
1979.   The American Folklore Society and folklore research in America,
                1888–1940. Ph.D. dissertation in folklore and folklife. University of
                Pennsylvania.
Dwyer-Shick, Susan, and Wilfred C. Bailey
1977   The development of the academic study and teaching of an-
                thropology. *Anthropology and Education Quarterly* 8:1–7.
Ehrenpreis, Irvin
1945   *The "types" approach to literature.* New York: King's Crown Press.
Ellis, A. B.
1895   Evolution in folklore. *Popular Science Monthly* 48:93–104.
Emrich, Duncan
1946   "Folklore": William John Thoms. *California Folklore Quarterly* 5:355–74.
Erasmus, Charles J.
1953   *Las dimensiones de la cultura: historia de la etnología en los Estados Unidos
                entre 1900 y 1950.* Bogotá: Editorial Iqueirna.
Espinosa, Aurelio M.
1930   Notes on the origin and history of the tar-baby story. *JAF* 43:129–209.
1985   *The folklore of Spain in the American Southwest.* Edited by J. M. Es-
                pinosa, Norman, OK: University of Oklahoma Press.
Espinosa, J. M.
1978   Spanish folklore in the Southwest: The pioneer studies of Aurelio M.
                Espinosa. *Americas, A Quarterly Review of Inter-American Cultural His-
                tory* 35:219–37.
1985   Aurelio M. Espinosa: New Mexico's pioneer folklorist. In J. M. Es-
                pinosa, ed., *The Folklore of Spain in the American Southwest*, 3–64.
                Norman: University of Oklahoma.
Farrand, Livingston
1904   The significance of mythology and tradition.*JAF* 17:14–22.
Fife, Austin E.
1960   Aurelio Macedonio Espinosa, Sr. (1880–1958). *WF* 19:98.
Fifty-first annual meeting of the American Folklore Society 1940 *JAF* 53:191–94.
Fifty-second annual meeting of the American Folklore Society, report of the
                Committee on Policy
1941   *JAF* 54:76–78.
Finnie, W. Bruce
1975   In Memoriam: Francis Lee Utley, 1907–1974. *Names* 23:127–29.
First annual meeting of the American Folk-Lore Society
1890   *JAF* 3:1–16.
Fischer, David H.
1970   *Historians fallacies: Toward a logic of historical thought.* New York:
                Harper and Row.

Fontenrose, Joseph
1971   *The ritual theory of myth.* Folklore Studies, no. 18. Berkeley: University of California Press.
Fortieth annual meeting of the American Folklore Society
1929   *JAF* 42:197–200.
Foster, George
1960   Edward Winslow Gifford, 1887–1959. *AA* 62:327–29.
Frank G. Speck (1881–1950)
1950   *Boletín bibliográfico de antropología americana* 13:312.
Freeman, John Finley
1965   University anthropology: Early departments in the United States. *KAS Papers* 32:78–90.
Gaidoz, M.
1885   Folklore in the United States. *Mélusine* 2:530–38.
Gay, E. Jane
1981   *With the Nez Percés: Alice Fletcher in the field, 1889–92.* Lincoln: University of Nebraska Press.
Geertz, Clifford
1973a   *The interpretation of cultures.* New York: Basic Books.
1973b   Thick description: Toward an interpretive theory of culture. In *The interpretation of cultures,* 3–30. New York: Basic Books.
1976   "From the native's point of view": On the nature of anthropological understanding. In *Meaning in anthropology,* edited by Keith Basso and Henry Selby, 221–37. Albuquerque: University of New Mexico Press.
Georges, Robert A.
1968   *Studies on mythology.* Homewood, IL: The Dorsey Press.
1980   Toward a resolution of the text/context controversy. *WF* 39:34–40.
Georges, Robert A., and Michael Owen Jones
1980   *People studying people. The human element in fieldwork.* Berkeley: University of California Press.
Gerould, G. H.
1936   Review of the *Motif-index of folk-literature.* *JAF* 49:275–76.
Gibson, Ann Judith, and John Howland Rowe
1961   A bibliography of the publications of Alfred Louis Kroeber 1876–1960. *AA* 63:1060–87.
Gilbert, G. K.
1902   John Wesley Powell. *Science* 16 (406):561–67.
Gillespie, Angus
1975   The contributions of George Korson. Ph.D. dissertation in American studies. University of Pennsylvania.
1980   *Folklorist of the coal fields.* Foreword by Samuel P. Bayard. University Park and London: The Pennsylvania State University Press.
Goddard, Pliny Earle
1915   The relation of folk-lore to anthropology. *JAF* 28:19–23.
Goldenweiser, Alexander A.
1910   Totemism, an analytical study. *JAF* 23:179–293.
1922   *Early civilization, An introduction to anthropology.* New York: Alfred Knopf.
Goldschmidt, Walter, ed.
1959   *The anthropology of Franz Boas. Essays on the centennial of his birth.* Memoirs of the AAA, no. 89. Washington, D.C.: AAA.
Goodenough, Ward H.
1956   Residence rules. *Southwestern Journal of Anthropology* 12:22–37.

Gordon, Dudley C.
1969   Charles L. Lummis: Pioneer American folklorist. *WF* 28:175–81.
Gossen, Gary
1971   Chamula genres of verbal behavior. *JAF* 84:145–67. Reprinted in Richard Bauman, *Verbal art as performance*, 81–115. Rowley, MA: Newbury House, 1977.
1974   *Chamulas in the world of the sun, Time and space in Maya oral tradition.* Cambridge: Harvard University Press.
Graduate study in folklore at the University of Texas
1972   *JAF* 84:229.
Green, Archie
1960   John Neuhaus: Wobbly folklorist. *JAF* 73:189–217.
1979   Charles Louis Seeger (1886–1979). *JAF* 92:391–99.
Greenway, John, ed.
1968   *MacEdward Leach memorial issue, JAF* 81.
Grobman, Neil
1974   Conceptual problems in writing a history of the development of folkloristic thought. *Folklore Forum* 12:56–63.
Hallowell, A. Irving
1951   Frank Gouldsmith Speck, 1881–1950. *AA* 53:67–87.
1957   The impact of the American Indian on American culture. *AA* 59:201–17.
1960   The beginnings of anthropology in America. In *Selected readings from the American Anthropologist, 1888–1920*, edited by Frederica de Laguna, 1–90. New York: Harper and Row.
1965   The history of anthropology as an anthropological problem. *Journal of the History of the Behavioral Sciences* 1:24–38.
1967   Anthropology in Philadelphia. In *The Philadelphia Anthropological Society: Papers presented on its golden anniversary*, edited by Jacob W. Gruber, 1–31. Philadephia: Temple University Press.
1976   *Contributions to anthropology, selected papers of A. Irving Hallowell.* Chicago: University of Chicago Press.
Halpert, Herbert, ed.
1982   *A folklore sampler from the Maritimes with a bibliographical essay on the folktale in English.* St. John's, Newfoundland: Memorial University Press.
Hand, Wayland D.
1943   North American folklore societies. *JAF* 56:161–91.
1946   North American folklore societies: A supplement. *JAF* 59:477–94.
1960   American folklore after seventy years: Survey and prospect. *JAF* 73:1–11.
1961   *Popular beliefs and superstitions from North Carolina. The Frank C. Brown Collection of North Carolina folklore.* Vol. 6. Durham: Duke University Press.
1964a   Folklore and mythology at UCLA. *WF* 23:35–38.
1964b   *Popular beliefs and superstitions from North Carolina: The Frank C. Brown Collection of North Carolina folklore.* Vol. 7. Durham: Duke University Press.
1965   Status of European and American legend study. *Current Anthropology* 6:439–46.
1966   *California Folklore Quarterly* and *Western Folklore:* An editorial survey, 1942–1966. *WF* 25:247–53.
1968   MacEdward Leach (1896–1967). *WF* 27:43–44.
1969   North American folklore studies, Supplement II. *JAF* 82:3–33.

1971　　　　*American folk legend: A symposium.* Berkeley: University of California Press.

1973　　　　Memories of Archer Taylor. *Folklore Forum,* 6 (4):iii.

1974　　　　Archer Taylor (1890–1973). *JAF* 87:2–9.

1976a　　　*American folk medicine: A symposium.* Berkeley: University of California Press.

1976b　　　Folk belief and superstition: A crucial field of folklore long neglected. In *Folklore Today,* edited by Linda Dégh, 209–19. Bloomington: Indiana University Press.

1980　　　　*Magical medicine.* Berkeley: University of California Press.

Hare, Peter

1985　　　　*A woman's quest for science: Portrait of anthropologist Elsie Clews Parsons.* Buffalo: Prometheus Books.

Haring, Lee

1981　　　　The Malagasy tale index. *Fabula* 22:96–99.

1982　　　　*Malagasy tale index.* FFC, no. 231. Helsinki: Suomalainen Tiedeakatemia.

Harkort, Fritz

1962　　　　Zür Geschichte der Typenindices. *Fabula* 5:94–98.

Hart, Walter Morris

1906　　　　Professor Child and the ballad. *PMLA* 21:755, 807.

Haskew, Eula

1928　　　　Charles Godfrey Leland: Collector of folk-lore. Master of Arts thesis in English. Columbia University.

Hatfield, Dorothy Blackman, and Eugene Current-Garcia

1961　　　　William Orrie Tuggle and the Creek Indian Folk Tales. *SFQ* 25:238–55.

Hautala, Jouko

1968　　　　*Finnish folklore research 1828–1918.* Helsinki: Tilgmann.

Hays, H. R.

1971　　　　*Explorers of man. Five pioneers in anthropology.* New York: Crowell-Collier Press.

Helm, June, ed.

1966　　　　*Pioneers of American anthropology: The uses of biography.* Seattle: University of Washington Press.

Henderson, M. Carole

1973　　　　Folklore scholarship and the sociopolitical milieu in Canada. *JFI* 10:97–107.

1975　　　　Many voices: A study of folklore activities in Canada and their role in Canadian culture. Ph.D. dissertation in folklore and folklife. University of Pennsylvania.

Henry, Joseph

1857　　　　*Smithsonian Institution annual report.* Washington, D.C.: U.S. Government Printing Office.

Herskovits, Melville J.

1943　　　　Some next steps in the study of Negro folklore. *JAF* 56:1–7.

1946　　　　Folklore after a hundred years: A problem in redefinition. *JAF* 59:89–100.

1951　　　　Folklore: Social sciences or humanistic discipline? *JAF* 64:129.

1953　　　　*Franz Boas: The science of man in the making.* New York: Scribners.

Herskovits, Melville, and Frances Herskovits

1936　　　　*Suriname folklore.* Columbia University Contributions to Anthropology, no. 27. New York: Columbia University Press.

1966 [1958]　*Dahomean narrative, a cross-cultural analysis.* Reprint. Evanston, IL: Northwestern University Press.

Hickerson, Joseph C.
1970   A tentative beginning toward a bibliography on the history of Amer-
              ican folkloristics and the American Folklore Society. *JFI* 10:109–11.
Higman, John
1979   The matrix of specialization. In *The organization of knowledge in modern
              America, 1860–1920*, edited by Alexandra Oleson and John Voss, 3–8.
              Baltimore: Johns Hopkins University Press.
Hinsely, Curtis M., Jr.
1981   *Savages and scientists*. Washington, D.C.: Smithsonian Institution
              Press.
Hodgen, Margaret
1936   *The doctrine of survivals*. London: Allenson and Co.
1942   Geographical diffusion as a criterion of age. *AA* 44:345–68.
Howe, James and Lawrence Hirschfeld
1981   The star girls' descent: A myth about men, women, matrilocality,
              and singing. *JAF* 94:292–322.
Howe, M. A. Dewolfe, and G. W. Cottrell, Jr.
1952   *The scholar-friends, Letters of Francis James Child and James Russell Lowell*.
              Cambridge: Harvard University Press.
Hultkrantz, Ake
1958   American "anthropology" and European "ethnology," a sketch and a
              program. *Laos* 7:99–106.
1976   Trends in Swedish folklore research. In *Folklore Today*, edited by
              Linda Dégh, 239–49. Bloomington: Indiana University Press.
Hummel, Arthur W.
1936   Berthold Laufer: 1874–1934. *AA* 38:101–11.
Hustvedt, Sigurd Bernhard
1912   The popular ballad in English and Danish. Master of Arts thesis in
              English. University of California, Berkeley.
1930   *Ballad books and ballad men*. Cambridge: Harvard University Press.
1970   *Ballad books and ballad men*. New York: Johnson Reprint Co.
Hyder, Clyde Kenneth
1962   *George Lyman Kittredge: Teacher and scholar*. Lawrence: University of
              Kansas Press.
Hyman, Stanley Edgar
1955   The ritual view of myth and the mythic. *JAF* 68:462–72.
1958   Reply to Bascom. *JAF* 71:152–55.
Hymes, Dell
1961   Alfred Louis Kroeber. *Language* 37 (1):1–28.
1962   On studying the history of anthropology. *Items* 16 (3):25–27.
1963   Notes toward a history of linguistic anthropology. *Anthropological
              Linguistics* 5:59–103.
1965   Some North Pacific Coast poems: A problem in anthropological
              philology. *AA* 67:316–41.
1971   The contribution of folklore to sociolinguistics research. *JAF* 84:42–
              50.
1974   *Studies in the history of linguistics, Traditions and paradigms*. Bloom-
              ington: Indiana University Press.
Ireland, Tom, and Jim Stovall
1974   Phenomenology and folklore. *Folklore Forum* 12:75–81.
Jacknis, Ira
1985   Franz Boas and exhibits, On the limitations of the museum method
              of anthropology. In *Objects and others, Essays on museums and material
              culture*, edited by George W. Stocking, 75–111. Madison: University
              of Wisconsin Press.

Jackson, Bruce
1976   Benjamin A. Botkin (1901–1975). *JAF* 89:1–6.
Jackson, Lillian Reeves
1929   The tale of the dog husband, A comparative study of a North American Indian folk tale. Master of Arts thesis in English. Indiana University.
Jacobs, Joseph, and Alfred Nutt
1892   *International folklore congress.* London: David Nutt.
Jacobs, Melville
1958   Clackamas Chinook texts, Part I. *International Journal of American Linguistics* 24 (2).
1959a   Clackamas Chinook texts, Part II. *International Journal of American Linguistics* 25 (2).
1959b   Folklore. In *The anthropology of Franz Boas,* edited by Walter Goldschmidt, 119–38. Memoirs of the AAA, no. 89.
1960   *The people are coming soon, Analysis of Clackamas Chinook myths and tales.* Seattle: University of Washington Press.
1966a   *The Anthropologist looks at myth. JAF* 79.
1966b   A look ahead in oral literature research. *JAF* 79:413–27.
Jason, Heda
1969   A multidimensional approach to oral literature. *Current Anthropology* 10:413–26.
Jennings, Jesse D.
1962   Fay-Cooper Cole 1881–1961. *American Antiquity* 27:573–75.
Jones, Steven
1979   Slouching towards ethnography: The text/context controversy reconsidered. *WF* 38:42–47.
Judd, Neil
1967   *The Bureau of American Ethnology: A partial history.* Norman: University of Oklahoma Press.
Kardiner, Abram, and Edward Preble
1961   *They studied man.* New York: Mentor Books.
Kemper, Robert Van
1977   *The history of anthropology: A research bibliography.* New York: Garland Publishing Co.
Kiefer, Emma Emily
1947   *Albert Wesselski and recent folktale theories.* Indiana University Publications. Folklore Series, no. 3. Bloomington: Indiana University Press.
Kinton, Jack F., and Evelyn Kinton
1972   *Seminal and contemporary leaders in anthropology, Their theories and methods.* Mt. Pleasant, IA: Social Science and Sociological Resources.
Kittredge, George Lyman
1885   Arm-pitting among the Greeks. *American Journal of Philology* 6:151–69.
1898   Francis James Child. In *English and Scottish Popular Ballads,* vol. 1, xxiii–xxxi. Boston: Houghton, Mifflin and Co.
1904   *The old farmer and his almanack.* Boston: William Ware and Co.
Kittredge, George Lyman, and J. W. Bright, eds.
1904   *The squyr of lowe degree.* The Albion Series of Anglo-Saxon and Middle English Poetry. Boston: Ginn and Co.
Kittredge, George Lyman, and J. B. Greenough, eds.
1904a   *The first book of Virgil's Aeneid with marked quantities.* (From Greenough and Kittredge's *Virgil.*) Boston: Ginn and Co.

1904b   *Cicero's orations for Milo Marcellus, and Ligarus and the fourteenth Philippic.* (From Allen and Greenough's *New Cicero.*) Boston: Ginn and Co.

Kittredge, George Lyman, and Helen Child Sargent, eds.
1904   *English and Scottish popular ballads.* Boston: Houghton Mifflin Co.

Kittredge, George Lyman, and C. T. Winchester, eds.
1904   *The sonnets of Shakespeare.* The Atheneum Press Series. Boston: Ginn and Co.

Kluckhohn, Clyde, and Olaf Prufer
1959   Influences during the formative years. In *The Anthropology of Franz Boas,* 4–28. Memoirs of the AAA, no. 89.

Klymasz, Robert B.
1976   Soviet views of American folklore and folkloristics, 1950–1974. In *Folklore Today,* edited by Linda Dégh, 305–12. Bloomington: Indiana University Press.

Kodish, Deborah
1978   Robert Winslow Gordon. *Quarterly Journal of the Library of Congress* 35 (4):218–33.

Krappe, Alexander H.
1930   *The science of folklore.* New York: The Dial Press.

Krause, Fritz
1911   *In den Wildnissen Brasiliens,* 346–347. Leipzig.

Kroeber, Alfred Louis
1899a   Animal tales of the Eskimos. *JAF* 12:17–23.
1899b   Tales of the Smith Sound Eskimo. *JAF* 22:166–82.
1900   Cheyenne tales. *JAF* 13: 161–90.
1906a   Folk-Lore Meetings in California. *AA* 8:435–36.
1906b   Berkeley Folk-Lore Club. *AA* 8:437–38.
1906c   Recent progress in anthropology at the University of California. *AA* 8:483–92.
1908a   Catch-words in American mythology. *JAF* 21:222–27.
1908b   *Ethnology of the Gros Ventre.* Anthropological Papers of the American Museum of Natural History, vol. 1, part 4.
1915   Frederic Ward Putnam. *AA* 17:712–18.
1923   *Phoebe Apperson Hearst memorial volume.* University of California Publications in American Archaeology and Ethnology, vol. 20. Berkeley: University of California Press.
1929   Pliny Earle Goddard. *AA* 31:1–8.
1935   History and science in anthropology. *AA* 37:539–69.
1937   Thomas Talbot Waterman. *AA* 39:527–29.
1940   The work of John R. Swanton. In *Essays in historical anthropology of North America,* 1–9. Washington, D.C.: Smithsonian.
1943a   Elsie Clews Parsons. *AA* 45:252–55.
1943b   Franz Boas: The man. In *Franz Boas 1858–1942,* edited by A. L. Kroeber, 5–26. Memoirs of the AAA, no. 61.
1952 [1950] A half century of anthropology. In *The nature of culture.* 137–143. Reprint. Chicago: University of Chicago Press.
1956   The place of Boas in anthropology. *AA* 58:151–59.
1957   Robert H. Lowie (1883–1957). *Year book of the American Philosophical Society,* 141–145.
1958   Robert H. Lowie. *Sociologus* (Berlin) 8 (1):1–3.
1976   *Yurok myths.* Berkeley: University of California Press.

Kroeber, A. L., and A. M. Tozzer
1936   Roland Burrage Dixon. *AA* 38:291–300.

Kroeber, Theodora
1970   *Alfred Kroeber: A personal configuration.* Berkeley: University of California Press.
1976   Foreword. In A. L. Kroeber, *Yurok myths,* xiii–xvii. Berkeley: University of California Press.
Krohn, Kaarle
1926   *Die folkloristische Arbeitsmethode.* Oslo: Ascheboug.
1971   *Folklore methodology.* Translated by Roger Welsch. Austin: The University of Texas Press.
Kuhn, Thomas S.
1970a   *The structure of scientific revolutions,* 2d ed., enlarged. Chicago: University of Chicago Press.
1970b   Postscript—1969. In *The structure of scientific revolutions,* 174–210. Chicago: University of Chicago Press.
1977   Second thoughts on paradigms. In *The essential tension, Selected studies in scientific tradition and change,* 293–319. Chicago: University of Chicago Press.
LaBarre, Weston
1948   Folklore and psychology. *JAF* 61:382–90.
Lamb, Daniel S.
1906   The study of the Anthropological Society of Washington. *AA* 8:564–79.
Lang, Andrew
1893   *Custom and myth.* London: Longmans, Green, and Company.
Langer, Susanne K.
1970 [1942] *Philosophy in a new key, A study in symbolism, rite, and art.* Reprint. Cambridge: Harvard University Press.
Leach, MacEdward
1968   The men who made folklore a scholarly discipline. In *Our living traditions,* edited by T. P. Coffin, 15–23. New York: Basic Books.
Leach, MacEdward, and Tristram P. Coffin
1961   *The critics and the ballad.* Carbondale: Southern Illinois University Press.
Leach, Maria, ed.
1949–50   *Funk and Wagnalls standard dictionary of folklore, mythology and legend.* 2 vols. New York: Funk and Wagnalls. Reprinted in 1972.
Lee, Dorothy D.
1949   Ruth Fulton Benedict (1887–1948). *JAF* 62:345–47.
Lesser, Alexander
1981   Franz Boas. In *Totems and Teachers,* edited by Sydel Silverman, 1–33. New York: Columbia University Press.
Lieut. Fletcher S. Bassett, U.S.N.
1893   *JAF* 5:319.
Lord, Albert
1948   Homer, Parry, and Huso. *American Journal of Archaeology* 52:34–44.
1960   *The singer of tales.* Cambridge: Harvard University Press.
Lowie, Robert H.
1908a   Catch-words for mythological motives. *JAF* 21:24–27.
1908b   The test-theme in North American mythology. *JAF* 21:97–148.
1909a   Additional catchwords. *JAF* 22:332–33.
1909b   Shoshone and Comanche tales. *JAF* 22:265–82.
1909c   Review of George Lawrence Gomme's *Folklore as a historical science.* *JAF* 22:99–101.
1911   The methods of American ethnologists. *Science* 34 (879):604–05.

| 1932 | Proverbial expressions of the Crow Indians. *AA* 34:739–40. |

1932   Proverbial expressions of the Crow Indians. *AA* 34:739–40.
1944a   Franz Boas (1858–1942). *JAF* 57:59–64.
1944b   Bibliography of Franz Boas in folklore. *JAF* 57:65–69.
1947   *Biographical memoir of Franz Boas 1858–1942.* Washington: National Academy of Sciences.
1948   Some facts about Boas. *Southwestern Journal of Anthropology* 4:69–70.
1956a   Boas once more. *AA* 58:159–64.
1956b   Reminiscences of anthropological currents in America half a century ago. *AA* 58:996.
1959   *Robert H. Lowie: Ethnologist.* Berkeley: University of California Press.
1960   Contemporary trends in American cultural anthropology. In *Lowie's selected papers in anthropology,* edited by Cora du Bois 461–71. Berkeley: University of California Press. Originally published in *Sociologus* 5 (1955):113–21.

Luomala, Katherine
1962   Martha Warren Beckwith. A commemorative essay. *JAF* 75:341–53.
1970   Introduction. In Martha Warren Beckwith, *Hawaiian mythology,* vii–xxix. Honolulu: University of Hawaii Press.

Lurie, Nancy Oestreich
1966   Women in early anthropology. In *Pioneers of American anthropology: The uses of biography,* edited by June Helm, 31–81. AES Monograph, no.43. Seattle: University of Washington Press.

Lynd, Robert, Margaret Mead, Alfred Kroeber, et al.
1949   *Ruth Fulton Benedict, A memorial.* New York: Viking Fund.

M.A. program in folklore, Berkeley
1965   *WF* 24:190.

McCown, Theodore D.
1961   Alfred Louis Kroeber (1876–1960). *Annual report of the Robert H. Lowie Museum of Anthropology,* 29–37. Berkeley: Robert H. Lowie Museum.

MacCurdy, George Grant
1899   The extent of instruction in anthropology in Europe and the United States. *Science* 10:910–17.
1902a   The teaching of anthropology in the United States. *Science* 15:211–16.
1902b   Twenty years of section H, Anthropology. *Science* 15:532–34.

McGee W. J.
1897   The Bureau of American Ethnology. In *The Smithsonian Institution, 1846–1896: The history of its first half-century,* edited by G. Brown Goode, 367–96. Washington, D.C.: Devine Press.
1898   Fifty years of American science. *Atlantic Monthly* 82:307–20.

McNeil, William K.
1974   Mary Henderson Eastman, Pioneer collector of American folklore. Folklore Preprint Series, vol. 11 (2). Bloomington, IN: Folklore Students Association.
1980   A history of American folklore scholarship before 1908. Ph.D. dissertation in folklore. Indiana University.
1985   The Chicago Folklore Society and the International Folklore Congress of 1893. *Midwestern Journal of Language and Folklore* 11 (1)15–19.

Mandel, Jerome, and Bruce A. Rosenberg, eds.
1970   *Medieval literature and folklore studies: Essays in honor of Francis Lee Utley.* New Brunswick, NJ: Rutgers University Press.

Maranda, Elli Köngäs
1963   The concept of folklore. *Midwest Folklore* 13:69–88.
1972   Theory and practice in riddle analysis. In *Toward new perspectives in folklore,* edited by Richard Bauman and Americo Paredes, 51–61. Austin: The University of Texas Press.

Mark, Joan
1980   *Four anthropologists: An American science in its early years.* New York: Science History Publications.
Martin, Peggy
n.d.   *Stith Thompson: His life and his role in folklore scholarship.* Folklore Monograph Series, vol. 2. Bloomington, IN: Folklore Publications Group.
Master's degree in folklore and mythology
1965   *WF* 24:41.
Mead, Margaret
1949   Ruth Fulton Benedict 1887–1948. *AA* 51:457–63.
1959a   *An anthropologist at work: Writings of Ruth Benedict.* Boston: Houghton Mifflin.
1959b   Apprenticeship under Boas. In *The anthropology of Franz Boas*, edited by Walter Goldschmidt, 29–45. Memoirs of the AAA, no. 89.
1960   A new framework for studies of folklore and survivals. In *Men and cultures*, edited by Anthony F. C. Wallace, 168–74. Fifth International Congress of Anthropological and Ethnological Sciences. Philadelphia: University of Pennsylvania Press.
1972   *Blackberry winter, My earlier years.* New York: William Morrow and Co.
1974   *Ruth Benedict.* New York: Columbia University Press.
Mead, Margaret, and Ruth Bunzel
1960   *The golden age of American anthropology.* New York: George Braziller.
Merriam, Alan P.
1964   Melville Jean Herskovits 1895–1963. *AA* 66:83–91.
Métraux, Alfred
1946   *Myths of the Toba and Pilaga Indians of the Gran Chaco.* Memoirs of AFS, no. 40. Philadelphia: AFS.
Michael, Marian Pendergrass
1960   Child, Sharp, Lomax, and Barry: A study in folksong collecting. Master of Arts thesis in English. University of Texas.
Midwestern Journal of Language and Folklore
1977   The history of folkloristics: An exchange of views 3 (2):41–53.
Miller, R. Berkeley
1975   Anthropology and institutionalization: Frederick Starr at the University of Chicago, 1892–1923. *KAS Papers* 51–52:49–60.
Mintz, Sidney
1981   Ruth Benedict. In *Totems and teachers*, edited by Sydel Silverman, 140–68. New York: Columbia University Press.
Mitchell, Rowland J.
1962   On studying the history of anthropology: Reflections of a historian. *Items* 16(3):27–29.
Modell, Judith
1975   Ruth Benedict, anthropologist: The reconciliation of science and humanism. In *Toward a science of man, Essays in the history of anthropology*, edited by Timothy H. Thoresen, 183–203. The Hague: Mouton.
1983   *Ruth Benedict, Patterns of a life.* Philadelphia: University of Pennsylvania Press.
Moedano, Gabriel
1963   El folklore como disciplina antropológica. *Tlatoani* 17:37–50.
Moneypeny, Anne, and Barrie Thore
1964   Bibliography of Melville J. Herskovits. *AA* 66:91–109.

Murphy, Robert F.
1972   *Robert H. Lowie*. New York: Columbia University Press.
National Research Council
1938   *International directory of anthropologists*. (January 1938) Multigraphed.
               Washington, D.C.
1940   *International directory of anthropologists*. (Section I, Western Hemi-
               sphere; Section II, Eastern Hemisphere) Multigraphed. Washington,
               D.C.
Newell, William Wells
1883   *Games and songs of American children*. New York: Harper and Brothers.
1888a   On the Field and Work of a Journal of American Folk-Lore. *JAF* 1:3–
               7.
1888b   Notes and queries. *JAF* 1:79–82.
1888c   Necessity of collecting the traditions of native races. *JAF* 1:162–63.
1888d   Folklore and mythology. *JAF* 1:163.
1890   The study of folklore. *Transactions of the New York Academy of Sciences*
               9:134–36.
1892   Folk-lore at the Columbian Exposition. *JAF* 5:239–40.
1895   Folk-lore studies and folk-lore societies. *JAF* 8:231–41.
1896   Review of *Indianische Sagen von der Nord-Pacifischen Kuste Amerikas*,
               Franz Boas. *JAF* 9:75–79.
1906   Individual and collective characteristics in folk-lore. *JAF* 19:1–15.
Niles, Susan A.
1981   *South American Indian narratives. Theoretical and analytical approaches,
               An annotated bibliography*. Garland Folklore Bibliographies, vol. 1.
               Alan Dundes, general ed. New York: Garland Publications.
Norton, C. E.
1897   Francis James Child. *Harvard Graduate Magazine* 6:163–69.
Notes and Queries
1893   *JAF* 6:228.
Officers of the American Folk-Lore Society
1892   *JAF* 5:352.
Oinas, Felix
1973   A visit with Archer Taylor. *Folklore Forum* 6 (4):iv–v.
1976   The problem of the notion of Soviet folklore. In *Folklore today*, edited
               by Linda Dégh, 379–97. Bloomington: Indiana University Press.
Oleson, Alexandra, and Sarborn Brown
1976   *The pursuit of knowledge in the early American republic*. Baltimore: Johns
               Hopkins University Press.
Oleson, Alexandra, and John Voss, eds.
1979   *The organization of knowledge in modern America, 1860–1920*. Baltimore:
               Johns Hopkins University Press.
Oring, Elliott
1977   The gratifications of history: A folkloristic example. *Midwestern Jour-
               nal of Language and Folklore* 3:47–50.
Ottenberg, Simon, ed.
1982a   *African religious groups and beliefs*. Delhi: Folklore Institute.
1982b   The anthropology of William R. Bascom. In *African religious groups
               and beliefs*, edited by Simon Ottenberg, 3–14. Delhi: Folklore Insti-
               tute.
Pandey, Triloki Nath
1972   Anthropologist at Zuni. *Proceedings of the American Philosophical So-
               ciety* 116 (4):321–37.
1975   "India man" among American Indians. In *Encounter and experience:*

            Personal accounts of fieldwork, edited by André Béteille and F. N.
            Madan, 194–213. Honolulu: University of Hawaii Press.
Paredes, Americo
1969   Concepts about folklore in Latin America and the United States. *JFI*
            6:20–38.
Parmenter, Ross
1966   Glimpses of a friendship: Zelia Nuttall and Franz Boas; Based on
            their correspondence in the library of the American Philosophical
            Society in Philadelphia. In *Pioneers of American anthropology: The uses
            of biography,* edited by June Helm, 83–147. Seattle: University of
            Washington Press.
Parsons, Elsie Clews
1923a   *Folk-lore from the Cape Verde Islands.* Memoirs of the AFS, no. 15.
1923b   *Folk-lore of the Sea Islands, South Carolina.* Memoirs of the AFS, no. 16.
1939   *Pueblo Indian religion.* 2 vols. Chicago: University of Chicago Press.
1940   *Taos tales.* Memoirs of the AFS, vol. 34. New York: J. J. Augustin.
Peabody, Charles
1915   Frederic Ward Putnam. *JAF* 28:302–06.
1916   Minutes of the twenty-seventh annual meeting of the AFS. *JAF* 29:
            297–98.
Pearce, Roy Harvey
1953   *The savages of America: A study of the Indians and the idea of civilization.*
            Baltimore: Johns Hopkins University Press.
Peri, David W., and Robert W. Wharton, eds.
1965a   Tributes to Samuel Alfred Barrett. *KAS Papers* 33:1–3.
1965b   Samuel Alfred Barrett 1879–1965. *KAS Papers* 33:3–28.
1965c   The works of Samuel Alfred Barrett. *KAS Papers* 33:29–35.
Pound, Louise
1921   *Poetic origins and the ballad.* New York: Charles Scribner's Sons.
1952   The scholarly study of folklore. *WF* 11:100–08. Reprinted in Louise
            Pound, *Nebraska folklore,* 222–33. Lincoln: University of Nebraska
            Press, 1959.
1959   *Nebraska folklore.* Lincoln: University of Nebraska Press.
Professor Child
1896   *Atlantic Monthly* 78:737–42.
Propp, Vladimir
1968   *Morphology of the folktale.* Austin: The University of Texas Press.
            Originally published in Russian in 1928. 1st edition and translation
            into English in 1958.
Putnam, Frederick Ward
1895   The history, aims and importance of the American Association for
            the Advancement of Science. *Science* 2:171–74.
1905   *The department of anthropology of the University of California.* Berkeley:
            University of California Press.
Rabinow, Paul
1977   *Reflections on fieldwork in Morocco.* Berkeley: University of California
            Press.
1979   *Interpretive social science: A reading.* Berkeley: University of California
            Press.
Radin, Paul
1958   Robert H. Lowie, 1883–1957. *AA* 60:358–75.
1972 [1956] *The Trickster, A study in American Indian mythology.* Reprint. New York:
            Schocken Books.
Rael, Juan B.
1959   Aurelio Macedonio Espinosa, Sr., 1880–1958. *JAF* 72:347–48.

Raglan, Lord
1936, 1949   *The hero, A study in tradition, myth and drama.* London: Methuen.
1955   Myth and ritual. *JAF* 68:454–61.
1957   Reply to Bascom. *JAF* 70:359–60.
1965 [1934]   The hero of tradition. In *The study of folklore,* edited by Alan Dundes,
              144–57. Reprint. Englewood Cliffs, NJ: Prentice-Hall.
Rank, Otto
1959   *The myth of the birth of the hero and other writings.* New York: Vintage
              Books.
Ranke, Kurt
1958   Review of the *Motif-index of folk-literature. JAF* 71:81–83.
Reichard, Gladys
1929   Secretary's report. [Fortieth annual meeting of the AFS.] *JAF* 42:197.
1934   *Spider woman, A story of Navajo weavers and chanters.* Glorieta, NM:
              The Rio Grande Press.
1941   Editor's report, 1940. [Fifty-second annual meeting of the AFS.] *JAF*
              54:82.
1943a   Elsie Clews Parsons. *JAF* 56:45–48.
1943b   Bibliography of Elsie Clews Parsons 1898–1903. *JAF* 56:45–48.
1943c   Franz Boas and folklore. In *Franz Boas 1858–1942,* edited by A. L.
              Kroeber, 52–57. Memoirs of the AAA, no. 61.
1947   *An analysis of Coeur d'Alene mythology.* Memoirs of the AFS, no. 41.
              Philadelphia: AFS.
1950   The Elsie Clews Parsons collection. *Proceedings of the American Philo-
              sophical Society* 94 (3):308–09.
1963 [1950]   *Navaho religion, A study of symbolism.* Reprint. Princeton, NJ: Prince-
              ton University Press.
Report of the Twenty-seventh Annual Meeting
1916   *JAF* 29:297.
Resolution on the death of William Wells Newell of the American Folk-Lore Society
1907   *JAF* 20:67–68.
Reuss, Richard A.
1971   American folklore and left wing politics: 1927–1957. Ph.D. disserta-
              tion in folklore. Indiana University.
1973   Introduction to *American folklore historiography. JFI* 10:3–5.
1974a   On folklore and women folklorists. *Folklore Feminists Communications*
              3:29–37.
1974b   "That can't be Alan Dundes! Alan Dundes is taller than that!" The
              folklore of folklorists. *JAF* 87:303–17.
Reuss, Richard, and Ellen Stekert
1971   The uses of folklore by the historian. *Historical Society of Michigan
              Chronicle* 7 (2):9–16.
Review of Francis James Child's *The English and Scottish popular ballads*
1886   *Mélusine* 4:206–11.
Richmond, Winthrop Edson, ed.
1957   *Studies in folklore, in honor of Distinguished Service Professor Stith
              Thompson.* Bloomington: Indiana University Press.
1970   The development of the popular ballad: A new theory. *Genre* 3:198–
              204.
1973   Archer Taylor. *Folklore Forum* 6 (4):vi.
Ried, Paul E.
1969   Francis J. Child: The fourth Boylston Professor on rhetoric and
              oratory. *Quarterly Journal of Speech* 55:268–75.

Riedl, Norbert F.
1966   Folklore and the study of material aspects of folk culture. *JAF* 79:557–
               63.
The Robert H. Lowie Museum of Anthropology.
1966   *The complete bibliography of Robert H. Lowie.* Berkeley: Robert H. Lowie
               Museum of Anthropology
Roberts, Warren E.
1965   Stith Thompson: His major works and a bibliography. *ARV* 21:5–20.
1977   Stith Thompson, 1885–1976. *Midwestern Journal of Language and
               Folklore* 3 (1):4–10.
Robinson, Fred Norris
1907   William Wells Newell. *JAF* 20:59–60.
1981   Irish proverbs and Irish national character. In *The wisdom of many,
               Essays on the proverb,* edited by Wolfgang Mieder and Alan Dundes,
               284–99. New York: Garland Publishers.
Rohner, Ronald P.
1966   Franz Boas: Ethnographer of the Northwest Coast. In *Pioneers of
               American anthropology: The uses of biography,* edited by June Helm,
               149–222. Seattle: University of Washington Press.
1969   *The ethnography of Franz Boas: Letters and diaries of Franz Boas written on
               the Northwest Coast from 1886–1931.* Chicago: University of Chicago
               Press.
Rooth, Anna Birgitta
1957   The creation myths of the North American Indians. *Anthropos*
               52:497–508.
Rosenberg, Charles
1961   *No other gods, On science and American social thought.* Baltimore: Johns
               Hopkins University Press.
Rosenberg, Rosalind
1982   *Beyond separate spheres: Intellectual roots of modern feminism.* New
               Haven: Yale University Press.
Rowe, John Howland
1962   Alfred Louis Kroeber 1876–1960. *American Antiquity* 27:395–415.
1978.   Anna Hadwick Gayton 1899–1977. *AA* 80:653–56.
Sapir, Edward
1961   Paul Radin, 1883–1959. *JAF* 74:65–67.
Sarton, George
1936   *The study of the history of science.* Cambridge: Harvard University
               Press.
1937   *The history of science and the new humanism.* Cambridge: Harvard
               University Press.
Schorer, C. E.
1962   Indian tales of C. C. Trowbridge: The star woman. *Midwest Folklore*
               12:17–24.
Seaburg, William R.
1978   Bibliography of Melville Jacobs. *AA* 80:646–49.
Sebeok, Thomas, ed.
1955   *Myth: A symposium, JAF* 68.
1957   *Folklore in literature: A symposium, JAF* 70.
Shils, Edward
1972   "Tradition, ecology, and institution in the history of sociology." In
               The twentieth century sciences, Studies in the biography of ideas, edited by
               Gerald Holton, 33–98. New York: Norton.
Siegel, Martin
1965   Science and the historical imagination: Patterns in French histo-

riographical thought, 1866–1914. Ph.D. dissertation in political science. Columbia University.

Silverman, Sydel, ed.
1981   *Totems and teachers, Perspectives on the history of anthropology.* New York: Columbia University Press.

Simpson, George Eaton
1973   *Melville J. Herskovits.* New York: Columba University Press.

Smith, Marian
1943   Centenary of the American Ethnological Society: Forward and brief history. *AA* 45:181–84.

1956   Gladys Amanda Reichard. *AA* 58:913–16.

1959   The importance of folklore studies to anthropology. *Folklore* 70:306–07.

1959   Boas' "natural history" approach to field method. In *The anthropology of Franz Boas*, edited by Walter Goldschmidt, 46–60. Memoirs of the AAA, no. 89.

Smithsonian Institution
1904   *An account of the Smithsonian Institution, Its origin, history, objects and achievements.* Washington, D.C.: Smithsonian.

Snow, C. P.
1964   *The two cultures, and a second look.* Cambridge: Cambridge University Press.

Spargo, John Webster
1930   Review of *The types of the folk-tales* (sic) *A classification and bibliography.* Stith Thompson. *JAF* 43:443–44.

Special Section: Historical Methodology in Folkloristics
1982   *WF* 41:28–61.

Speck, Frank
1935   *The Naskapi, The savage hunters of the Labrador peninsula.* Norman: University of Oklahoma Press.

1940   *The Penobscot man; The life history of a forest tribe in Maine.* Philadelphia: University of Pennsylvania Press.

Spier, Leslie
1939   Edward Sapir, Bibliography. *AA* 41:469–77.

1943   Elsie Clews Parsons. *AA* 45:244–51.

1959   Some central elements of the legacy. In *The anthropology of Franz Boas*, edited by Walter Goldschmidt, 146–55. Memoirs of the AAA, no. 89.

Starr, Frederick, and Ernest W. Clement
1893   Resolutions of respect: Lieutenant F. S. Bassett. *The Folk-Lorist* V:257.

Stekert, Ellen J.
1975   Benjamin Albert Botkin: 1901–1975. *WF* 34:335–38.

Stern, Gwen, and Paul Bohannan
1970   American Anthropologist: The first eighty years. *Newsletter of AAA* 11 (December):1, 6–12.

Steward, Julian H.
1961   Alfred Louis Kroeber, 1876–1960. *AA* 63:1038–60.

1974   Robert Harry Lowie 1883–1957 *Biographical Memoirs* 44:1175 211. Washington, D.C.: The National Academy of Sciences of the United States of America.

Stocking, George
1960   Franz Boas and the founding of the American Anthropological Association. *AA* 62:1–17.

1965a   "Cultural Darwinism" and "philosophical idealism" in E. B. Tylor: A special plea for historicism in the history of anthropology. *Southwestern Journal of Anthropology* 21:130–47.

1965b   From physics to ethnology: Franz Boas' Arctic expedition as a prob-
             lem in the historiography of the behavioral sciences. *Journal of the
             History of the Behavioral Sciences* 1:53–66.
1965c   On the limits of "presentism" and "historism" in the historiography
             of the behavioral sciences. *Journal of the History of the Behavioral
             Sciences* 1:211–18.
1966   The history of anthropology: Where, whence, whither? *Journal of the
             History of the Behavioral Sciences* 2:281–90.
1968   *Race, culture, and evolution; Essays in the history of anthropology.* New
             York: Free Press.
1974a   The Boas plan for the study of American Indian languages. In *Studies
             in the history of linguistics*, edited by Dell Hymes, 454–84. Bloom-
             ington: Indiana University Press.
1974b   Some comments on history as a moral discipline: "Transcending
             textbook chronicles and apologetics." In *Studies in the history of lin-
             guistics*, edited by Dell Hymes, 511–512. Bloomington: Indiana Uni-
             versity Press.
1974c   *The shaping of American anthropology, 1883–1911; A Franz Boas reader.*
             New York: Basic Books.
Sutherland, Edwin Van Valkenburg, ed.
1964   The diaries of John Gregory Bourke: Their anthropological and
             folklore content. Ph.D. dissertation in folklore. University of Penn-
             sylvania.
Swanton, John R.
1907   A concordance of American myths. *JAF* 78:220–22.
1910   Some practical aspects in the study of myths. *JAF* 23:1–7.
Taylor, Archer
1927   *The black ox, A study in the history of a folk-tale* FFC, no. 70. Helsinki:
             Suomalainen Tiedeakatemia.
1928   Precursors of the Finnish method of folklore study. *Modern Philology*
             25:481–91.
1931   *The proverb.* Cambridge: Harvard University Press.
1940   Some trends and problems in studies of the folktale. *Studies in
             Philology* 37:1–25.
1952   Tom Peete Cross, 1879–1951. *JAF* 65:138.
1953   Trends in the study of folksong, 1937–1950. *SFQ* 17:97–113.
1959   Review of *Studies in honor of Distinguished Service Professor Stith
             Thompson*, W. Edson Richmond, ed. *JAF* 72:67–68.
1964   The classics of folklore. *ARV* 20:113–24.
1965   Folklore and the student of literature. In *The study of folklore*, edited
             by Alan Dundes, 34–42. Englewood Cliffs, NJ: Prentice Hall. Orig-
             inally published in *The Pacific Spectator* 2 (1948): 216–23.
1972   *Comparative studies in folklore, Asia-Europe-America.* Asian Folklore and
             Social Life Monographs. Lou Tsu-K'uang and Wolfram Eberhard,
             eds. vol. 41. Taiwan: The Orient Cultural Service.
Taylor, Archer, and Wayland Hand
1966   Twenty-five years of folklore study in the West. *WF* 25:229–43.
Thompson, Laurence C.
1978   Melville Jacobs (1902–1971). *AA* 80:640–46.
Thompson, Stith
1915   Local meeting, Texas Folk-Lore Society. *JAF* 28:307.
1919   *European tales among the North American Indians: A study in the migra-
             tion of folk-tales.* Colorado Springs: Colorado College.
1928   *The types of the folk-tale, A classification and bibliography; Antti Aarne's
             Verzeichnis der Marchentypen (FF Communications no. 3).* Translated and

enlarged. FFC, no. 74. Helsinki: Suomalainen Tiedeakatemia.

1929   *Tales of the North American Indians.* Cambridge: Harvard University Press.

1932–36   *Motif-index of folk-literature.* 6 vols. Bloomington: Indiana University Press.

1936a   Folktale congress in Sweden. *JAF* 49:171.

1936b   Personal notes on a folktale congress. *Indiana University Alumni Quarterly* 23:1–17.

1949   The future of folklore research in the United States. *American Philosophical Society Proceedings* 93 (3):244–47.

1951   *The folktale.* New York: Dryden Press.

1952   Problems in folklore. In *An introduction to research in English literary history,* edited by Chauncey Sanders, 253–76. New York: Macmillan.

1953   *Four symposia on folklore.* Indiana University Folklore Series, no. 8. Bloomington: Indiana University Press.

1955   Narrative motif-analysis as a folklore method. *FFC,* no. 161:3–9. Helsinki: Suomalainen Tiedeakatemia.

1955–58   *Motif-index of folk-literature.* 6 vols. Bloomington: Indiana University Press.

1956   *Folklorist's progress.* Multigraphed. Bloomington: Indiana University.

1957   Recollections of an itinerant folklorist. In *Mesquite and willow,* edited by Mody C. Boatright, 118–28. Dallas: Southern Methodist University Press.

1961   *The types of the folktale, A classification and bibliography; Antti Aarne's Verzeichnis der Marchentypen (FFC no. 3).* 2d rev. ed. Translated and enlarged. FFC, no. 184. Helsinki: Suomalainen Tiedeakatemia.

1965a   J. Frank Dobie 1888–1964. *JAF* 78:62–63.

1965b   The star husband tale. In *The study of folklore,* edited by Alan Dundes, 414–74. Englewood Cliffs, NJ: Prentice-Hall. Originally published in *Studia Septentrionalia* 4 (1953):93–163.

1966   *Second wind; a sequel after ten years to folklorist's progress.* Multigraphed. Bloomington: Indiana University.

1968 [1929]   *Tales of the North American Indians.* Reprint. Bloomington: Indiana University Press.

1977 [1951]   *The folktale.* Reprint. Berkeley: University of California Press.

Thoresen, Timothy

1973   Folkloristics in A. L. Kroeber's early theory of culture. *JFI* 10:41–55.

1975a   Paying the piper and calling the tune: The beginnings of academic anthropology in California. *Journal of the History of the Behavioral Sciences* 11:257–75.

1975b   *Toward a science of man.* Paris, The Hague: Mouton.

1976   Kroeber and the Yuroks, 1900–1908. In A. L. Kroeber, *Yurok Myths,* xix–xxviii. Berkeley: University of California Press.

Thorpe, James

1948   *A bibliography of the writings of George Lyman Kittredge.* Cambridge: Harvard University Press.

Tinkle, Lon

1978   *An American original, The life of J. Frank Dobie.* Boston: Little, Brown.

Tozzer, A. M.

1909   Permanent secretary's report to council, Twentieth annual meeting of the AFS. *JAF* 22:85–86.

Twentieth annual meeting of the AFS

1909   *JAF* 22:82–89.

Twenty-second annual meeting of the American Folk-Lore Society

1911   *JAF* 24:21–25.

Twenty-sixth annual meeting of the American Folk-Lore Society
1915   *JAF* 28:99–102.
Tylor, Edward Burnett
1871   *Primitive culture: Researches into the development of mythology, philosophy,
                religion, art, and custom.* 2 vols. London: John Murray.
1874   American aspects of anthropology. *Popular Science Monthly* 26:152–68.
                Reprinted in Regina Darnell, *Readings in the history of anthropology,*
                218–34. New York: Harper and Row, 1974.
United States Congress
1976   Public law 94–201. 94th Congress, H. R. 6673 (January 2, 1976): 1–6.
University of California
1913   *Register 1912–13.* Berkeley: University of California Press.
1939   *General catalogue,* vol. 33. Berkeley: University of California Press.
Upadhyaya, Hari S.
1968   Reminiscences of an octogenarian folklorist. *Asian Folklore Studies*
                27:1–65.
Utley, Francis Lee
1952   Conflict and promise in folklore. *JAF* 65:111–19.
1961   Folk literature: An operational definition. *JAF* 74:193–206.
1965   Folk literature: An operational definition. In *The study of folklore,*
                edited by Alan Dundes, 7–24. Englewood Cliffs, NJ: Prentice-Hall.
                Originally published in *JAF* 74 (1961):193–206.
1970   The academic status of folklore in the United States. *JFI* 7:110–15.
1974   The migration of folktales: Four channels to the Americas. *Current
                Anthropology* 15:5–27.
1978   The folktale: Life history vs. structuralism. In *Varia folklorica,* edited
                by Alan Dundes, 1–22. The Hague: Mouton.
Vance, Robert Lee J.
1893   Folk-lore study in America. *Popular Science Monthly* 43:586–98.
1896–97   The Study of Folk-Lore. *The Forum* 22:249–56.
van Gennep, Arnold
1943   *Manuel de folklore français contemporain.* Vol. I, part 1. Paris: Editions
                Auguste Picard.
Voegelin, Erminie
1949–50   Folklore. In *Funk and Wagnalls Standard Dictionary of Folklore, My-
                thology and Legend,* edited by Maria Leach, vol. 1: 403. New York:
                Funk and Wagnalls.
1958   Robert Harry Lowie, 1883–1957. *JAF* 71:149–50.
Voegelin, Erminie, ed.
1943   *Elsie Clews Parsons memorial number, JAF* 56.
1944   *Franz Boas memorial number, JAF* 57.
Voigt, Vilmos
1976   Towards a theory of genres in folklore. In *Folklore Today,* edited by
                Linda Dégh, 485–96. Bloomington: Indiana University Press.
Wagley, Charles
1940   World view of the Tapirape Indians. *JAF* 53:256.
Wake, C. Staniland, ed.
1894   *Memoirs of the International Congress of Anthropology.* Chicago: The
                Schulte Publishing Company.
Walens, Stanley
1981   *Feasting with cannibals, An essay on Kwakiutl cosmology.* Princeton, NJ:
                Princeton University Press.
Waterman, Thomas Talbot
1914   The explanatory element in the folk-tales of the North-American
                Indians. *JAF* 27:1–54.

White, Leslie A.
1963   *The ethnography and ethnology of Franz Boas.* Bulletin of the Texas
            Memorial Museum, no. 6. Austin: Texas Memorial Museum.
Wilgus, D. K.
1959   *Anglo-American folk-song scholarship since 1898.* New Brunswick, NJ:
            Rutgers University Press.
1967   *Folklore international; Essays in traditional literature, belief, and customs in
            honor of Wayland Debs Hand, professor of German and folklore, UCLA.*
            Hatboro, Pennsylvania: Folklore Association.
1973a   The future of American folksong scholarship. *SFQ* 37:315–29.
1973b   The "text is the thing." *JAF* 86:241–52.
1974   Francis Lee Utley: 1907–1974. *WF* 33:202–04.
William Wells Newell Memorial Meeting
1907   *JAF* 20:59–66.
Williams, Marcelle
1982   Male first, female second; Sexism in the Aarne-Thompson type
            index. Manuscript. University of California, Berkeley.
Willis, William S., Jr.
1973   Franz Boas and the study of black folklore. In *The New Ethnicity,*
            edited by John W. Bennett, 307–34. Proceedings of the American
            Ethnological Society. St. Paul: West Publishing Co.
Wilson, William A.
1976   *Folklore and nationalism in modern Finland.* Bloomington: Indiana Uni-
            versity Press.
Wirth, Louis
1953   The social sciences. In *American scholarship in the twentieth century,*
            edited by Merle Curti, 33–82. Cambridge: Harvard University Press.
Witthoft, John
1950   Frank G. Speck, 1881–1950, Ethnologist and teacher. *Southern Indian
            Studies* 2 (1):2, 39–44.
1951   Frank Gouldsmith Speck, 1881–1950; Anthropological bibliography
            1903–1950. *AA* 53:75–87.
Wolf, Eric
1969   American anthropologists and American anthropology. In *Reinvent-
            ing anthropology,* edited by Dell Hymes, 251–63. New York: Random
            House.
1981   Alfred L. Kroeber. In *Totems and teachers,* edited by Sydel Silverman,
            35–65. New York: Columbia University Press.
Yoder, Don, ed.
1976   *American folklife.* Austin: The University of Texas Press.
1976   Folklife studies in American scholarship. In *American folklife,* edited
            by Don Yoder, 3–18. Austin: The University of Texas Press.
Zan, Yigal
1982   The text/context controversy: An explanatory perspective. *WF* 41:1–
            27.
Zumwalt, Rosemary
1978   The enigma of Arnold van Gennep (1873–1957); The master of French
            folklore and the hermit of Bourg-la-Reine. Master of Arts thesis in
            folklore. University of California, Berkeley.
1979   Henry Rowe Schoolcraft, 1793–1864: His collection and analysis of
            the oral narratives of American Indians. *KAS Papers* 53-54:44–57.
1982   Arnold van Gennep: The Hermit of Bourg-la-Reine. *AA* 84:299–313.
1985   Roots of conflict in folklore studies: The literary and the anthropo-
            logical. In *Social contexts of American ethnology, 1840–1984,* edited by
            June Helm, 73–82.

Index

folklore graduate program, 7; AFS resurgence, 12; MacEdward Leach, 63; Stith Thompson's motif work, 105; Afro-American folktales, origin of, 130–31, 134; death of, 135; Franz Boas, remarks on, 135–36, 137–38; anthropologists and folklore, 135–37; performance theory, 139; folklore courses, 141; folklore theories, 142, 143
DuBois, Cora: AFS Committee on Membership, 42
Dundes, Alan: 8–9, 144; anthropological and literary orientation to folklore, 8; William Wells Newell on folklore and mythology, 19; black folklore, 100; devolution, 103; folklore, discipline of, 124; hero pattern, 126; Afro-American folktales, origin of, 130; European scholarship, 142–43
Dwyer-Shick, Susan: 144; anthropological and literary folklorists' conflict, 8; JAF editors, 31

Eggan, Fred, x
English and Scottish ballads, 45, 46–49, 50
English and Scottish Popular Ballads, The, 9, 100
English Folklore Society: founding of, 16
Erixon, Sigurd, 101
Espinosa, Aurelio: 63; AFS president, 37, 65; Elsie Clews Parsons's funding of, 89
Ethnography and folklore, 7
European folklore societies, 16–17

Fewkes, Jesse Walter, 116
Fieldwork, 10–11
Finland: folklore studies, center for, 101
Finnish historic-geographic method, 107–11
Fischer, David: chronic fallacy, xi
Fletcher, Alice, 116
Folk: 17, 18, 100
Folklore: comparative study, x; study of, psychological, x; European orientation to, 5, 16, 17, 143; American orientation to, 5, 16, 17, 20; collection, 11, 14, 22, 59–60, 101, 110, 122; fieldwork, 11; discipline of, 12, 124, 142; oral emphasis, 17; scientific study of, 18; affiliation of, 22; interdisciplinary nature, 23; literature, 23, 25; independent discipline, 26; anthropology, part of, 25, 26, 30, 43; archiving of, 59; context of, 138–39
Folklore graduate programs, 7–8
Folklore recording: wax cylinders, 30; aluminum discs, 62; Ediphone, 83
Folklorist: identity of, xi, 128, 129, 135, 142, 143, 144
Folk-Lorist, The: Journal of the Chicago Folk-Lore Society, 22–23
Folktales: 58–59, 65, 84–85, 91, 130–35; negro, 15; Asiatic-American, 71; Afro-American, origin of, 130–35
Fontenrose, Joseph, 125, 126, 129

Fortier, Alcee: AFS president, 36
Foster, George, 68
Frank C. Brown Collection of North Carolina Folklore, 54, 55
Frazer, James George, 129

Gayton, Anna: x; 1940 Committee on Policy, 40
Geertz, Clifford, xii
Genres, 10, 99, 102, 103, 139
Georges, Robert, 140, 143
Glassie, Henry: MacEdward Leach, 23, 147n
Goddard, Pliny Early: 75, 87; courses, 77–78, 98; AFS president, 87
Goldenweiser, Alexander, 69, 73, 84, 89
Grimm, Jacob and Wilhelm: Francis James Child, influence on, 46
Grimm, Wilhelm: ballad origin, 103–104
Grundtvig, Svend: 100–101, Francis James Child, 46, 48, 146n
Gummere, Francis, 52
Gunther, Erna, 92

Hale, Horatio, 32
Hallowell, A. Irving: x; JAF editor, remarks on, 40; AFS president, 40, 42; Frank Speck, 82
Hand, Wayland: 54–55, 66, 140, 143; Chicago Folk-Lore Society, 24; AFS, AAA treatment of, 38; folk beliefs, folk medicine, legends, 45; AFS president, 55; JAF editor, 55; Dictionary of American Popular Beliefs and Superstitions, 55; MacEdward Leach, 65
Harris, Joel Chandler, 131, 134
Harrison, Jane, 125, 128, 129
Hart, Walter Morris: 52, 55; ballads, 45; Child's ballad concept, 102
Harvard University, 10, 45, 52, 53, 55, 60, 61, 62, 97
Hearst, Phoebe Apperson: 77; Alfred Louis Kroeber, job offer, 76
Herskovits, Frances Shapiro, 84
Herskovits, Melville: 9, 75, 82, 84, 85, 100, 130, 131, 132, 136, 138; 1940 Committee on Policy, 40; Franz Boas and dissertation topics, 73–74; folktale collecting, 84
Herzog, George, 39, 40, 82, 101
Holmes, W. H.: 1893 World's Fair Congress of Anthropology, 27
Humanities: in academia, 3–4
Hurston, Zora Neale, 75
Hustvedt, Sigurd: 52–53; ballads, 45
Hyman, Stanley Edgar, 127, 128–30, 135
Hymes, Dell, 95

Indiana University: 12, 45, 52, 57; folklore graduate program, 7
International Folk-Lore Congress, 22

Jacobi, Abraham, 70
Jacobs, Melville: 68, 75, 82–83, 120; Franz